PAUL'S THEOLOGY IN CONTEXT

Paul's Theology in Context

Creation, Incarnation, Covenant, and Kingdom

James P. Ware

William B. Eerdmans Publishing Company

Grand Rapids, Michigan

Wm. B. Eerdmans Publishing Co.
4035 Park East Court SE, Grand Rapids, Michigan 49546
www.eerdmans.com

Published 2019
Printed in the United States of America

28 27 26 25 24 23 22 21 20 19   1 2 3 4 5 6 7 8 9 10

ISBN 978-0-8028-7678-2

Library of Congress Cataloging-in-Publication Data

Names: Ware, James P. (James Patrick), 1957- author.
Title: Paul's theology in context : creation, incarnation, covenant, and
    kingdom / James P. Ware.
Description: Grand Rapids : Eerdmans Publishing Co., 2019. | Includes
    bibliographical references and index.
Identifiers: LCCN 2018039318 | ISBN 9780802876782 (pbk. : alk. paper)
Subjects: LCSH: Paul, the Apostle, Saint—Theology. | Church
    history—Primitive and early church, ca. 30-600. | Christianity and other
    religions.
Classification: LCC BS2651 .W37 2019 | DDC 227/.06—dc23
    LC record available at https://lccn.loc.gov/2018039318

For Abraham Malherbe

Contents

Contents

CONTENTS

Abbreviations

AB	Anchor Bible
AJA	*American Journal of Archaeology*
BECNT	Baker Exegetical Commentary on the New Testament
BGBE	Beiträge zur Geschichte der biblischen Exegese
BLE	*Bulletin de littérature ecclésiastique*
BSac	*Bibliotheca Sacra*
CBQ	*Catholic Biblical Quarterly*
CH	*Church History*
CJ	*Concordia Journal*
ExAud	*Ex Auditu*
HNT	Handbuch zum Neuen Testament
HTR	*Harvard Theological Review*
ICC	International Critical Commentary
Int	*Interpretation*
JBL	*Journal of Biblical Literature*
JETS	*Journal of the Evangelical Theological Society*
JR	*Journal of Religion*
JSNT	*Journal for the Study of the New Testament*
JSNTSup	Journal for the Study of the New Testament Supplement Series
JSOTSup	Journal for the Study of the Old Testament Supplement Series
JTS	*Journal of Theological Studies*
LNTS	The Library of New Testament Studies
LXX	Septuagint
MDAI	*Mitteilungen des Deutschen archäologischen Instituts*
MT	Masoretic Text
NIB	*The New Interpreter's Bible*
NICNT	New International Commentary on the New Testament
NIGTC	New International Greek Testament Commentary
NovTSup	Supplements to Novum Testamentum

NTS	*New Testament Studies*
PSTJ	*Perkins School of Theology Journal*
RQ	*Restoration Quarterly*
SANT	Studien zum Alten und Neuen Testaments
SBLSS	Society of Biblical Literature Symposium Series
SBT	Studies in Biblical Theology
StPatr	Studia Patristica
TS	*Theological Studies*
TU	Texte und Untersuchungen
WBC	Word Biblical Commentary
WTJ	*Westminster Theological Journal*
WUNT	Wissenschaftliche Untersuchungen zum Neuen Testament
ZNW	*Zeitschrift für die neutestamentliche Wissenschaft und die Kunde der älteren Kirche*

Introduction

This book is for clergy, students, and laypeople who wish to enrich their understanding of the letters of Paul within the New Testament. This little book by no means claims to offer a complete treatment of Pauline theology, nor does it undertake a passage-by-passage commentary on each letter. Rather, it aims to provide a basic "map" or guide to Paul's theology that will illumine and enliven the study, preaching, and teaching of all his letters. It seeks to uncover the "big picture" of Paul's theology, in order that any passage in his letters may be read with new insight. This book is not written for specialists, but for the average reader interested in the serious study of Paul. However, through the way in which it illuminates key areas of Paul's theology in fresh ways, I hope this book will also be of interest to my fellow biblical scholars, as well as to theologians who wish to work in a way conversant with Scripture.

One way in which this book will differ from many others of its kind is in its basic approach or emphasis in the study of Paul. Paul's gospel announced the fulfillment of the promises of the God of Israel for the whole world; he called himself "the apostle to the gentiles"; and he claimed to bring "good news" to them.[1] The approach of this book will therefore be *twofold*.

First, we will study Paul's gospel—just as he presented it to his gentile hearers—as *the fulfillment of Israel's hopes and Scriptures in Jesus Christ*. We will discover that the Jewish character of Paul's thought, its foundations in the Old Testament Scriptures, is key to unlocking the riches of his theology.[2] Reading Paul's letters

---

1. See Rom 1:5; 11:13; 15:8–12, 15–21; 16:25–27; 1 Cor 15:1–2; Gal 1:15–16; 2:7–10; Eph 3:1–13; 1 Thess 1:5; 2:8–9; 1 Tim 2:4–7; cf. Acts 14:15.

2. Among the many scholars who have shown the critical importance of reading Paul within his Jewish and biblical context, Richard Hays deserves special mention. His groundbreaking book *Echoes of Scripture in the Letters of Paul* (New Haven: Yale University Press, 1989) demonstrated that Paul's allusions to the Scriptures in his letters reveal that his thought is firmly rooted in the overarching Old Testament narrative. We will find in the course of this book that grasping the context of Paul's allusions within the larger Old Testament story will be crucial to a full understanding of his theology.

in this ancient Jewish and biblical context will illumine every area of his thought, and provide fresh insight into important questions in the study of Paul's theology, including the most debated issue in contemporary Pauline study—the "new perspective" on Paul and the law.

Second, we will ask *how Paul's gospel would have been heard in the ancient gentile world into which it came.* How would Paul's message of the reign of the God of Israel now come in Jesus Christ have struck its first hearers among the welter of gods and goddesses, philosophers and sages, popular beliefs and shared assumptions of the ancient world to which it was addressed?[3] We will view Paul's theology against a wide background, considering not only ancient religion but also ancient philosophy, and among the philosophers not only movements more familiar within the Greco-Roman world such as the Stoics, the Epicureans, and the followers of Plato, but also other ancient perspectives such as the teachings of the Buddha and of the Hindu sages.[4] If we study Paul and his theology not in isolation, but in comparison with the other great thinkers and systems of the ancient pagan world to which Paul believed he had been sent, what will we find?[5] It is the premise of this book that if we ask what the average intelligent gentile or pagan would have found

---

3. In the comparative study of Paul and the philosophers of the Greco-Roman world, the work of Abraham J. Malherbe remains in my view unsurpassed. Malherbe's work is distinctive in both the scholarly rigor with which it situates Paul's gospel in its ancient context, and the theological insight with which it reveals the uniqueness of Paul's gospel within that context. For an introduction to Malherbe's approach, see the classic collection of essays: Abraham J. Malherbe, *Paul and the Popular Philosophers* (Minneapolis: Fortress, 1989). To Abraham Malherbe, who was my teacher, my own study of Paul in his ancient context is indebted in a thousand ways. To him this book is dedicated.

4. Paul's gospel is not usually compared with ancient Buddhist and Hindu thought, but Buddhism and Hinduism were important philosophical movements contemporary with Paul, and as we will see, the comparison will be most illuminating. On the knowledge of the Hindu and Buddhist sages and their teaching within the ancient Greco-Roman world into which Paul's gospel first came, see Clement of Alexandria, *Miscellanies* 1.15 ("the sages of India . . . some called Brahmins, and others Sramanas . . . [and] . . . those in India who follow the teachings of Buddha"); 2.20; 4.7; Origen, *Against Celsus* 1.24 ("the Brahmins and Sramanas among the philosophers of India"); Porphyry, *On Abstinence* 4.17–18 ("in India . . . the sages who teach of divine things, whom the Greeks customarily call gymnosophists"); Cicero, *Concerning Divination* 1.47; Philo, *That Every Good Person Is Free* 74; 93–96; Lucian, *The Runaways* 6–7; *The Passing of Peregrinus* 25; Aristotle, fragments 35; Arrian, *Anabasis* 7.1–3; Plutarch, *Alexander* 64–65; 69; Dio Chrysostom, *Orations* 49.7; Diogenes Laertius, *Lives* 9.61–63; Aelian, *Various History* 5.6; Pliny the Elder, *Natural History* 6.22; Diodorus Siculus, *History* 2.40; 17.107; Strabo, *Geography* 15.1.65–73; 16.2.39; Dio Cassius 44.9; and Jerome, *Against Jovinianus* 1.43.

5. I use the term "pagan" throughout this study in a neutral and descriptive sense (customary among scholars of antiquity) with reference to the polytheistic gentile world that Paul engaged with his gospel. That this world was not monolithic, but embraced a great diversity of beliefs, practices, and thought systems, will be evident throughout this book.

different, startling, or unique about Paul's gospel, we will discover what was truly *new* about the message Paul called the "good news." We will discover the heart of Paul's gospel. We will be reading Paul in his ancient context and in full perspective.

It is the thesis of this book that from this vantage point we will be able to view four key pillars of Paul's gospel, which make up the conceptual infrastructure of the whole. The body of this book is divided into four parts, reflecting these four pillars of Pauline theology: creation, incarnation, covenant, and kingdom. These provide the essential "map" of Paul's thought as a whole, in the light of which we can grasp all its various parts. To be sure, these dimensions of Paul's thought are intertwined and interrelated, and taking them up separately and individually is somewhat artificial. As we will see, Paul believed the kingdom has come through the incarnation of God's Son, and his mighty acts in Zion whereby he sealed the covenant. And the kingdom is the restoration and fulfillment of creation. The fourfold division of this book is only a practical one. But I believe the student of Paul will find it extremely helpful and illuminating.

As we seek to unpack Paul's gospel as the fulfillment of Israel's hopes in Christ and in the context of the ancient pagan world into which it came, one or the other aspect of this twofold approach to Paul's letters may predominate in individual chapters or segments of this book. But the goal throughout the book will be the same—to shed light on Paul's theology in new and exciting ways.[6] Of course, there is no room in a book of this size for anything like a complete treatment of all the issues debated among Paul's modern interpreters, nor does space permit detailed interaction with the scholarly literature on Paul. I have purposely kept notes and references to an absolute minimum. However, the book does provide a general introduction for the nonspecialist to most of the key issues and debates in the contemporary scholarly study of Paul. The book aims to provide readers of Paul a sort of compass to help them navigate through the maze of often-conflicting scholarly views, appreciating genuine advances and insights while avoiding unsupported claims and false trails.

Among the Pauline epistles are some letters whose direct authorship by Paul himself is undisputed among contemporary scholars of Paul (Romans, 1 Corinthians, 2 Corinthians, Galatians, Philippians, 1 Thessalonians, Philemon); for the

---

6. The contemporary scholar best known for seeking to elucidate Paul's theology through the twofold angle of his Jewish and pagan contexts is N. T. Wright. The best introduction to Wright's work on Paul is in my opinion his excellent little book *What Saint Paul Really Said: Was Paul of Tarsus the Real Founder of Christianity?* (Grand Rapids: Eerdmans, 1997). See also Wright's magnum opus on the apostle: *Paul and the Faithfulness of God*, vol. 4 of *Christian Origins and the Question of God* (Minneapolis: Fortress, 2013). I have learned much from Wright's seminal work, am in fundamental agreement with his approach to Paul, and follow a very similar approach in this book.

other letters, it is debated whether they were authored by Paul or by one of his disciples (Ephesians, Colossians, 2 Thessalonians, 1 Timothy, 2 Timothy, Titus). Nothing in the pages that follow, where I attempt to uncover the "big picture" of Paul's theology that underlies all the letters, depends upon this question. I regard all thirteen epistles as Pauline, in the sense that they were written either solely and directly by Paul (the undisputed letters, plus Ephesians, Colossians, and 2 Thessalonians) or by Paul in concert with a coworker authorized by the apostle to write on his behalf (1 Timothy, 2 Timothy, Titus). The discussion of Pauline theology in the pages that follow will therefore draw upon the entire canonical corpus of Paul's letters. But I will focus on the undisputed epistles of Paul, together with the prison epistles Ephesians and Colossians, because of the foundational role of these letters within the larger corpus. All translations in this book of Paul's letters, other biblical texts, and ancient sources outside the Bible are the author's.

The main body of the book, in four parts and twelve chapters, focuses on Pauline theology. Part 5, consisting of two chapters, explores the historical role of Paul within Christian origins. Contrary to popular but profoundly unhistorical theories casting Paul as "the second founder of Christianity," these chapters show that Paul functioned collaboratively with the earliest apostles and eyewitnesses of Jesus as one member of a college of apostles, with a shared body of fixed core teachings, but that he, along with Peter, James, and John, also had a distinctive status and role as one of the core pillars of this apostolic body. Readers with a strong interest in exploring the astounding evidence Paul's letters as historical sources provide regarding the beginnings of Christianity, the eyewitness origins of the Gospels, and the earliest apostolic message may wish to read these chapters first. But I have placed them last on the assumption that most readers will want to turn first to chapter 1 and the heart of this book—the theology.

Part One

Creation

Chapter One

The Apostle of Creation

The great majority of Pauline scholars today agree that the theme of creation, of God as creator, is evident in Paul's letters. They disagree only on the relative importance of the doctrine of creation in Paul's overall thought. Some scholars of Paul have argued that creation was not an important aspect of his teaching. Ernst Käsemann, for instance, claimed that "creation is not an independent doctrine in the authentic Pauline epistles."[1] Other scholars maintain not only the presence but also the critical significance of God's creating activity and the goodness of creation within Paul's thought.[2] However, a recent small but influential faction of interpreters moves in a radically different direction, arguing (against all previous Pauline scholarship) that Paul did not believe in one creator God at all but was in fact a polytheist (a worshiper of many gods).[3]

1. Ernst Käsemann, *Commentary on Romans* (Grand Rapids: Eerdmans, 1980), 40. Likewise, according to John Reumann, Paul's expectation of Jesus's second coming "scarcely made creation a matter of importance to him" (*Creation and New Creation: The Past, Present, and Future of God's Creative Activity* [Minneapolis: Augsburg, 1973], 90).

2. See especially John G. Gibbs, *Creation and Redemption: A Study in Pauline Theology* (Leiden: Brill, 1971); Jonathan D. Worthington, *Creation in Paul and Philo*, WUNT 2.317 (Tübingen: Mohr Siebeck, 2011); Nebe Gottfried, "Creation in Paul's Theology," in *Creation in Jewish and Christian Tradition*, ed. Henning Graf Reventlow and Yair Hoffman, JSOTSup 319 (Sheffield: Sheffield Academic, 2002), 111–37; N. T. Wright, *Paul and the Faithfulness of God*, vol. 4 of *Christian Origins and the Question of God* (Minneapolis: Fortress, 2013), 638–41; Wright, *What Saint Paul Really Said: Was Paul of Tarsus the Real Founder of Christianity?* (Grand Rapids: Eerdmans, 1997), 85–92; and James Ware, "The Salvation of Creation: Seneca and Paul on the Cosmos, Human Beings, and Their Future," in *Paul and Seneca in Dialogue*, ed. Joseph R. Dodson and David E. Briones (Leiden: Brill, 2017), 285–306. For a partial move in this direction, see Steve Kraftchick, "Paul's Use of Creation Themes: A Test of Romans 1–8," *ExAud* 3 (1987): 72–87.

3. So Paula Fredriksen, *Paul: The Pagans' Apostle* (New Haven: Yale University Press, 2017), 12, 138, 144, 238–39n15; Fredriksen, "Mandatory Retirement: Ideas in the Study of Christian Origins Whose Time Has Come to Go," in *Israel's God and Rebecca's Children: Christology and Community in Early Judaism and Christianity*, ed. David B. Capes et al. (Waco: Baylor University Press, 2007), 35–38; and Bart Ehrman, *How Jesus Became God: The Exaltation of a Jewish Preacher from Galilee* (New York: HarperOne, 2014), 39–54.

What did Paul really teach regarding creation? What would lead interpreters to such radically diverse readings of the theology of creation in Paul's letters? Answers to these questions are crucial for any serious student of Paul, and will be the focus of this chapter.

In this chapter I will show that God as creator was the very foundation of Paul's thought, that Paul's letters reveal a full and rich theology of creation, and that an appreciation of the vital role within Paul's theology of God as creator, and of the God-given and good creation, is critical for understanding his letters. In so doing, I will not only show that the recent revisionist view that denies the presence of the theme of the one creator God in Paul is mistaken, but also uncover the key interpretive misstep that leads capable scholars to what I believe is a radical misreading of Paul. In making this case, I will be writing in agreement with the standard scholarly view that the theme of the one creator God is evident in Paul's letters, and in particular with those scholars who have argued for the importance of the theme of God as creator in Pauline theology.

But I will also be doing something quite different than is usually done, for I will begin our study by asking *how Paul's message about the creator God would have been heard by his gentile hearers in the context of ancient beliefs regarding the cosmos and the divine.* This question, so vital for understanding Paul's teaching about creation within its ancient context, has in my view not been given the attention it deserves within Pauline scholarship. An exception is the important and insightful work of N. T. Wright.[4] But there is more often a general assumption that creation was a belief Paul held in common with his pagan hearers.[5] This is one reason why some interpreters have minimized the importance of creation in Paul's thought— the assumption that, rather than belonging to Paul's gospel proper, creation was merely a common starting point between Paul and his ancient audience. But this assumption is mistaken. As we will see, for his ancient hearers Paul's announcement of the creator God was in fact astonishing news. It was part of the good news Paul had for them.

---

4. See Wright, *Paul and the Faithfulness of God,* 619–773; Wright, *What Saint Paul Really Said,* 91–92.

5. James D. G. Dunn, *The Theology of Paul the Apostle* (Grand Rapids: Eerdmans, 1998), 38, for example, thinks that creation was a "less controversial" part of Paul's preaching for his pagan audience. "The concept of creation and of a creator . . . could easily hold its place within the range of Greco-Roman religion and philosophy."

The Gods and the Cosmos in Ancient Thought and Worship

In the ancient gentile world into which Paul's gospel came, the concept of one creator God—that is, a transcendent, personal being, distinct from the cosmos, who had brought the cosmos into existence—was unknown. All ancient peoples for whom we have evidence (with the exception of the Jewish people) worshiped many gods. Moreover, the multiple gods and goddesses of the ancient Greco-Roman world—Apollo, Artemis, Aphrodite, Hermes, even the highest god, Zeus—were not considered to be *outside* nature and the cosmos, but were believed to be products or aspects of it (Hesiod, *Theogony* 1–962; Ps.-Homer, *Hymn to Aphrodite* 1–246; Ovid, *Metamorphoses* 1.1–261). Their powers were great but not unlimited. Ancient *polytheism*, the universal religion of the ancient world outside Israel, contained no conception of one almighty creator God.

The ancient philosophers and sages did not oppose this traditional worship of the gods, but sought to modify it by what they considered a higher and more rational conception of the universe and of the divine. The Epicureans (followers of the philosopher Epicurus, who founded this influential movement in the early third century BCE) were the materialists or physicalists of their day. According to Epicurean *materialism*, all things were the result of blind time and chance, of atoms falling through an infinite void (Lucretius, *On the Nature of the Universe* 1–2; 5). The gods, immortal creatures who, like everything else, had resulted from this process, lived in blissful unconcern for human beings (Epicurus, *Letter to Menoeceus* 123; *Fundamental Propositions* 1; Cicero, *On the Nature of the Gods* 1.43–56; Lucretius, *On the Nature of the Universe* 3.1–30). Likewise for the Buddha (who lived and taught in the fifth century BCE, founding the philosophical and religious movement we know as Buddhism), the universe had no creator, and the gods were finite parts of the cosmic whole (*Digha Nikāya* 1; 27; *Anguttara Nikāya* 10.29).

The Stoics (followers of the most influential school of philosophical thought in Paul's day, founded by Zeno of Citium in the third century BCE) were also materialists, like the Epicureans, but of a very different sort. For the Stoics held that the material cosmos, embracing all of nature, human beings, and the gods, was itself divine, a conscious, living being, the highest divinity. According to this Stoic *pantheism*, the cosmos in all its aspects is the self-unfolding, indeed the visible manifestation, of the highest deity. This Stoic belief in one highest divinity comes closer than anything we find in pagan religion to the concept of one almighty creator. And yet the Stoics had no conception of a God who transcends the material cosmos and had brought it into being. For the Stoics, God and the world were one and the same (Zeno, *Stoicorum Veterum Fragmenta* 1.111, 158, 163; Seneca, *Natural Questions* 1, praef. 13–14; 2.45–6; *Letters* 92.30; *On Benefits* 4.7.1; Marcus Aurelius,

Meditations 8.54).[6] This pantheistic mode of thought was shared by many ancient Hindu sages, who taught that the universe was an emanation (that is, an outgrowth or outflow) of divine being, and itself divine (*Rigveda* 10.90; *Bhagavad Gita* 9).

Within the ancient pagan world, the philosopher who came closest to the conception of a transcendent creator God was Plato (c. 429–347 BCE). Plato, to be sure, was a polytheist, believing in multiple divinities. However, Plato envisioned among the many gods a highest divinity, immaterial, distinct from the material universe, the creator of the soul or spirit within each human being. But existing eternally and independently of this divinity was the unformed matter of the cosmos. In this Platonic *dualism*, all being has its source in two equally eternal and independent principles, matter and God. But matter in its coarser forms is inferior and unreceptive to the purposes of the highest God. Thus, within the work of "creation" as Plato conceived it—that is, the transformation of the eternal, unformed matter into the ordered cosmos that we know—the highest divinity delegated the earthly and bodily aspects to lesser gods of limited powers. The most celebrated account of creation in antiquity, Plato's *Timaeus*, explained that, whereas the world-soul, the divine stars and planets, and the celestial aspect of the human soul were all the work of the highest divinity, the human body, the lower parts of the soul, and the plants and animals of the earthly realm were the work of lesser deities (*Timaeus* 41a–42e; 69b–d; 76e–77c).[7]

In summary, then, the ancient pagan world addressed by Paul's gospel had no knowledge of a transcendent creator. Within the traditional polytheistic worship, and in the materialism of Epicurus and the Buddha, the gods were products or as-

6. I provide a more detailed analysis of the Stoic conception in James Ware, "Moral Progress and Divine Power in Seneca and Paul," in *Passions and Moral Progress in Greco-Roman Thought*, ed. John T. Fitzgerald (New York: Routledge, 2008), 267–83.

7. Historians of the ancient world debate to what extent the conception we have explored within Stoic pantheism and Platonic dualism of a single highest divinity, uniquely superior to all other gods, may be loosely called a form of "pagan monotheism." Although a minority view advocates the usefulness of the term "monotheism" in these philosophical contexts, the majority of ancient historians reject the applicability of the term, on the ground that both Stoics and Platonists acknowledged the existence and worship of subordinate gods. For this standard view, see the classic treatments of Martin P. Nilsson, *Geschichte der griechischen Religion*, 2nd ed. (Munich: Beck, 1961), 569–78, and Ramsay MacMullen, *Paganism in the Roman Empire* (New Haven: Yale University Press, 1981), 83–89. For the continuing debate, see Stephen Mitchell and Peter Van Nuffelen, eds., *One God: Pagan Monotheism in the Roman Empire* (Cambridge: Cambridge University Press, 2010). In any case, whether the Stoic and Platonic notions of a highest divinity may usefully be termed "monotheistic" in some limited sense or not, all historians of antiquity agree that, as we have seen, the notion of one transcendent creator, distinct from the cosmos and the source of all that exists, was not present in these philosophical systems nor anywhere else in the pagan world of the first century CE.

pects of the cosmic system. In the pantheism of the Stoics and the Hindu sages, the universe was the unfolding or emanation of the highest divinity. Within Platonic dualism, the material realm existed eternally, in independence from the highest divinity, who had delegated the fashioning of earthly creatures to lesser beings. Thus, even the semitranscendent deity conceived by Plato was but one aspect of a larger cosmic whole.

A Different God

Paul's gospel proclaimed a different God, the God of the Jews, the God of Abraham, Isaac, and Jacob. This God was not only a different God, but a different *kind* of God altogether. As we have seen, the gods of ancient worship and philosophy were either identified with the cosmos, considered aspects or features of it, or regarded as but one part of a total cosmic system. Both the gods of ancient worship and the philosophical divinities were, accordingly, considered to be limited in their powers. Constrained by necessity, fate, or material forces, there were spheres of reality outside their control.

The God whom Paul proclaimed, by contrast, was the God of Israel, the transcendent creator, unlimited in power, and the cosmos was his good and perfect handiwork (Rom 1:20–25; 4:17; 11:33–36; 1 Cor 8:4–6; 1 Thess 1:9–10; 1 Tim 1:17; 6:15–16). He was not a product or aspect of the cosmos, as were the gods of ancient pagan worship. Nor was he identified with the cosmos, like the highest divinity of the Stoics. Instead, he had *created* it. Transcendent (that is, not a part of nature and the cosmos) and everlasting (that is, without beginning and without end), the creator God had made a world distinct from himself, like a painter paints a painting or a sculptor sculpts a sculpture. The God of Israel's Scriptures was the everlasting God, the creator of heaven and earth (see Isa 40:12–31; Jer 10:1–16; Amos 4:13; 5:8; Pss 33:6–9; 95:1–7; 121:2; 124:8; 134:2). The power of the God proclaimed in Paul's gospel was *unlimited* (Rom 1:20; cf. Gen 18:14; Jer 32:17; Ps 135:5–6).

Unlike Plato's quasi-transcendent deity, the creator God whom Paul announced had not formed the cosmos from eternally preexisting matter, but had created all things from nothing. The technical term for this in Christian theology is *creatio ex nihilo*, or "creation out of nothing." That the God of Abraham, Isaac, and Jacob had created all things out of nothing is implicit from the first pages of the Bible. In Genesis 1:1, "In the beginning God created the heavens and the earth," the phrase "heavens and earth" is a *merism* (that is, the use of contrasting terms to express the whole) indicating the totality of all that exists. However, although I believe *creatio ex nihilo* is implicit in Genesis 1, it is not expressed overtly. God's creation of all things out of nothing is implied with even greater force in the Psalms (Pss 33:6–9; 102:25–27; 147:4; 148) and in the book of Isaiah (Isa 40:21–26; 42:5; 44:24; 45:18; 48:12–13). But the concept is given explicit expression for the first time in 2 Maccabees 7.28 (second century BCE). Thereafter overt references to creation out of nothing are common in ancient Jewish texts (e.g., 1QS [Rule of the Community] 3.15; 2 Enoch 24.2; Joseph and Aseneth 12.1–3; 2 Baruch 21.4; 48.8; and Philo, *On the Special Laws* 4.187). The conception is powerfully present, as has been recently shown, in the prologue of John's Gospel (John 1:1–18).[8]

However, within the entire Bible this aspect of creation is expressed most frequently and directly in Paul's epistles. Paul makes the merism of Genesis 1:1 explicit: for when speaking of God's creation, in place of "heavens and earth" he generally prefers to speak of "all things" (Greek: *ta panta*; cf. Eph 3:9; Col 1:16–17; 1 Tim 6:13). In Paul's formula "from him and through him and to him are all things" (Rom 11:36), the prepositional phrase "from him" (*ex autou*) explicitly describes God as the source of all being. So, too, in 1 Corinthians 8:6 ("one God, the Father, from whom [*ex hou*] are all things") and 1 Corinthians 11:12 ("all things are from God [*ek theou*]"), God is affirmed not only as the *fashioner* of all things, but also as the *source* of their existence.

In Romans 4:17, arguably the most powerful expression of the concept of *creatio ex nihilo* in his letters, Paul describes the God in whom Abraham believed as "the God . . . who calls that which does not exist into existence" (Greek: *theou tou . . . kalountos ta mē onta hōs onta*). Within the context, God's power to create out of nothing is demonstrated in his miraculous fulfillment of the promise that the childless Abraham would become the father of many nations (Rom 4:18–22). Some would therefore suggest that God's calling "that which does not exist into existence" has no reference to creation, but only to the calling of the gentiles to faith.[9] However, two factors make it evident that, in describing God in this way, Paul is thinking primarily of the original creative act whereby God brought all things into being. First, the wording of Paul's formula corresponds closely to other formulaic descriptions of the divine act of creation elsewhere in ancient Jewish literature, such as Philo, *On the Special Laws* 4.187: in creation God "called that which had no existence into existence" (*ta mē onta ekalesen eis to einai*).[10] Second, Paul's language of God "calling" that which does not exist into being has its origins in Isaiah's majestic description of God "calling" sun, moon, stars, heaven, and earth

8. See Ian A. McFarland's insightful treatment in *From Nothing: A Theology of Creation* (Louisville: Westminster John Knox, 2014), 18–24, 85–107.

9. So Käsemann, *Commentary on Romans*, 122–24.

10. Cf. Philo, *On the Creation of the World* 81; *On the Change of Names* 46; *On the Migration of Abraham* 183; *Who Is the Heir?* 36; and 2 Baruch 21.4.

into existence (Isa 40:26; 41:4; 48:13; cf. Ps 147:4). But Paul's formulation goes beyond even Isaiah in its explicit affirmation that God called all things "from non-being into being" (*ta mē onta hōs onta*). That is, God did not fashion the cosmos from preexisting material, but brought all things into existence from nothing.[11]

Creatio ex nihilo is not an insignificant detail regarding the mechanics of creation, but is central to the biblical and Pauline conception of God as creator. Unlike the gods of ancient worship and philosophy—the divinities of the Epicureans, the Stoics, the Hindu sages, the Buddha, and Plato—the creator God preached by Paul was not one part or aspect of a larger reality, but the unique source of all reality. Within the varied philosophies and religions of pagan antiquity, material reality is the ultimate Fact, either itself the highest divinity, or containing the various divinities, or existing independently of the highest divinity.[12] But in Paul, the ultimate Fact is the creator God, who brought all things into existence.[13] Creation out of nothing is thus the foundation and correlate of biblical monotheism. In providing perhaps the fullest exposition of *creatio ex nihilo* within the Bible, Paul's letters make an important contribution to the biblical doctrine of God. In continuity with this witness of the Scriptures, the creator God's creation of all things out of nothing would become an explicit and staple element of the church's teaching.[14]

Contemporary persons often regard the exclusive claims of Paul's gospel, to bring to the gentile world the message of the one, true creator God, as misguided, even offensive. Aren't all gods and religions equal and alike? Was it not arbitrary and intolerant for Paul to claim that, of all the gods in the ancient world, his god alone was the unique creator God? But this point of view is founded on a historical

11. On the explicit witness of Rom 4:17 to the doctrine of *creatio ex nihilo* in Paul, see Jaroslav Pelikan, "Creation and Causality in the History of Christian Thought," *JR* 32 (1960); Dunn, *Theology*, 40n59. It is commonly argued that the doctrine of creation out of nothing is strictly a postbiblical phenomenon, first taught by Theophilus of Antioch in the late second century CE (see Gerhard May, *Creatio ex Nihilo: The Doctrine of "Creation out of Nothing" in Early Christian Thought* [Edinburgh: T. & T. Clark, 1994]). However, as I have attempted to show in this brief discussion, this claim is founded upon an inadequate reading of the biblical witness, especially the Pauline evidence.

12. A modern counterpart is the limited deity of process theology, an amalgam of Platonic dualism and Christian theism espoused in recent decades by such figures as John B. Cobb, David Ray Griffin, and Ian Barbour. For the rejection within process theology of the notion of *creatio ex nihilo*, and thus of the concept of a transcendent creator God, see John B. Cobb and David Ray Griffin, *Process Theology: An Introductory Exposition* (Philadelphia: Westminster, 1976), 63–75.

13. I borrow this language of the "ultimate Fact" from C. S. Lewis, *Miracles: A Preliminary Study* (New York: Macmillan, 1947), 98. See also McFarland, *From Nothing*, 87–91.

14. See Shepherd of Hermas, *Mandate* 2.1; Theophilus, *Autolycus* 2.4; Irenaeus, *Against Heresies* 3.10.3; *Apostolic Constitutions* 8.12.7; Augustine, *Confessions* 11.5.7; 12.7. For the doctrine's rich implications for all of Christian theology, see McFarland, *From Nothing*.

misunderstanding. For, as a point of historical fact, the God Paul proclaimed *was* unique. As we have seen, the varied religions and philosophies within the ancient world had no conception of one transcendent creator God. "The idea of Creation was a striking Christian innovation in philosophy."[15] Paul did not proclaim the same kind of limited divinity or divinities with which his gentile hearers were familiar. Thus, when Paul claimed to reveal the "unknown God" to the Athenians (Acts 17:22–34), he knew whereof he spoke. Paul proclaimed to his gentile hearers a new God, a new *kind* of God, previously unknown—the *creator* God.

A Different Cosmos

In proclaiming a new God, the creator, the source of all that exists, Paul brought the good news of a different *cosmos* than his gentile hearers had previously known. Within ancient *polytheism*, the cosmos was the ultimate reality, greater than the gods, its meaning and purpose (if there be any) indecipherable (Hesiod, *Theogony* 36–138). So too in Epicurean *materialism*, the multiple universes were the product of atoms colliding in an infinite void, without plan or purpose (Lucretius, *On the Nature of the Universe* 1–2). Within Stoic *pantheism* the cosmos was likewise the ultimate reality, but in Stoic thought the material universe was itself a living, sentient, and rational divine being (Zeno, *Stoicorum Veterum Fragmenta* 1.158, 163; Cicero, *On the Nature of the Gods* 2.19–46). In Platonic *dualism*, physical reality, necessarily flawed because of its materiality, existed eternally alongside the highest divinity, and in its formed state was the inferior work of intermediate, limited divine beings (*Timaeus* 30; 41a–42e; 47e–48a; 68e–69d). Similarly for the Buddha, physical existence was the "wheel of sorrow," a positive evil and the source of all suffering (*Saṃyutta Nikāya* 2.1.10; *Anguttara Nikāya* 3.58–61). The Hindu philosophers of the East, like the Stoics, deemed the universe a necessary outflow and emanation of the divine being (*Bhagavad Gita* 9). But similarly to Plato and the Buddha, they taught that this material world was *maya*, or "illusion," a shifting sea of deceptive reality from which the wise sought escape (*Māṇḍukya Upanishad* 2–12; *Bhagavad Gita* 7; Porphyry, *On Abstinence* 4.18).

Paul's gospel brought with it a new and radically different understanding of physical existence and of the cosmos. The material world was not a mere brute fact, with no larger meaning or purpose (as in Greco-Roman polytheism, Epicureanism, and Buddhism). It was the creation of God. Nor was it a necessary

15. Georges Florovsky, "The Concept of Creation in St. Athanasius," ed. F. L. Cross, StPatr 6, TU 81 (Berlin: Akademie Verlag, 1962), 36.

emanation (and thus a declension and fall) from the divine being (as in Stoic or Hindu pantheism). Instead, the cosmos came into being by the *free decision* of a holy and transcendent creator God (Rom 4:17; Acts 14:17; 17:26–27; cf. Ps 33:6–9; Isa 40:26; Amos 4:13; 5:8).[16] The cosmos was not itself the ultimate reality, but distinct from its creator, his workmanship. Nor was the cosmos the work of inferior, intermediary deities (as in Platonic dualism). Rather, all things came into being by the *direct creative act* of the one, almighty God, "who created all things" (Eph 3:9; cf. Rom 11:36; 1 Tim 6:13; Acts 14:15; Isa 44:24). And therefore the physical cosmos and material existence were not illusory or evil, something to be escaped, as in Hinduism, Buddhism, or Platonic dualism. Instead, they were the holy and good creation of a good creator God. Matter was his invention. The body was his handiwork. The very fact that it was the direct creation, out of nothing, by the free decision of a holy creator, endowed the world and everything in it with an indelible goodness and sacredness. Paul's gospel thus brought with it an essential cosmic optimism (that is, a conviction of creation's essential goodness) that would have been startling to his pagan hearers. "The earth is the Lord's, and its fullness," proclaimed Paul (1 Cor 10:26, quoting Ps 24:1). The world and everything in it— whether the body itself (1 Cor 6:13–14), marriage and sexuality (1 Cor 7:1–7), food and wine (1 Cor 10:26–31; 1 Tim 4:3–4; 5:23), and even the very matter of which the cosmos was composed—were the good creation of a benevolent creator. In place of the grave and eternal cosmos his hearers had known, Paul brought the good news of the God-given and good creation.

Creation, Reason, and Argument

Within the intricate theological argument that makes up Paul's letter to the Romans, creation is the very beginning and foundation:

> [18]For the wrath of God is revealed from heaven against all godlessness and unrighteousness of human beings who suppress the truth in unrighteousness. [19]Because that which may be known of God is plain within them; for God has made it plain to them. [20]For ever since the creation of the world his invisible attributes, that is, his eternal power and deity, are manifestly visible, being comprehended through the things that have been made, so that they are without defense or excuse. (Rom 1:18–20)

16. Cf. Florovsky, "Creation," 37.

The foundational role of creation within the argument of Romans obviously belies the recent revisionist claim of those scholars who deny the presence of the theme of the one creator God in Paul. But it also belies the claim that this concept played only a minor role in Paul's thought. Romans 1 reveals not only the presence, but also the fundamental importance, of the theme of God as creator in Paul's teaching.

Here I wish to focus on the nature of Paul's argument. Paul claims that reason joins hands with faith in pointing to the reality of the creator God proclaimed in his gospel. We see here an important aspect of Paul's understanding of faith: in Paul's theology faith is not (as often supposed) opposed to reason, nor to logic, nor to knowledge, nor to certainty—but rather to *sight* (2 Cor 5:7, "for we walk by faith, not by sight"; cf. Rom 8:24–25; 2 Cor 4:16–18). Paul affirms that faith in the good news of Christ is fully *reasonable*. In fact, in this passage Paul makes the quite radical claim that, when hearers are confronted with the apostolic announcement concerning the creator God, the decision of faith is fully rational, grounded in the evidence of the creator within his creation (Rom 1:20), but the choice to disbelieve is grounded in an irrational suppression of the truth (Rom 1:18). In Acts we see Paul in his missionary preaching pointing to the evidence of creation as reasonable grounds for conversion and faith (Acts 14:14–17; 17:22–28); here in Romans he highlights the culpability of those who disbelieve the gospel despite this evidence. Some scholars have strained to find a contradiction here between Acts and Romans.[17] But the two concepts are quite obviously different sides of the same coin.

In what way did Paul understand the truth of the creator to be "manifestly visible" (Rom 1:20) by means of the creation? We should first be clear about what Paul is *not* doing. He is not, as the ancient philosophers did, employing reason in order to arrive at the knowledge of a previously unknown deity. Rather, Paul is claiming that the truth of the creator God, who has made himself known by revelation, is rationally evident to all through the creation he has made. Unlike the philosophers, who seek knowledge of the divine through *reason*, Paul employs reason to corroborate the truthfulness of the knowledge of God that is given by divine *revelation*—in Israel's sacred Scriptures, and climactically in the person of Christ.

Although functioning in this very different context, Paul's thought here appears to have a close kinship with two arguments known among the ancient philosophers. The *argument from design*, also known as the *teleological argument*, reasons from the evidence of purposeful design within nature—its intricacy, complexity, variety, and beauty—to the truth of a God who created it. Stoic and Platonist philosophers, as we have seen, did not conceive of a creator God in the

---

17. The classic case for the contradiction is Philipp Vielhauer, "On the 'Paulinism' of Acts," *PSTJ* 17 (1963): 5–18 (originally published in 1951 as "Zum 'Paulinismus' der Apostelgeschichte").

same sense that Paul did, but came the closest to this conception within the ancient pagan world, and believed in a divine origin of the universe. They used the argument from design tellingly against ancient materialists such as the Epicureans (see Plato, *Laws* 10; *Philebus* 28d–30b; Cicero, *On the Nature of the Gods* 2.3–4, 13–44, 86–153; *Concerning Divination* 2.148). Paul here likewise claims that the evidence of design within creation ("the things that have been made," Rom 1:20) points to the reality of a divine Designer.

The kinship of Paul's thought here with the Stoic and Platonist argument from design is one indication among many in his letters that, although he believed that the fullness of truth is found only in the true God revealed in Christ, he regarded many aspects of pagan religion and philosophy in a positive light, as a sincere but incomplete search for the creator God, and a divinely ordained preparation for the good news of Christ. This concept is classically expressed in the account of Paul's speech in the book of Acts before Stoic and Epicurean philosophers in Athens on Mars Hill, an ancient center of philosophical discussion (Acts 17:16–34). Discovering among the sacred precinct's objects of worship an altar to an "unknown god," the apostle proclaimed to the Athenians, "What, therefore, you worship but do not know, this I announce to you" (Acts 17:23)—whereupon Paul proceeded to announce the good news of Jesus, and call his hearers to salvation through faith in the gospel (Acts 17:24–34). This concept of pagan philosophy and religion as a preparation for the gospel is another striking instance of the coherence between Paul's own letters and Luke's portrayal of Paul's teaching in the book of Acts.

But Romans 1:18–20 also seems to presuppose a second way whereby the creation reveals its creator. For Paul's language indicates that he is contemplating not only a creation that reveals God through its beauty and design, but also a creation whose beginning at a point in the finite past ("ever since the creation of the world," 1:20) necessarily points to a creator who is without beginning and of infinite power ("his eternal power and deity," 1:20). Paul's thought here appears to be closely akin to the *cosmological argument*, the most common version of which goes like this:

1. Major Premise: Whatever begins to exist has a cause of its existence.
2. Minor Premise: The universe began to exist.
3. Conclusion: The universe has a cause of its existence—the creator God.[18]

---

18. The most influential contemporary discussion of this argument is found in William Lane Craig, *The Kalam Cosmological Argument* (New York: Macmillan, 1979). The syllogism here follows his formulation, and the discussion below is much indebted to his presentation and elaboration of the argument. For a classic statement of the other main version of the cosmological argument, which argues from the contingency of the universe rather than its finite past, see Aquinas, *Summa theologiae* I, q. 2, a. 3.

Already in Plato (who came nearest of all the ancient philosophers to the biblical concept of a transcendent creator) we find a form of the cosmological argument:

> Now in regard to the whole heaven, or cosmos . . . we must first investigate (and this is the primary question which must first be asked regarding anything whatsoever) whether it has always been, having no beginning of its existence, or whether it has come into existence, having had some kind of beginning. The cosmos has come into existence. For it is visible and tangible and material; and all things that are such are perceptible. And all perceptible things, apprehended by opinion and perception, have come into existence and had a beginning, as we saw. And we affirm that whatever has come into existence necessarily has a cause of its existence. But to find the maker and Father of this universe is a difficult task, and having found him, it is impossible to speak of him to all human beings. (Plato, *Timaeus* 28)[19]

The thought in Romans 1 differs from that in *Timaeus* 28 in two crucial respects. First, Plato seeks by reasoning to arrive at a knowledge of a previously unknown creator (hence Plato's reserve regarding the ability even to speak of this being); Paul argues that reason corroborates the truth of the creator who has made himself known in the Scriptures, and in his fullness in the person of Jesus Christ (Rom 1:1–5; 3:21–26; 16:25–27). Second, when Plato speaks of the universe having a beginning, he is thinking of the formed and ordered cosmos. As we saw, Plato believed that the matter of the universe, in its unformed state, had an infinite past. In Plato's thought, the material world in one form or another has always existed. Paul's argument is different—and new in an important way. For when Paul speaks of the beginning of the universe ("since the creation of the world," Rom 1:20), he is thinking of the creator God's creation of all things, including matter itself, out of nothing (*creatio ex nihilo*). Paul argues from the universe having had an *absolute* beginning to the truth of the creator God. This is something new in philosophy. In Paul's argument, the creational monotheism of the Bible has met the cosmological argument of the philosophers, and transformed it.

Modern science, rather than lessening the relevance of Paul's cosmological argument, has added immeasurably to its power. For scientific discoveries over the previous century have shown that the material universe is not eternal, but had a cosmic beginning (the event cosmologists describe as $t = 0$). The logical

19. Other ancient versions of the cosmological argument are found in Plato, *Laws* 888–99, and Aristotle, *Metaphysics* 12.

implications of this discovery are breathtaking. If the cosmos—matter, energy, time, and space—had a beginning, it must have a cause, which is itself uncaused, without beginning, distinct from the cosmos, a being of "eternal power and deity" (Rom 1:20).

To be sure, these scientific findings are not entirely consistent with Plato's version of the argument. Indeed, these discoveries are, in an important respect, inconsistent with all the varied philosophies and religions of Paul's day that we surveyed—whether polytheism, materialism, pantheism, or dualism—as well as their modern counterparts. For all these various systems assume, as did Plato, that the matter of the universe is eternal. This is contradicted by the now standard scientific model of cosmic origins, which tells us that matter, space, and time had a beginning (t = 0). But these discoveries are in startling convergence with the unique biblical and Pauline conception of a transcendent creator God, who not only formed and ordered the cosmos, but brought all things into being—including matter, space, and time—from nothing. The cosmos revealed by Hubble's law is not the eternal universe envisioned by the materialist, pantheist, or dualist, but the created and contingent cosmos of the biblical creator God. Although unfortunately overshadowed by often-confused debate regarding the precise relationship of the opening chapters of Genesis to evolutionary theory, the discovery of modern science regarding an absolute beginning of the universe, and the remarkable concurrence of this discovery with the biblical revelation of God as creator, is surely the most significant development in the history of the interaction between theology and science.

These discoveries of modern science have brought about a sea change in the debate regarding the cosmological argument. In the past, physicalists or materialists (thinkers who believe that the universe is the sum of reality) generally countered the cosmological argument by rejecting its minor premise: that the universe had a beginning. The universe, they claimed, had existed forever, was self-existent, and was thus itself the primary cause of all things. The famed skeptical philosopher David Hume, for instance, had Cleanthes take this tack in his *Dialogues* (pt. 9). But our best current science now indicates that the cosmos had an absolute beginning. Therefore contemporary materialists now generally reject, in one way or another, the major premise: the law of cause and effect. The universe may have come into being, they claim, through no cause whatsoever. To enter into this contemporary debate is beyond my purpose here, which has been to explore the nature of Paul's argument from creation for the reasonableness of faith in the creator. But the power of Paul's groundbreaking version of the cosmological argument in light of modern scientific discoveries should be noted. In attempting to refute Paul's argument, its opponents are driven to deny the law of cause and effect. This is an astonishing claim, for the notion of causality is an essential component of rational thought. To deny the principle of cause and effect is to abandon reason. Whether this escape into irrationality can be defended, or is the result of what Paul calls "the suppression of the truth in unrighteousness" (Rom 1:18), I will leave to the reader to decide.

The Creator God as the Foundation of Pauline Theology

I have tried to show that, contrary to the view in some quarters, the theme of creation is not a minor feature of Paul's gospel, but a vital element within his thought. But that is hardly putting the matter strongly enough. For creation and, as we will see, incarnation, covenant, and kingdom make up the conceptual "infrastructure" of Paul's theology. To be sure, creation is not the very center of Paul's thought. Another of these four pillars (we will find) is the epicenter of Paul's theology. But of these four pillars it is the most fundamental, for it is the presupposition of all the rest. Here, then, is my claim regarding Paul's theology: *the creator God, distinct from his creation, is the fundamental conception within Paul's thought.* The reader may ask what practical impact this suggestion has on the reading of Paul's letters. Here I have a concrete proposal in terms of method, which I believe can serve to wonderfully illumine Paul's epistles. I propose that from Paul's fundamental notion of God as creator arises an essential relation or distinction, which may be illustrated this way:

$$\frac{\text{Creator}}{\text{Creation}}$$

This is, I would argue, the fundamental category within Paul's *ontology*—that is, his understanding of the whole of reality. It is the fulcrum upon which all of Paul's thought pivots.[20] And here is my proposal regarding method or approach in reading Paul: this duality or distinction, which grows directly out of Paul's fundamental doctrine of God as creator (together with three related distinctions that will be discussed in the following chapters), provides the interpretive key to Paul's thought. On the other hand, the attempt to read Paul's letters *outside this creational context* can only result in radical misinterpretation of Paul. That is why the view that creation is of minimal importance in Paul's thought must inevitably lead to a lessened understanding of *every aspect* of Pauline theology.

20. I am much indebted to discussions with Charles Reed for developing my grasp of the critical role of this distinction within the structure of Paul's theology.

The power of this fundamental category to illumine Paul's thought will become clear as this book proceeds. But one example can be given here. As we saw earlier in this chapter, the claim has recently been put forward by eminent New Testament specialists that Paul was not a monotheist, but a polytheist.[21] They point out that Paul assumes the existence, not of a single celestial being, but of many celestial, supernatural beings—angels, demons, thrones, dominions, principalities, and powers (Rom 8:38–39; 1 Cor 2:6–8; 4:9; 15:23–28; Eph 1:20–23; 6:11–12; Phil 2:9–11; Col 1:16; 1 Tim 5:21). What is this, they ask, but polytheism? Even the uninformed may sense that this is mistaken. After all, Paul tells us emphatically that there is only one God (Rom 3:30; 1 Cor 8:4–6; Eph 4:5–6; 1 Tim 2:5). And readers of this chapter know that this is a profound misinterpretation of Paul. But what would compel intelligent scholars to make such a radical misreading? The root cause, I contend, is the misprojection onto Paul of categories of thought familiar to educated twenty-first-century Westerners, which have their roots in the philosophies of Plato, Descartes, Kant, and Hegel. These scholars are reading Paul in light of some such distinctions or dualities, I would propose, as these:

Spirit	Invisible Realm	Supernatural	Immaterial	Noumenal
Matter	Visible Realm	Natural	Material	Phenomenal

If we ask where the celestial and demonic beings in Paul fit in this diagram, in each case they find their place in the *upper* story. The diagram looks like this:

Invisible Realm	God
	Angels
	Demons
	Thrones
	Dominions
	Principalities
	Powers
Visible Realm	Human Beings
	Animals
	Plants
	Inanimate Matter

---

21. See Fredriksen, *Paul*, 12, 138, 144, 238–39n15; Fredriksen, "Mandatory Retirement," 35–38; Ehrman, *How Jesus Became God*, 39–54.

If these are the master categories we bring to Paul (and for many contemporary readers they are), the conclusion that Paul believed in many divine beings appears inescapable. But what happens if we situate these beings within what I have proposed is Paul's own master category, creator/creation? Then the diagram looks like this:

Creator	God
Creation	Human Beings
	Angels
	Demons
	Thrones
	Dominions
	Principalities
	Powers
	Animals
	Plants
	Inanimate Matter

Now the supernatural and celestial entities of which Paul speaks in his letters are found firmly in the *lower* story—created beings having the source of their existence in the one creator God.

I am not, of course, claiming that such oppositions or contrasts as invisible realm/visible realm, or immaterial/material, have no place in Paul's thought. What I am claiming is that these distinctions must be understood within the context of Paul's more fundamental distinction between creator and creation. Colossians 1:16 helpfully indicates how this works:

> In him all things were created, in the heavens and upon the earth, the visible things and the invisible things, whether thrones or dominions or principalities or powers; all things have been created through him and for him.

Paul's thought in this passage includes several contrasts or oppositions: heaven/earth, visible/invisible, and so forth. But all these are subsumed under, and relativized by, a far more crucial distinction: the distinction between these created beings and the One in, through, and for whom they were created.[22] It is the con-

---

22. Cf. Aquinas, *Summa theologiae* III, q. 16, a. 10: "All that is, is either the creator or the creation." Of course, in Col 1:16 the One in, through, and for whom all things were created is the Son

ceptual "map" on which the other distinctions find their proper place. The contrast between creator and creation is the fundamental distinction in Paul's thought.

Conclusion: Apostle of a Different God

By examining how Paul's gospel would have been heard in the ancient pagan world to which it was addressed, we have discovered the fundamental place of creation within Paul's thought. The world into which Paul's gospel came had no conception of a transcendent creator. The gods of ancient worship, and the philosophical divinities of the Epicureans, the Stoics, the Hindu sages, the Buddha, and Plato, were either identified with the cosmos, or considered products or aspects of it, or believed to coexist alongside an independent and eternal material realm. To this world Paul brought the news of a different God, a different *kind* of God, previously unknown—the creator God, the source of all reality, the transcendent creator who brought all things into being.

In announcing a new God, the creator, Paul brought the good news of a different *cosmos* than his hearers had previously known. It was not a mere material fact without meaning or purpose, nor a degeneration from purer divine being, nor the work of inferior divinities. It was a world that had come into being by the direct creative act of a holy creator, and was thus endowed with an essential goodness and sacredness.

Moreover, Paul claimed that the reality of the creator God, made known in the gospel of Christ, is rationally evident to all through the creation he has made. Paul's version of the cosmological argument, in its premise of an absolute beginning of the universe, was an innovation in philosophy, and its stunning convergence with the modern scientific discovery of an absolute beginning of matter, space, and time has added immeasurably to its remarkable power. However, unlike the philosophers, who sought knowledge of the divine through reason, Paul believed in a living God known through his own self-revelation. He employed reason to corroborate the truthfulness of the knowledge of God that is given by divine revelation and proclaimed in his gospel.

In short, Paul's gospel brought to his ancient hearers the good news that the cosmos was in fact the creation. Indeed, as I have sought to show, the creator God, distinct from his creation, is the fundamental conception within Paul's theology. The apostle to the gentiles was the apostle of creation.

---

of God, Jesus Christ (Col 1:12–20). Here we come to the center of Paul's gospel, which we will explore in part 2.

Chapter Two

The Good News of the Fall

As we saw in the last chapter, to a world with no knowledge of a transcendent creator, Paul brought the startling news of the creator God, and of the God-given and good creation. And yet it would be a mistake to think that Paul's doctrine of the good creation ignored the stark reality of suffering and evil. After all, Paul wrote several of his letters while imprisoned and in chains, awaiting trial (and eventual execution) under the Roman emperor Nero. Comfortable modern scholars sometimes fail to appreciate Paul's life-and-death struggle in prison on behalf of the gospel as the backdrop of many of his epistles. As Robin Scroggs notes of Paul's letter to the Philippians: "The desperate ambiguity of life or death explicitly permeates the first section of the letter and must infiltrate every topic Paul addresses; however, some commentators seem to think Paul was on a Sunday outing while he wrote."[1] Unlike the great sages and philosophers with whom we compare Paul in these pages (with the exception of Socrates), Paul confronted evil and experienced great suffering firsthand, sealing his doctrine with a martyr's death.

But if the cosmos is the good creation of a good creator, what is the origin of evil, sorrow, suffering, and death? Here too Paul's gospel announced an astonishingly different answer to this searching human question. And that answer was good news indeed. It was the good news of the Fall.

The Origin of Evil, Suffering, and Death

Paul's proclamation of the God of Abraham, Isaac, and Jacob, the one, almighty creator God, brought to his hearers a radically new understanding of the origin

---

1. Robin Scroggs, "Paul the Prisoner: Political Asceticism in the Letter to the Philippians," in *Asceticism in the New Testament*, ed. Leif E. Vaage and Vincent L. Wimbush (New York: Routledge, 1999), 187.

of suffering, of evil, and of death. In the ancient world into which Paul's gospel came, suffering and death were believed to be an eternal and unchangeable reality of the cosmic order. Death and suffering, it was believed, were the fated lot of humanity, an eternal decree even the immortal gods were powerless to alter (Homer, *Odyssey* 3.229–38; *Iliad* 16.433; Aeschylus, *Eumenides* 647–49; Cicero, *Concerning Divination* 2.25). So, too, for the philosophers and sages, sorrow, pain, and bodily death were an everlasting fixture of the cosmic scheme. Within Epicurean and Buddhist *materialism*, impermanence and death were eternal features of a universe that had come into being apart from any divine providence or control (Lucretius, *On the Nature of the Universe* 1–3; Gautama Buddha, *Mahavagga* 1). Within Platonic *dualism*, the physical world was the work of lesser, intermediary divinities. Because of the limited power of these lesser gods, and the limitations of matter, human beings were by necessity subject to physical evils and death (Plato, *Timaeus* 41a–42e; 69c–73d). Within Stoic *pantheism*, suffering, pain, and death were unavoidable by-products of the coarse material nature of the body and of the cosmos, a flaw within creation itself, beyond the power of even the highest divinity to forestall (Seneca, *On Providence* 6.5–8; *Letters* 58.27; 107.9–10; Epictetus, *Discourses* 1.1.10–12). In the understanding of life and of the cosmos within the world Paul addressed, suffering, evil, and death were woven from all eternity into the fabric of the universe. In the heart of the nature of things were impermanence and death.

According to Paul's gospel, by contrast, evil, suffering, and death were no part of the original God-given and good creation. They are the result of an event within creation's history, the catastrophic disruption of the original cosmic order through human rebellion (Gen 3). Through this primeval rupture of life-giving communion with God and willing enslavement to evil, suffering and bodily death entered into the creation (Rom 5:12–14; 1 Cor 15:21–22, 56), and the entire cosmos was made subject to futility and decay (Rom 8:19–20, 22).

It is impossible to overstress the importance of this marked contrast between Paul's message and the beliefs of his ancient pagan hearers regarding suffering and death. According to Paul's gospel, the world as it is now is *not* the world a loving and good creator created it to be. Evil, suffering, and bodily death are *enemies* (1 Cor 15:25–26), intruders into the good creation, due not to limitations upon God, the almighty creator, but to cosmic and human rebellion. Death is not (as in the philosophers) a necessary by-product of creation, but the result of the ancient curse that came through humanity's fall (Gen 3:17–19). The great theme of the book of Ecclesiastes within the Old Testament is the vanity, meaninglessness, and futility of human life: "Futility of futilities, all is futility!" (Eccles 1:2). Paul takes up the central term of Ecclesiastes, *mataiotēs*, or "futility," in order powerfully to describe this present blighted condition of the created order: "for the creation has been subjected to futility (Greek: *mataiotēs*)" (Rom 8:20). But in Paul this is an *inversion* of creation, not the original purpose of its design. For Paul's ancient pagan hearers, the cosmos was a world flawed by necessity; according to Paul's gospel, the cosmos is a good world spoiled.[2]

The ancient philosophers and sages were in agreement that the ultimate Reality was either indifferent to human suffering and death or powerless to alter it. They differed only as to the proper way to cope with this tragic reality. Against this background, the philosophical implications of Paul's characterization of death as God's "enemy" (1 Cor 15:26) are enormous. This was a striking and *new* philosophical claim, which put all of reality in a new light. It affirms that this world is neither an alien place, to be escaped (as in Platonism and Buddhism), nor a dark and tragically flawed homeland, to be endured with resignation (as in Stoicism), but *enemy-occupied territory*. It distinguishes (in a way the ancient philosophers could not have imagined) between the God-given and good creation, and the death and evil that now infect it. And it proclaims an almighty and good creator who is neither the author of death, nor indifferent to it, but its implacable enemy—and, as we will see, its ultimate conqueror. A crucial part of Paul's good news was the good news of the Fall.

The primordial act of human rebellion against their creator that brought about the present altered state of the creation is called by theologians the fall of humanity. This event is narrated in the first pages of Israel's Scriptures, and is implicit throughout. But within the Bible, the nature and implications of this event are fleshed out most fully in Paul's letters. In what did the Fall consist, and in what sense according to Paul is humanity "fallen" from its original creation? To understand this, we must first explore Paul's teaching regarding humanity as originally created by God.

Pauline Anthropology: Human Beings as Originally Created

To delineate Paul's anthropology (that is, his doctrine of humanity), we must explore Paul's understanding of human beings in regard to their bodies, their souls, their differentiation as men and women, and their identity as image-bearers of God.

---

2. I owe the analogy to C. S. Lewis, *Miracles: A Preliminary Study* (New York: Macmillan, 1947), 125–26.

The Body

The ancient sages generally viewed human embodiment—the fact that human beings are physical creatures with bodies of flesh and bones—in a negative light. The Stoic philosopher Seneca considered the body the prison of the soul, by which it is encumbered and from which it longs to be freed (*Letters* 65.16–17, 21; 71.16; 92.33–34; 102.22–23). So, too, for Cratippus the Aristotelian philosopher, the soul was weighed down by "the chains of the body" (in Cicero, *Concerning Divination* 1.70, 110–15, 129). The Buddha regarded personal physical existence as the source of all sorrow and suffering, and taught his followers how they might escape it (*Anguttara Nikāya* 3.90, 103–5, 116). Porphyry described the negative view of the body that underlay the ancient practice of suicide by immolation among the sages of India (Porphyry, *On Abstinence* 4.18; cf. Arrian, *Anabasis* 7.2–3; Cicero, *Concerning Divination* 1.47). According to Plato's teaching, the body was the work of inferior, lesser divinities (*Timaeus* 41a–42c; 69b–d; 76e–77c). In striking contrast with such views, Paul's gospel proclaimed that not only the soul, but also the physical body, was the direct, immediate work of the creator. "And the Lord God formed Adam from the dust of the earth, and breathed into his nostrils the breath of life, and the man became a living soul" (Gen 2:7, quoted by Paul in 1 Cor 15:45). The body, therefore, was the good and holy work of God (1 Cor 6:13–14; 7:34). In Paul's thought, firmly founded in the Jewish Scriptures, physical embodiment is a part of the good creation.

The Soul

Alongside this important difference between Paul and the philosophers regarding the human body was a significant point of agreement regarding the soul. In the world Paul's gospel addressed, both the common person and the philosopher assumed that human beings were made up of not only a body but also a soul (or spirit), the inner principle of life, consciousness, feeling, thought, and will. Contemporary philosophers call this *substance dualism*—the belief that the human being consists of not only a body but also a soul. Here we see an important point of agreement or contact with Paul's gospel, for Paul also speaks of the soul (*psychē*) or spirit (*pneuma*), distinct from the body, within each person (1 Cor 2:11; 7:34; Phil 2:30; Col 3:23; 1 Thess 5:23; cf. Acts 17:16; 20:10). The ancient philosophers produced elaborate theories about the soul, dissecting its varied parts and functions (see, for example, Aristotle, *Soul*; Plato, *Republic* 4; *Phaedrus* 245–46; *Timaeus* 69c–72d; Lucretius, *On the Nature of the Universe* 3; Chrysippus, in *Stoicorum Veterum Fragmenta* 2.790–911). Paul, by contrast, does not provide a systematic doctrine or analysis of the soul (although many interpreters have tried to find one!), but is content to employ the terms "soul" and "spirit" in their common, everyday meaning.[3]

Body and Soul

However, Paul's understanding of the soul *is* very different from three philosophical views of the soul with which in our contemporary world it is sometimes confused. The first is the doctrine of the Stoics and the Hindu sages that the soul is itself divine, a fragment or offshoot of the highest divinity (Seneca, *Letters* 31.11; 66.12; *Brihadaranyaka Upanishad* 1.4.7–10; *Bhagavad Gita* 6.24–32). The second is Plato's teaching that the soul is uncreated and eternal, without beginning or end (Plato, *Phaedrus* 245–46; cf. *Bhagavad Gita* 2.12–25). By contrast, in Paul's teaching, as throughout the Bible, the soul is distinct from God, created together with the body as the handiwork of the creator (Rom 1:9; 1 Cor 15:45; 1 Thess 5:23; cf. Gen 2:7; Isa 42:5; Zech 12:1). A third philosophic view of the soul in contrast with Paul's understanding also belongs to Plato. In Platonic dualism, as we have seen, the supreme divinity was the source of the highest, divine aspect of the human soul, whereas the body and the lower, body-related aspects of the soul were the work of inferior beings (Plato, *Timaeus* 41a–42e). Plato therefore held to a radical version of substance dualism that philosophers sometimes call *self-body dualism*. On this view, the real person or self is the soul, which uses the body as its instrument. Many people in our society today are default self-body dualists, believing the physical body to be extraneous to an individual's personhood and true identity. Many assume that this is the understanding implicit in Paul's letters.

But although Paul's anthropology is a form of substance dualism (recognizing the distinction between the body and the soul), it is entirely incompatible with body-self dualism. For in Paul's teaching the person or self *includes* the body as well as the soul. Thus Paul always speaks of the person as a *composite being* made up of a body as well as a spirit or soul (Rom 1:9; 1 Cor 2:11; 1 Thess 5:23). In Paul's teaching, the body, as the good creation of God, is an integral aspect of the fullness of the human being. Body and soul were made for each other.

3. For further discussion, see Herman Ridderbos, *Paul: An Outline of His Theology*, trans. John Richard De Witt (Grand Rapids: Eerdmans, 1975), 120–21; Joseph Fitzmyer, *Pauline Theology: A Brief Sketch* (Englewood Cliffs, NJ: Prentice-Hall, 1967), 61–62.

Sex and Gender

This dimension of Paul's teaching is controversial within our contemporary cultural climate. But it is crucial for grasping Pauline anthropology. The disagreement of Paul and Plato regarding the goodness of human embodiment and its relation to personhood involves another key difference. In the Platonic view, sexual differentiation (that is, the bodily distinction between man and woman) came about as a deterioration from humanity's original creation, the result of human wickedness (Plato, *Timaeus* 90e–91d). Moreover, within Plato's self-body dualism, one's biological sex, being a bodily and visible feature, is no part of one's true personhood or identity. Similarly for many contemporary persons, one's identity as a man or a woman is a psychological state that may or may not correspond to the visible body. On this view, binary sex difference (that is, human identity as either male or female) is a mere social construct, and gender identity in reality belongs on a fluid spectrum of multiple possibilities—I may choose or be inwardly impelled to identify as a man, a woman, or something different altogether, irrespective of my physical embodiment as male or female.

According to Paul's gospel, by contrast, binary sexual difference is an intrinsic and indelible feature of the original and good creation. "And God created human beings in his image, in the image of God he created them, male and female he created them" (Gen 1:27; echoed by Paul in Rom 1:26–27; 1 Cor 11:7; Eph 4:24; Col 3:10). Because in Pauline and biblical anthropology the self includes the body, one's bodily and visible identity as a man or a woman is an essential aspect of one's human identity. It is the sacred gift of God (1 Cor 11:11–12).[4] So sacred is this gift of embodied manhood and womanhood that, as we will see in chapter 12, Paul understands the physical complementarity of male and female as a mysterious foreshadowing within the created order of the union of Christ with the church (Eph 5:31–32). And this gift of sexual complementarity, through its attendant gift of procreation, made possible that feature of human life that Plato wished to

---

4. Modern science's discovery of the body's chromosomal structure, which reveals that human identity as male or female is not merely a matter of different sexual organs but pervades every cell of the human body, is in notable agreement with this Pauline and biblical conception of gender as an intrinsic aspect of the human person. The phenomenon of intersex persons (individuals of potentially ambiguous physical sex due to a rare congenital defect) is not a new discovery, but was well known in antiquity (Matt 19:12; Cicero, *Concerning Divination* 1.98; Pliny the Elder, *Natural History* 7.34; Lucian, *Parliament of the Gods* 23.1). Within the Bible, intersex persons are always treated with dignity and welcomed fully into the redeemed community (Isa 56:3–5; Jer 38:7–13; 39:15–18; Acts 8:26–39). However, the argument that this congenital abnormality calls into question the reality of binary sex difference has no scientific or logical basis.

obliterate for the philosophic class (Plato, *Republic* 5) but that Paul proclaimed Christ had come to renew and sanctify: marriage and the family. For Plato, human identity as male or female (and in particular as female [*Timaeus* 90e]) is a restriction, a declension, and a fall. Paul's gospel, by contrast, affirmed the goodness of the created world of men and women, husbands and wives, mothers and fathers, and brothers and sisters (1 Cor 7:1–16; Eph 6:1–4; Col 3:20–21; Titus 2:2–5). Just as Plato's erasure of embodied sexual difference from the essence of the human person was rooted in his negative view of the body and of the material world, Paul's belief in the God-given and good nature of embodied sexual difference is the necessary corollary of his belief in the essential goodness of the human body and of all creation.

The Image of God

Within the Genesis narrative, human beings are the pinnacle of God's creation (Gen 1:26–31), distinguished from all the rest of God's creatures by their creation "in the image of God" (Gen 1:26–27). In what did this "image of God" consist, according to Pauline theology?[5] Here the key Pauline theme of the renewal of the divine likeness in those who believe (which we will explore in chapter 11) provides the crucial data. In light of Paul's description of the restoration of the divine image in Christ (2 Cor 3:17–18; 4:4–6; Eph 2:14–18; 4:20–24; Col 3:9–11), it becomes apparent that in Paul's thought the "image of God" consisted in humanity's creation in *an original state of union with the creator, sharing in the divine glory, life, righteousness, and holiness.* Through this union with the creator, body and soul were in harmonious unity. And through this participation in God, the source of all life, human beings were endowed with the fullness of life, free from suffering, sorrow, and death (Rom 5:12).

There is yet another dimension of the image of God that, although regularly overlooked, is crucial within Paul's thought (and in biblical thought as a whole): humanity's original creation in a state of union with their maker was not static but dynamic, for it was a state to be perfected through humanity's free response of trust in and devotion to the creator. Thus, in both the Genesis narrative and Paul's exposition of that narrative, Adam and Eve were created with bodies that were free from death (Gen 2:17; 3:2–3; so Rom 5:12), but not in permanent possession

---

5. I am especially indebted in the paragraphs that follow to the insights into the Pauline (and larger biblical) theology of the Fall in John S. Romanides, *The Ancestral Sin*, trans. George S. Gabriel (Ridgewood, NJ: Zephyr, 2002).

of imperishability or immortality (Gen 3:19; so 1 Cor 15:45–49). Immortality or everlasting life (the "tree of life," Gen 2:9; 3:22) was a gift to be bestowed as a result of their free decision of communion with God (2 Cor 11:2–3).[6] This dynamic conception of the image of God reveals the crucial place, within Paul's conception of humanity, of human free will or self-determination. The divine image, and the divine communion and life it enabled, was a gift of the creator, but a gift that could only be fulfilled and perfected through humanity's free decision to partake of the fullness of this divine life. The divine-human relationship was thus in Paul's thought from the beginning a *covenantal* relationship, a mutual intercommunion of love between creature and creator.

Just as Paul brought the good news of the creator God to an ancient world with no prior conception of a transcendent creator, so this fundamental premise of Pauline theology—that the fulfillment of human existence is found in a fellowship of love with its creator—has no parallel in the ancient world. Epicurean and Buddhist *materialism*, in which there is no creator and the gods are finite parts of the cosmic whole without concern for human beings, obviously precludes any such notion. According to Platonic *dualism*, human beings (or at least ordinary human beings) can have no knowledge of the supreme being. In Stoic and Hindu *pantheism*, the human soul is itself eternal and divine, a fragment of deity dwelling in the mortal human body, and thus identical with God (Seneca, *Letters* 31.9–11; 48.11; 66.12; 73.16; 120.14; Posidonius, in Cicero, *Concerning Divination* 1.64; *Brihadaranyaka Upanishad* 4). But identity precludes the possibility of relationship. In Paul's anthropology, by contrast, human beings are creatures called to a communion of love with their creator. Distinct from God, human beings are created for friendship with God. Augustine classically expressed this central biblical and Pauline conception when he wrote: "O God, you have made us for yourself, and our heart is restless, until it finds its rest in you" (*Confessions* 1.1) .

Pauline Anthropology: Human Beings as Fallen

According to Paul's gospel, the fall of humanity belonged to a larger cosmic narrative, in which the context and source of humanity's temptation to original evil was a prior rebellion of Satan, a personal spiritual being of great power, good in his original creation by God but now in malevolent opposition to the creator and to his creation (Rom 16:20 [echoing Gen 3:15]; 2 Cor 11:3; 1 Thess 3:5; 1 Tim 3:6).

---

6. For recognition of this key element of the Genesis narrative and of Pauline theology, see Theophilus, *To Autolycus* 2.27; Aquinas, *Summa theologiae* I, q. 97.

Paul portrays the Fall, humanity's free decision to follow Satan in rebellion against God (Rom 5:12), as a betrayal of the covenant of love with the creator (2 Cor 11:3). Paul also depicts this rebellion as an act of idolatry—that is, giving trust or worship to someone or something other than the creator (Rom 1:22–23, echoing Gen 3:6). In the Fall, humanity rejected communion with God for the sake of that which is not God.[7] And, according to Paul, this inversion of the proper relation between creature and creator brought about a radical change in human nature (Rom 5:12–18). In what did this change consist?

A key passage is Paul's synopsis of the state of post-Fall humanity in Romans 3:23: "all have sinned and are bereft of the glory of God." The first clause ("all have sinned") affirms that the fall of Adam is replicated in the life of each human being (cf. Rom 3:10–20; 5:12–14; Gal 3:10–12). All human beings "share in Adam's loss, but as those who willingly follow the same path."[8] The second clause ("are bereft of the glory of God") points to an alteration in human nature that came through Adam's transgression, and is at the roots of this universal replication of Adam's sin (cf. Rom 5:19, "through the one man's disobedience all were made sinners"). "Adam's transgression was more than the pattern for future transgressions: it *made* Adam's progeny sinners."[9] In what sense were all made sinners by Adam's fall? Romans 3:23 is often translated as: "for all have sinned and fall short of the glory of God." For many English readers, such a translation implies that the dilemma of post-Fall human beings is their failure to attain to the standard ("fall short of") of God's righteous requirements (rather confusingly described, on this reading, as "the glory of God"). But Paul's Greek cannot mean this. The verb usually translated "fall short" is *hystereō*, which means to be in lack or destitution. What Paul affirms in Romans 3:23 is that all "fall short" in the sense that they are *destitute* or *bereft* of the glory of God. Elsewhere Paul closely relates the glory of God and the divine image (1 Cor 11:7; 2 Cor 3:18; 4:4, 6). According to Romans 3:23, then, the fallen nature of humanity involves precisely the *loss* or *effacement* of the image of God, that is, rupture of the glorifying, sanctifying, and life-giving communion with the Spirit of God with which humanity was originally created (cf. Rom 5:12, 17–21; 8:2–8; Gal 3:21–22). This loss of communion with God was replaced by active enslavement to Satan and demonic powers subordinate to him, created but powerful and malevolent spiritual beings opposed to God and hostile to humanity (Rom 8:38–39; 1 Cor 2:6–8; 15:24–28; 2 Cor 4:4; Gal 4:3, 8–9; Eph 2:1–3; 1 Tim 4:1).

---

7. For this way of putting the matter I am indebted to Stephen E. Fowl.

8. Anthony C. Thiselton, *The Living Paul: An Introduction to the Apostle's Life and Thought* (Downers Grove: InterVarsity, 2009), 79.

9. Frank J. Matera, *God's Saving Grace: A Pauline Theology* (Grand Rapids: Eerdmans, 2012), 92.

Theologians use the term "original sin" to denote this Pauline conception of fallen human nature, deprived of union with God, as the *origin* of all sinful acts. Although some would object to this term, the concept it expresses is clearly present in Paul's letters. When Paul uses the word "sin" (Greek: *hamartia*), he uses it most frequently in the singular ("sin," not "sins"), in order to describe, not sinful *actions*, but this *state* or condition of separation from the Spirit of God and enslavement to demonic powers that is the source of sinful acts (Rom 3:9; 5:12, 20–21; 6:12; 7:7–25; 8:2; Gal 3:22).

Estranged from union with God, the whole human being, body and soul, is enslaved to moral evil (Rom 6:6, 19–21; 7:1–25). And the result of this bondage to sin is *dehumanization*—the corruption and defacement, through moral evil, of the humanity originally given by God (Rom 1:24–32; Eph 4:17–19; 1 Thess 4:5; Titus 3:3).[10] In Paul's theology, if you separate humanity made in God's image from its creator, the result is not the merely human—it is the inhuman. Consistent with his doctrine of the body as an intrinsic component of the human person, a prominent feature of the dehumanization Paul describes is the misuse of the body through sexual immorality (Rom 1:24–27; 1 Cor 6:9–11; Gal 5:19–21; Eph 5:3–7; Col 3:5–7). Through original sin (the rupture of life-giving communion with God), all human beings now share a nature that is hostile to God, enslaved to evil, and under divine judgment (Rom 3:9–20, 22–23; 5:12–14; 6:20–21; 8:5–8; Gal 3:21–22; Eph 2:1–3; Col 1:21; 2:13–14).[11]

Paul frequently describes this divine judgment as "the wrath of God" (Rom 1:18; 2:5, 8; 3:5; 5:9; Eph 2:3; 5:6; Col 3:6; 1 Thess 1:10). Modern persons often find this concept troubling, because they believe it conflicts with God's love. But, fortunately, this is a misunderstanding of Paul's teaching. God's love belongs to his very *nature* (2 Cor 13:11, "the God of love and peace"; Gal 5:22, "the fruit of the Spirit is love"; cf. 1 John 4:16, "God is love"). God's wrath, by contrast, does not belong to his nature, but is *consequent* upon human sin and rebellion (Rom 1:18; Eph 2:3; 5:6; Col 3:6). Paul in Romans 2 defines this wrath by synonymous parallelism as "the righteous judgment of God" (Rom 2:5; cf. 2 Thess 1:5–10). It is the necessary response of a holy God to evil. Indeed, if God were not implacably opposed to evil, he would not be good. And yet God's love *delights in* neither evil nor his wrath. As we will see, the central mystery of Paul's gospel is the love of God who sent his Son to *save* fallen humanity from his wrath (Rom 5:8–9; Eph 2:3–7; Titus 3:3–7).

---

10. See N. T. Wright, *What Saint Paul Really Said: Was Paul of Tarsus the Real Founder of Christianity?* (Grand Rapids: Eerdmans, 1997), 136–40.

11. For an excellent summary of these various aspects of the state of post-Fall humanity as they are developed in Paul's individual letters, see Matera, *God's Saving Grace*, 88–102.

In Romans 1 Paul describes the idolatry of fallen humanity in words borrowed from the creation account in Genesis 1 ("they exchanged the glory of the ever-living *God* for the *likeness* of an *image* of a corruptible *human being*, and of *birds* and of *cattle* and of *creeping things*," Rom 1:23 [cf. Gen 1:26]), in order to depict humanity's alienation from its creator as the *inversion* of the good and divinely intended created order. According to Paul's theology, as we have seen, this inversion or reversal was cosmic in its effects. Through the rupture of creation brought about by the Fall, physical, bodily death received its power over humanity (Rom 5:12; 1 Cor 15:21–22) and the good created order became infected with disorder and futility (Rom 8:19–20).

Paul's Doctrine of Original Sin in Its Ancient Context

We have seen that Paul's proclamation of a good cosmos spoiled had no parallel in the world into which his gospel came. Paul's ancient hearers would have likewise found his doctrine of universal human sin startling, but not in the way we might expect. The ancient philosophers in general readily acknowledged the universal or near-universal moral corruption and wickedness of humankind (see, for instance, the Platonist philosopher Cotta's searing indictment of humanity in Cicero, *On the Nature of the Gods* 3.65–79). But they believed that this moral darkness and propensity to evil was an outworking of human nature as it had always been—and always will be. Even the Epicureans and Stoics, who held that humanity had declined from a past "golden age" of relative innocence and blessedness (Lucretius, *On the Nature of the Universe* 5.925–1135; Seneca, *Letters* 90; 95.13–35), did not attribute this decline to any change or corruption of human nature. They would have been astonished by Paul's claim that moral evil was not natural, but unnatural; that it did not belong to the nature of human beings as originally created, but belonged to the corrupted nature of human beings now fallen. Paul's gospel announced that moral evil did not have its source in the creator, nor any place in the original creation. Paul's sober news about the Fall brought with it the good news of a holy creator and his good creation.

Paul's hearers would have been arrested not only by Paul's message regarding evil as a usurper, but also by the radical character of evil in Paul's preaching. The philosophers one and all believed that the universe and human beings are deeply flawed, but offered therapeutic methods to improve human nature and cope with a flawed cosmos. The Stoics counseled noble resignation, Buddha taught detachment, Plato recommended education. The philosophers conceived a world of everlasting and unchanging gray, but suggested methods to make the bleak picture more bearable. Paul's gospel proclaimed a world created bright and luminous, but now shrouded in deep darkness. It proclaimed a humanity made in the image of God, the pinnacle of God's creation, but now corrupted by sin and under God's wrath. His diagnosis of the human condition was stark: fallen humanity was under the dominion of Satan and demonic powers, estranged from its creator, without hope, and without God in the world (Rom 6:17–23; Eph 2:1–3, 11–12; Col 1:21; Titus 3:3). As we will see, Paul's "good news" did not offer palliatives or coping mechanisms for a world tinged with gray, but offered the promise of a pitch-dark world made shining and luminous once again.

And Paul's hearers would have been struck by an entirely new and different vision of the purpose of human existence, which has but a shadowy parallel in Plato's conception of the moral life oriented toward desire of "the good beyond being" (Plato, *Republic* 6, 504d–509b). For Paul's proclamation of original sin, rooted deeply in his doctrine of the Fall, had a corollary, rooted deeply in his doctrine of creation. It was the good news that human beings, however much now estranged from God, were created for fellowship with their creator. His gospel was a call to enter that fellowship.

Creation and Fall as the Map for Paul's Theology

In the previous chapter, I proposed that from Paul's conception of the creator God, distinct from his creation, there arises a fundamental distinction or relation within his thought, which may be illustrated thus:

Creator
—
Creation

This, I argued, is the fundamental category within Paul's *ontology*—that is, his understanding of the whole of reality. Related to this is a second major relation or distinction within Paul's thought, having to do with the intended relationship of the creator to the human creatures made in his image. It is the key to Pauline *anthropology*—that is, his understanding of the nature and destiny of humanity. Paul's conception of humanity as originally created, in contrast with humanity as fallen, focuses upon the following distinction or opposition:

Union with the Creator
—
Separation from the Creator

The two dualities or distinctions delineated above, which grow directly out of Paul's fundamental doctrines of creation and fall, provide the proper interpretive map or guide for navigating Paul's letters. All of Paul's varied distinctions or contrasts (flesh/spirit, heavenly/earthly, church/world, etc.) "map" onto these fundamental categories. As in the previous chapter I gave an example of the power of the first category, the distinction between creator and creation, to illumine Paul's thought, I will give here an example of the second. This example will take us beyond creation and fall to provide a glimpse of the redemptive work of Christ that will be the subject of the rest of this book.

A dominant and recurring motif in Paul's epistles is the contrast or opposition between flesh and spirit (Rom 2:28–29; 7:4–6; 8:3–14; 1 Cor 3:1–4; Gal 3:2–3; 5:16–25). Given its importance in Paul, a proper understanding of this feature of Paul's thought is absolutely crucial for a genuine grasp of Paul's theology. It is clear that when Paul *contrasts* flesh and spirit, "spirit" has a positive value and "flesh" normally has a negative value. Some Pauline scholars regard Paul's negative evaluation of the "flesh" as obvious evidence that Paul disparaged the body and the material world as inherently evil and sinful. As a result, they believe that Paul regarded the created order in its bodily and material aspects as less than fully good, and the physical creation as something to be escaped.[12] Average readers of Paul's letters often assume that Paul's opposition of flesh and spirit denotes at least *some* kind of negative judgment of the body and of physical, space-time existence, with the presumed goal of salvation therefore being some form of existence that is "spiritual" in the sense of nonbodily, angelic, or immaterial.

But, as this and the previous chapter have shown, Paul's doctrine of the goodness of the cosmos, of matter, and of the human body—as the direct handiwork of a holy creator—reveals that this is a profoundly mistaken reading of his theology. And I would propose that the mistake is the result of mapping Paul's language of "flesh" and "spirit," perhaps without realizing it, onto a master grid that is not Pauline at all, but rather (following philosophic categories of thought that have filtered down to all of us whether we know it or not) Platonic, Cartesian, or Hege-

---

12. See, for example, Nikolaus Walter, "Leibliche Auferstehung? Zur Frage der Hellenisierung der Auferweckungshoffnung bei Paulus," in *Paulus, Apostel Jesu Christi*, ed. Michael Trowitzsch (Tübingen: Mohr Siebeck, 1998); Andreas Lindemann, *Der Erste Korintherbrief* (Tübingen: Mohr Siebeck, 2000), 324–73; Mark D. Given, "Paul and Writing," in *As It Is Written: Studying Paul's Use of Scripture*, ed. Stanley E. Porter and Christopher D. Stanley, SBLSS 50 (Atlanta: Society of Biblical Literature, 2008), 255–56; Peter Lampe, "Paul's Concept of a Spiritual Body," in *Resurrection: Theological and Scientific Assessments*, ed. Ted Peters, Robert John Russell, and Michael Welker (Grand Rapids: Eerdmans, 2002), 103–14; and Hans Grass, *Ostergeschehen und Osterberichte* (Göttingen: Vandenhoeck & Ruprecht, 1962), 146–73.

lian. As a result, we map Paul's distinction between flesh and spirit to some such antithesis or contrast as these:

"Spirit"		Spirit		Immaterial
————————	*maps to*	————————	*or*	————————
"Flesh"		Matter		Material

I wish to propose an entirely different way of reading Paul's contrast of flesh and spirit: Paul's contrast is one way in which he expresses the master contrast or opposition that informs his entire anthropology:

"Spirit"		Union with the Creator
————————————————	*maps to*	————————————————
"Flesh"		Separation from the Creator

Paul's contrast, then, is between the life of fallen humanity untouched by the Spirit and power of God, and union with God in Christ through the gift of the Holy Spirit. Reading the relevant Pauline passages in this creational context, rather than in a context foreign to them, illumines them immediately. Consider the following passages:

> Did you *receive the Spirit* through works of the law or by hearing with faith? Are you so foolish? Having begun with the Spirit, are you now being perfected by the flesh? (Gal 3:2–3)

> For we are the circumcision, who worship *in the Spirit of God*, and boast in Christ Jesus, and put no trust in the flesh. (Phil 3:3)

> But you are not in the flesh, but in the Spirit, *if indeed the Spirit of God dwells in you.* (Rom 8:9)

The point, then, of Paul's contrast of flesh and the Spirit has nothing to do with a contrast between bodily and nonbodily existence, with the implication that the body is to be discarded, to facilitate some nonphysical mode of being. Rather, the "flesh" refers to a state of *privation*, bereft of the transforming power of the Spirit (cf. Rom 3:23, "*destitute of* the glory of God"). It is Paul's shorthand for human nature marred by the Fall. And Paul contrasts this with the restoration of human nature through the communion of the whole composite human being, body and soul, in the life-giving Spirit of God.[13] This is the union with their creator for which human beings were made, and which, as we will see, the Son of God came to restore.

Conclusion: The Fallen Creation and the Good Creator

Paul's gospel of creation brought a new understanding of the origin of evil, suffering, and death. To an ancient world that believed suffering and death were necessary and eternal realities of the natural order, Paul proclaimed that death and suffering were unnatural intruders into the good creation, the result of a catastrophic disruption of the original cosmic order through a primordial act of human rebellion against the creator. And to a world that considered moral darkness and evil an essential and divinely given aspect of human nature, Paul's doctrine of original sin announced that moral evil had no place in human beings as originally created, but belonged to the corrupted nature of human beings now fallen. Paul's gospel thus proclaimed not only creation but also fall. But the flip side of Paul's grave news regarding the Fall was the good news of the holy creator, human beings made in his image, and the God-given and good creation.

Paul's gospel also brought a new understanding of the human person. To a world that generally viewed the soul as the true self and disparaged the body, Paul's gospel proclaimed that the body, including its gendered nature as male and female, was the good and holy creation of God, and an integral aspect of the fullness of the human being. According to Paul's gospel, humanity was created in an original state of union with the creator, but through the loss of this sanctifying and life-giving communion with God fallen humanity was now corrupted by sin and under God's wrath. All this was new for Paul's ancient gentile hearers. But they would perhaps have been struck most of all by a claim at the heart of Paul's doctrine of the Fall, a claim without parallel in pagan religion and philosophy. It was the claim of Paul's gospel that the fulfillment of existence is found in a fellowship of love with its creator—and the invitation of his gospel to enter into that communion of love through Jesus Christ.

I have proposed that from Paul's fundamental conceptions of creation and fall arise two essential distinctions or oppositions that structure all of Paul's thought, and provide an interpretive key that illumines all of Paul's letters. The first moves

---

13. For insightful reading of "flesh and Spirit" in Paul along similar lines, see David Wenham, *Paul: Follower of Jesus or Founder of Christianity?* (Grand Rapids: Eerdmans, 1995), 230–32.

on the level of creation, and is the distinction between creator and creation. The second belongs on the level of both creation and fall, and is the contrast between union with the creator (humanity as originally created) and separation from the creator (humanity as now fallen). The two halves of this latter counterpole are a collision and a contradiction. The Fall marred human nature, created for union with God, and opened an unbridgeable gulf between humanity and its creator. But the other Pauline binary, that of creator and creation, is not a contradiction, but a distinction. Or rather, it is a relation. And within that relation lies the possibility that the One who created all things, the unlimited and almighty creator, would, in some unfathomable way, act to bridge the unbridgeable gulf, restore fallen humanity, heal fallen human nature, and renew the entire creation.

Paul's gospel is the good news of how that possibility became reality in Jesus Christ. And that is why creation is the foundation, but not the very heart and center, of Paul's gospel. The heart of Paul's gospel presupposes his doctrine of creation but involves an even more startling claim. It involves a claim that had no equivalent or parallel in the ancient gentile world, for that world had no conception of a transcendent creator. It was the claim that the creator has entered his creation. It was the good news of the incarnation.

Part Two

Incarnation

Chapter Three

The Two Streams of Expectation

I n the historic Christian creeds, as in Paul's theology, the creation is fundamental: "I believe in one God, the Father almighty, maker of heaven and earth, of all things visible and invisible." But the central affirmation of these creeds is the incarnation: the entrance of the creator into his creation in the person of Jesus of Nazareth. Jesus the Nazarene, born of the Virgin Mary, is "the only-begotten Son of God, eternally begotten of the Father, God from God, Light from Light, true God from true God." The core claim of the Christian faith is that Jesus is the creator God come in the flesh. Intimately joined to this, as we see in the Trinitarian structure of the creeds themselves, is the revelation of the mysterious triune nature of the one God: Father, Son, and Holy Spirit.

Historically, the chief sources among the biblical authors for the language and categories of the church's Christology (the branch of theology that seeks to explore the person and identity of Jesus Christ) were the writings of John and Paul. Ironically, however, in the previous century it was widely held by scholars of Paul that the doctrine of Jesus's divinity was a post-Pauline invention, and that the church's traditional Trinitarian reading of Paul's Christology was a false imposition upon his writings. But in the past few decades the actual evidence of Paul's letters has led to a welcome revolution in scholarly understanding of Pauline Christology. The majority of Pauline scholars today hold that Paul's letters, like John's Gospel, reveal what is called a "divine" or "high" Christology in essential continuity with the great creeds. However, a small minority of scholars still argue (as did many scholars in the previous century) that Paul's epistles evince a "low" Christology identifying Jesus as God's chief messenger or servant, but not God himself.[1]

In this chapter I will be writing in strong agreement with the majority scholarly view, but will also seek to bring greater depth and clarity to the discussion, unlocking the riches of Paul's divine and incarnational Christology. In this book we are seeking to illumine Paul's thought using a twofold method, studying his gospel

---

1. For the relevant scholarly literature reflecting each of these views, see the notes in chapter 4.

in light of its Jewish and biblical context, and in comparison with the religious and philosophical beliefs of the ancient gentile world into which his gospel came. But in this chapter and throughout part 2 of this book, our predominant focus will be the first of those two lenses, the study of Paul's gospel in the context of Israel's hopes and Scriptures. For unlocking Paul's theology of the incarnation, and the uniqueness of that message for the gentile world, will involve grasping the foundations of that message in the revelation previously given to ancient Israel. And so we will begin this chapter by exploring the theology of God and expectations of his coming reign in the Old Testament. Placing Paul's letters firmly within their ancient Jewish and biblical context will enable us to grasp Paul's answer to Jesus's question to his disciples, "Who do you say that I am?"

The Exodus and Its Climax: The Name and Presence of God

Throughout the Old Testament, the distinction between the creator and his creation is foundational. An infinite metaphysical gulf differentiates the creator God from the creation that is his handiwork (Gen 14:19; 2 Kings 19:15; 2 Chron 2:12; Neh 9:6; Isa 40:28; 42:5; 44:24; 66:2). But it would be a bad mistake to suppose that this affirmation of God's transcendence involves the idea of a distant, unknowable, or indifferent God. Instead, as we saw in chapter 2, within the biblical conception human beings were created for fellowship with God (Gen 1–2), and the tragedy of the Fall consists in the separation of humanity from its creator (Gen 3–11). The entire biblical narrative of redemption that follows, from Genesis 12 onward, may be described as the story of the work of God to restore this union and fellowship between the creator and human beings made in his image.

In the opening scene of this redemptive story, the creator God reveals himself as the *covenant* God to Abraham, Isaac, and Jacob (Gen 12–50). In this Abrahamic covenant God promises to make Abraham's family a great nation and to give them a land of plenty as their inheritance (Gen 12:1–3; 15:1–21; 17:1–27; 22:15–18). Moreover, the creator God enters into an intimate union of covenantal love with Abraham and his family to come, a relationship summed up in what scholars call the "covenant formula": "I will be your God, and you will be my people" (Gen 17:7–8; Exod 6:6–7; 19:5–6; Lev 26:12; Jer 7:22–23; Ezek 37:27). But the Abrahamic covenant has a wider horizon, for its climactic promise reveals that its ultimate purpose is the redemption of all humanity: "in your seed all the peoples of the earth will be blessed" (Gen 12:3; 22:18). The curse that came through the Fall (Gen 3:17–19) will be undone by the blessing promised to Abraham. The Abrahamic covenant is foundational for the whole Bible, including Paul's letters, and will be the focus of part 3 of this book.

A crucial moment in God's self-revelation to his covenant people occurs on the verge of the exodus, at the burning bush, where Moses asks God to reveal to him his name:

> [13]And Moses said to God, "Behold, I am going to the sons of Israel, and I will say to them, 'The God of your fathers has sent me to you.' And they will say to me, 'What is his name?' What shall I say to them?" [14]And God said to Moses, "I AM WHO I AM." And he said, "Thus you shall say to the sons of Israel, 'I AM has sent me to you.'" [15]Then God spoke again to Moses: "Thus you shall say to the sons of Israel, 'The Lord, the God of your fathers, the God of Abraham, the God of Isaac, and the God of Jacob has sent me to you.' This is my name forever, my name of remembrance to all generations." (Exod 3:13–15)

God's initial answer, essentially a rejection of Moses's request, is grounded in the unfathomable mystery of God, beyond all human comprehension—"I AM WHO I AM" (3:14). But then, without diminishing the mystery, God in his grace reveals his name to Moses: "The Lord, the God of your fathers, the God of Abraham, the God of Isaac, and the God of Jacob" (3:15). Lying beneath the designation "the Lord" in the original Hebrew of verse 15 is a *name*, the sacred name "Yahweh" (hereafter YHWH). Even more hallowed than the divine title "God" was the divine name YHWH. Over the course of centuries the Jewish people ceased to pronounce this sacred name of God aloud, substituting the Hebrew word *Adonai* (in Greek translation *kyrios*), which means "Lord." (This is why throughout the Old Testament most English translations of the Bible render the Hebrew name YHWH as "the Lord.") When used in this way, the word "Lord" (whether in its Hebrew form *Adonai* or its Greek form *kyrios*) functioned no longer as a title, but as the very name of God.

In revealing to Moses his name, the creator God truly *makes himself known* to Israel. Although it is hidden from the English reader, in the original Hebrew the name YHWH in verse 15 is the third person form of the verb "I AM" in verse 14, and thus means "The One Who Is." The name "The One Who Is" expresses that God's existence, his dynamic, living being, belongs to his very nature or essence. He is the Existing One, the living God. He alone can give life, creating out of nothing, bringing being out of nonbeing from the fullness of his own being. The name YHWH thus identifies Israel's God as the one true creator God. Yet the name YHWH, in being drawn from the preceding words "I AM WHO I AM," also recalls that statement's declaration of the creator God's transcendence and incomprehensibility. Thus, in giving his name, God truly reveals himself—and yet the unfathomable mystery of God remains.

The most important occurrence of the divine name in the Old Testament is found in the book of Deuteronomy, which recounts the renewal of the covenant between God and Israel on the eve of their entry into the promised land. This central passage in the life of ancient Israel, Deuteronomy 6:4, was in Paul's day recited daily by faithful Jews: "Hear, O Israel: The Lord our God is one Lord!" This passage is known as the Shema (from its opening word "hear" in Hebrew). In this core confession of Israel's belief in the one creator God, Israel's God is identified both by the divine title ("God") and by the sacred divine name ("the Lord"). The word here translated "the Lord" is in the Hebrew text the divine name YHWH. The confession thus affirms that YHWH, the Lord, is the one and only God. There is one God, one Lord. Moreover, the words "our God" (an abbreviated form of the covenant formula) identify the Lord, the only true God, as the covenant God of Israel.

When God in the exodus takes Israel to himself, to be his covenant people, he does so that he might dwell among them forever. The climax of the exodus, and the overwhelming theme of the Old Testament thereafter, is the personal dwelling and presence of YHWH among his people in his sanctuary (Exod 29:45–46; Lev 26:11–12; 2 Chron 6:41–42). The centrality of the Lord's presence with his people is the reason for the lengthy, detailed instructions (so off-putting to modern readers) regarding the construction of the tabernacle (Exod 25–31; 35–40) and of the temple (1 Kings 6–7; 1 Chron 15–16; 2 Chron 2–5). It is at the heart of the great pilgrimage feasts (Exod 34; Lev 23; Deut 16; 26) and of ancient Israel's psalmody and liturgy (1 Kings 8; 2 Chron 6–7; Pss 68; 84; 87; 116; 120–134; 150). At the very epicenter of Israel's life was the dwelling of the Lord in Zion: "Blessed be the Lord from Zion, who dwells in Jerusalem. Praise the Lord!" (Ps 135:21).

The First Major Stream of Jewish Expectation

When Israel forsakes the covenant, divine judgment inexorably follows: Jerusalem is captured, Israel is taken into exile, and the temple, God's dwelling place, is destroyed (2 Kings 18–19; 25; Ps 89). As the dwelling of the Lord in Zion had been the center of his people's life, so the deepest tragedy of the exile was the departure of God's presence from Israel (see Ps 74; Ezek 1; 8:3–4; 10:4–5; 11:22–24). Yet the prophets also envision a time beyond the exile, when the Lord would act, out of the unfathomable love, mercy, and faithfulness at the mysterious foundations of his covenant with Abraham, to wondrously redeem Israel (Lev 26:40–45; Mic 7:18–20) and bring salvation to all nations (Isa 2:1–5).

This Jewish hope in a coming kingdom and reign of God is absolutely unique in the ancient world. All other ancient peoples for whom we have evidence had a *cyclical* view of history—history is simply one event after another, repeating in an endless cycle. Among the philosophers and sages, Epicurus envisioned the eternal formation and destruction of infinite universes (Lucretius, *On the Nature of the Universe* 2.1023–1174), Plato affirmed the eternal continuation of the universe in its present state (*Timaeus* 37c–38c), Buddha taught a never-ending "sorrowful wheel" of death and reincarnation (*Anguttara Nikāya* 3.58–61, 103–5), and the Stoics maintained an everlasting cyclical recurrence of all things (Cicero, *On the Nature of the Gods* 2.118; Seneca, *On Consolation to Marcia* 21.2). The people of Israel alone had a *linear* understanding of history—YHWH is the Lord of history, and history is moving toward a great climax, the kingdom of God. The prophetic picture involved a kaleidoscope of expectations: a new exodus (Jer 32; Hos 2:14–23; Amos 9:7–15; Hab 2:1–9), a new covenant (Jer 31:27–34; Ezek 36:16–36), the inclusion of the nations (Isa 11:10; 45:20–25; Jer 3:16–18; 16:19–21), the resurrection of the dead (Isa 25:6–9; 26:11–19; Dan 12:1–2), and the renewal of the whole creation (Isa 11:6–9; 35:1–10; 66:22–24). The very heartbeat of the prophetic Scriptures are these promises of God's mighty acts in Zion in the time of his saving reign.

But uniting all these varied promises were two major streams of expectation. The first was the expectation of a coming king from the lineage of David the son of Jesse, who would deliver Israel and reign as king over all nations—the Messiah or the Christ (Isa 9:1–7; 11:1–10; Ps 2; Amos 9:7–15; Mic 5:1–5; Zech 9:9–10). Paul's letters are filled—all Pauline scholars agree—with the joyous announcement that the first major stream of Jewish expectation, the advent of the messianic king from the line of David, has been fulfilled in Jesus. This is clear from Paul's repeated application, through quotation, allusion, and echo, of multiple messianic prophetic texts to Jesus. An example is Romans 15:12, where Paul cites the climactic acclamation of Israel's second messianic oracle (Isa 11:1–10) as fulfilled in Jesus: "And again Isaiah says: 'And there shall come the root of Jesse, the one who arises to rule the nations; in him the nations shall put their hope'" (Rom 15:12, citing Isa 11:10). Jesus's fulfillment of the messianic hope is also strikingly evident in Paul's constant references to Jesus as "Christ Jesus" or "Jesus Christ." For the word "Christ" is not a name, but a *title*, and means "Messiah," and thus identifies Jesus as the promised anointed king from the seed of David. To be sure, some scholars hold that in this Pauline usage the title "Christ" has lost its messianic meaning and become no more than a proper name. But I believe this view fails to adequately grasp Paul's Jewish context. That a first-century Jew such as Paul could apply the epithet "Christ" without full consciousness of the messianic claim involved is simply not credible historically. It is true that in Paul's formulations "Christ" does not normally occur as a predicate (i.e., "Jesus is the *Christ*"), but in apposition with the name of Jesus (i.e., "*Christ* Jesus"). But this is not because the messianic title has metamorphosed into a proper name. Rather, as has recently been shown, in Paul's formulation the messianic title is employed in the style of an *honorific* (i.e., "Messiah Jesus").[2]

Paul thus believed that in Jesus Christ, the promised King from the line of David, the long-awaited kingdom of God had now come. Within Paul's thought, Jesus brings the messianic kingdom in two stages. Through his first coming he has *inaugurated* the messianic kingdom (Rom 1:3–4; 9:5; Gal 4:4; 1 Tim 3:16; Titus 2:11–12); through his second coming he will *consummate* it (Phil 3:20–21; 1 Thess 1:10; 4:16–17; 2 Thess 1:7–10; 1 Tim 6:13–16; Titus 2:13–14). In Paul's theology of the kingdom we find that Jewish and biblical *linear* understanding of history that we have seen is so different from the cyclical view of history in the pagan world into which Paul's gospel came. We also find here a third fundamental distinction or contrast that structures Paul's thought. In chapter 1 we discussed the Pauline distinction between creator and creation, and in chapter 2 the contrast between union with the creator and separation from the creator. Paul's theology of the kingdom involves a third binary contrast:

Inaugurated Kingdom
_____
Consummated Kingdom

Paul's theology of the kingdom thus moves on a twofold plane, affirming (to use the words of the ancient Muratorian Canon [c. 170 CE]) Christ's "double advent, the first, which has taken place, when he came in humility and was despised, and the second, which is to come, when he comes in royal power and glory."[3]

Paul's belief that Jesus is the promised Messiah, the human king from the seed of David, has an important corollary. The "Christ" that Paul preached was therefore truly human, an earthly human being, and this was important for Paul. This may seem too obvious to need mention. However, a certain minority stream within New Testament scholarship regards it as axiomatic that the "Christ" of Paul's preaching was solely Jesus now exalted as (on this scenario) a heavenly, ethereal being, and claims that Paul had little or no interest in the earthly Jesus. As H. J. Schoeps put it, for Paul "the Jesus of the flesh belongs to the past; the Christ is no longer an earthly figure. . . . The earthly life of Jesus is no longer rel-

---

2. See Matthew V. Novenson, *Christ among the Messiahs: Christ Language in Paul and Messiah Language in Ancient Judaism* (Oxford: Oxford University Press, 2015). So also (following Novenson) Paula Fredriksen, *Paul: The Pagans' Apostle* (New Haven: Yale University Press, 2017), 135.

3. Muratorian Canon 19.

evant."[4] The focus of Paul's preaching, these scholars claim, was not the earthly *Jesus* but the heavenly, exalted *Christ*. But this claim, when it comes to a grasp of Pauline theology, is drastically (and disastrously) mistaken. For Paul's firm belief that "Christ" (Rom 1:1, *Christos*) was "born of the seed of David" (Rom 1:3, *genomenou ek spermatos Dauid*; cf. 2 Tim 2:8) necessarily involved the equally firm belief that he was "born of a woman" (Gal 4:4, *genomenon ek gunaikos*). As Paul is fond of repeating, "Christ" (*Christos*) came *kata sarka*, or "according to the flesh" (Rom 9:5; cf. 1:3), that is, he is fully human (Rom 8:3; Phil 2:7; Eph 2:17–18; Col 2:22). And, of course, Paul's constant references to the cross of *Christ* (1 Cor 1:17; Gal 6:12–14; Phil 3:18), the death of *Christ* (Rom 5:6–8; 14:15; 1 Cor 11:26; 15:3; Col 1:22; 1 Thess 5:9–10), and the blood of *Christ* (Rom 3:25; 5:9; Eph 2:13; Col 1:20) simply make no sense unless he identified the Christ with the earthly, historical Jesus. The Christ of Paul's theology is truly and fully human. Contrary to the view that Paul's thought sunders the human Jesus from the heavenly Christ, it is at the heart of Paul's theology that Jesus *is* the Christ.

In the messianic expectation within the Old Testament, there is a sort of mysterious tension. Israel is to have no king but God (Judg 8:22–23; 1 Sam 8:6–7; Isa 33:22; Zech 14:9). This is why, when Israel first enters the promised land, they are ruled not by a king but by judges (Judg 1–21; Ruth 1:1; 2 Sam 7:11), and why the people's request for a king in the days of Samuel is portrayed in the Bible as sinful and misguided (1 Sam 8–12). And yet, through the subsequent Davidic covenant and its promise of an everlasting Davidic throne (2 Sam 7; Pss 2; 72; 78; 89; 132; Ezek 37:24–25), the coming reign of this human messianic king is given a central role in the divine plan. This is a point of tension and mystery never resolved in the Old Testament. One thing is clear. Although the average reader of the Bible might assume that the messianic expectation is the central prophetic hope of the Old Testament, this is simply mistaken. The expectation of the Messiah's advent plays an important role in the Old Testament, but it is not central. It is to that central hope that we now turn.

The Second Major Stream of Jewish Expectation

The second major stream of expectation is the central hope of the Old Testament—the expectation that, in a fashion beyond imagining, the Lord himself

---

4. H. J. Schoeps, *Paul: The Theology of the Apostle in the Light of Jewish Religious History*, trans. Harold Knight (Philadelphia: Westminster, 1961), 108. In the same vein is Wilhelm Heitmüller, "Zum Problem Paulus und Jesus," *ZNW* 13 (1912): 320–37.

would come to dwell among his people in the fullness of his presence, life, and glory, to restore and renew all things, filling all creation with his presence and glory (Isa 35; 40:1–11; Ps 96; Ezek 37:21–28; 43:1–9; 48:35; Zech 14:1–19; Mal 3:1–5). The personal presence and dwelling of YHWH with his people, which we have seen was at the heart of Israel's life in the time of promise, was thus also the central expectation of the time of fulfillment.[5] In his presence among Israel in the tabernacle and in Solomon's temple, the Lord dwelt behind the veil of the most holy place, accessible only to the high priest once a year on the Day of Atonement (Exod 40; Lev 16; 2 Chron 5). The prophetic expectation of the coming of YHWH, by contrast, envisioned the Lord's presence among his people in a fullness of which his dwelling in Solomon's temple was only a foreshadowing (Isa 25:6–9; Ezek 40–48; Zech 14:16–21). The central expectation of the Old Testament was the coming of YHWH himself, and his mighty, saving acts in Zion when he came:

> Let the heavens rejoice, and the earth be glad; let the sea roar, and all within the sea. Let the field exult with joy, and all that is in it. Then all the trees of the forest will sing for joy. Let them rejoice in the presence of the Lord! For he is coming! For he is coming to bring justice to the earth! (Ps 96:11–13)

> My dwelling will be among them, and I will be their God, and they will be my people. And the nations will know that I am the Lord who makes Israel holy, when my holy dwelling place is in their midst forever. (Ezek 37:27–28)

> Go up to a lofty mountain, you who bring the gospel to Zion! Lift up your voice with strength, you who bring the gospel to Jerusalem! Lift up your voice, do not fear; say to the cities of Judah, "Behold, your God!" Behold, the Lord YHWH will come with power, his mighty arm reigning for him. Behold, his reward is with him, his recompense before him. As a shepherd he will tend his flock, with his arm he will gather the lambs, and in his bosom he will carry them, gently leading those with young. (Isa 40:9–11)

---

5. This theme is well known to scholars of the Old Testament. The scholar primarily responsible for bringing the importance of this theme to the attention of New Testament interpreters is N. T. Wright. See his *Jesus and the Victory of God*, vol. 2 of *Christian Origins and the Question of God* (Minneapolis: Fortress, 1996), 612–53, and *Paul and the Faithfulness of God*, vol. 4 of *Christian Origins and the Question of God* (Minneapolis: Fortress, 2013), 653–90.

This saving advent of the Lord would not only bring salvation for Israel, but, as promised in the covenant with Abraham, would also bring blessing and salvation for all the peoples of the earth (Gen 12:1–3; 22:15–18; Pss 47; 67; 96; Isa 2:1–5; 49:1–6; 60:1–3; Jer 3:17; 16:19–21). In that day, the prophet Joel envisions, "everyone who calls on the name of the Lord will be saved" (Joel 3:5 [Eng 2:32]). The presence and coming of the creator God would thus bring about the restoration of the union of humanity with its creator lost in the Fall. YHWH's advent would also bring about the creator God's final victory over evil, bringing deliverance and salvation for those who turn to him, but just judgment on those who forsake the Lord, turn to false gods, and cling to evil (Isa 2:10–22; 66:15–24; Obad 15–21; Mal 3:1–5). YHWH's coming, his saving acts in Zion, and the fullness of his presence would bring about the full revelation to all nations of the divine name once made known to Moses at the burning bush. The "one Lord" of Deuteronomy 6:4 would reveal himself in power as the one true living God: "For from the rising to the setting of the sun, my name will be great among the nations, and in every place incense will be offered to my name, and a pure offering; for my name will be great among the nations, says the Lord of hosts" (Mal 1:11).

The Name and Presence of God in Paul's Theology

We saw above how Paul's application of the prophetic messianic oracles to Jesus reveals his conviction that Jesus is the promised messianic king from the line of David. But it is Paul's application of the central biblical texts concerning Israel's God, and especially his application of the prophetic texts involving the second great stream of expectation, the advent, saving activity, and enduring presence of YHWH, that offers the startling and truly central key to his Christology.

1 Corinthians 8:4–6

In 1 Corinthians 8:4, Paul writes, "We know that no idol in the world has any real existence, and there is no God but one." In so doing Paul repeats the teaching at the heart of the Bible, which we saw in chapter 1 was fundamental to his gospel: there is one, living, creator God. But note how Paul fleshes this out in verses 5 and 6:

> [5]For although there are so-called gods whether in heaven or on earth, just as there are many gods and many lords, [6]yet for us there is one God, the

Father, from whom are all things, and we for him, and one Lord, Jesus
Christ, through whom are all things and we through him.

The key to the passage is the recognition that, as virtually all Pauline scholars
agree, Paul's language echoes the most important occurrence of the divine name
in the Old Testament. This is the central monotheistic confession of ancient Israel,
the Shema, found in Deuteronomy 6:4: "Hear, O Israel, the Lord our God is one
Lord!" As we saw earlier in the chapter, this confession employs both the divine
title "God" and the divine name "the Lord" to affirm that YHWH, the Lord, is the
one and only God.

Within this ancient Jewish context, Paul's use of this confession is explosive.
In echoing Deuteronomy 6:4, Paul ascribes the divine title to "the Father" ("one
God, the Father") and the sacred divine name to "Jesus Christ" ("one Lord, Jesus
Christ"). Not only in Deuteronomy 6:4 but also in every Jewish text known to us
from antiquity, the phrase "one Lord" refers without exception to the one God
of Israel. But Paul here identifies the "one Lord" as Jesus Christ.[6] The Son is not a
created being outside the identity of the one God, but the "one Lord" proclaimed
in Israel's ancient confession of faith. Paul's confession identifies the unique and
incomparable "one God, one Lord" of Israel's central affirmation as the Father, and
his Son, the Lord Jesus Christ.[7]

And the words Paul adds to this confession of Jesus as the one Lord—"through
whom are all things"—are in the Bible and elsewhere in ancient Jewish literature
used always and only of God as creator (cf. Rom 11:36, "from him and *through him*
and to him are all things"). Paul in 1 Corinthians 8:6 affirms these words of the
one Lord, Jesus Christ ("one Lord, Jesus Christ, through whom are all things"). As
we saw in chapter 1, the foundation of Paul's theology is the distinction between

6. Cf. Erik Waaler, *The Shema and the First Commandment in First Corinthians: An Intertextual
Approach to Paul's Rereading of Deuteronomy*, WUNT 2.253 (Tübingen: Mohr Siebeck, 2008), 445:
"The implication of Paul's allusion . . . [to Deut 6:4], applying it directly to Jesus Christ, is tremendous
in a first century Jewish context. No existing non-Christian Jewish text in the centuries prior and
posterior to this comes close to using the phrase 'one Lord' with reference to any divine or semi-divine
beings alongside God." Richard Bauckham notes incisively: "In the confession of 'one Lord, Jesus
Christ,' Paul is not adding to the one God of the Shema a 'Lord' the Shema does not mention. He is
identifying Jesus as the 'Lord' whom the Shema affirms to be one" (*God Crucified: Monotheism and
Christology in the New Testament* [Grand Rapids: Eerdmans, 1998], 38).

7. The seminal modern study of 1 Cor 8:4–6 is N. T. Wright, "Monotheism, Christology and
Ethics: 1 Corinthians 8," in *The Climax of the Covenant: Christ and the Law in Pauline Theology* (Minneapolis: Fortress, 1991), 120–36. Other penetrating treatments include Waaler, *The Shema and the
First Commandment in First Corinthians*; Bauckham, *God Crucified*, 36–40; and Wesley Hill, *Paul and
the Trinity: Persons, Relations, and the Pauline Letters* (Grand Rapids: Eerdmans, 2015), 112–20.

creator and creation. All things have come into being by the direct creative act, without intermediary, of the one transcendent creator, "who created all things" (Eph 3:9). In 1 Corinthians 8:6 Paul expresses this conception of the creator God, distinct from his creation, as powerfully as anywhere in his letters. But he identifies the author of creation as both the Father, "from whom are all things," and his Son, the Lord Jesus Christ, "through whom are all things."

Colossians 1:16–17

Paul likewise writes in Colossians of Jesus, the "beloved Son" of the Father (Col 1:13), as the eternal creator, maker, and goal of all creation:

> [16] In him all things were created, in the heavens and upon the earth, the visible things and the invisible things, whether thrones or dominions or principalities or powers; all things have been created through him and for him. [17] And he is prior to all things, and all things in him have their existence. (Col 1:16–17)

Paul's twofold use in this passage of the word *ktizō*, or "create" (1:16a, "were created"; 1:16b, "have been created"), is extremely significant. As we explored in chapter 1, it is a foundational principle of the biblical and Pauline teaching that creation is the direct act of the creator alone, without angelic or creaturely mediation (Isa 44:24; cf. Rom 11:36; 1 Tim 6:13; Acts 14:15). The divine work of creation is shared with no creature. That is why the specialized verb *ktizō* (create) is used throughout the New Testament and early Christian literature only of the action of God, never of angels, human beings, or other creatures. And thus when Paul in Colossians 1:16 uses the verb *ktizō* of the action of *Christ*, he identifies him unambiguously as the creator of all things.[8]

The relation of Father and Son in the activity of creation is suggested by Paul's affirmation that all things were created *in* the Son (1:16, "*in him* all things were created"; 1:17, "all things *in him* have their existence") and *through* the Son (1:16, "all things have been created *through him*"). Paul's language points to a distinction between the Father and the Son in the work of creation, in which the Father is the *source*, the Son the *agent*, of creation. This is also the implication of the formulation in 1 Corinthians 8:6: "one God, the Father, *from* whom are all things . . . one Lord, Jesus Christ, *through* whom are all things."

---

8. On the activity of creation within Paul's biblical context as a marker, unshared with any creature, of the God of Israel's unique identity, see Bauckham, *God Crucified*, 35–40.

The Father, as the creator, is described in 1 Corinthians 8:6 as the goal or purpose of creation ("from whom are all things, and we *for him* [Greek: *eis auton*]"). Using the same language, Colossians 1:16 describes the Son as creation's goal or purpose: "all things have been created through him and *for him* (Greek: *eis auton*)." In Colossians 1:16–17, Paul identifies the Son, together with the Father, as the eternal creator, the One through whom and for whom all things exist.

Romans 10:12–13

In Romans 10 Paul sums up "the word of faith which we proclaim" (Rom 10:8): "If you confess with your mouth that Jesus is the Lord (Greek: *kyrios*) and believe in your heart that God raised him from the dead, you will be saved" (Rom 10:9). Romans 10:10–13 consists of a commentary and expansion on Romans 10:8–9, which climaxes in this way: "For there is no difference between Jew and gentile, for the same Lord is Lord (*kyrios*) of all, rich toward all who call upon him. For 'everyone who calls on the name of the Lord (*kyrios*) will be saved'" (Rom 10:12–13). Paul here understands the prophet Joel's vision of YHWH's coming salvation for "all humanity" (Joel 2:28 [MT/LXX 3:1]) as fulfilled in the worldwide spread of the gospel (Rom 10:12–13). But what is especially striking is Paul's quotation of Joel 2:32 (MT/LXX 3:5): "everyone who calls on the name of the Lord will be saved." Paul's quotation is taken from the Septuagint (LXX), the ancient Greek translation of the Old Testament, where "the Lord" functions as God's personal name. The original Hebrew of Joel 2:32 (3:5) reads "everyone who calls on the name of YHWH will be saved." In the prophetic vision, "the Lord" is YHWH, Israel's God. But Paul understands this prophetic promise as fulfilled in the confession of *Jesus* as the Lord. It is simply not possible to understand "the Lord" here as some sort of lesser lord, for the word *kyrios* in Paul's quotation translates the very name of YHWH. And in describing the faithful as *calling on* the name of Jesus, Paul depicts Jesus as receiving the worship that in Paul's Jewish and biblical context is due to YHWH alone. Jesus is "Lord of all" (Rom 10:12). Once again, Paul identifies Jesus as YHWH, the creator God of Israel.

Philippians 2:9–11

Likewise, in the climactic verses of what scholars call the "Christ hymn" in Philippians 2:5–11, Jesus through his resurrection and exaltation is given the name above every name, and receives the worship of all creation:

[9]For this reason God in response highly exalted him, and gave to him the name which is above every name, [10]that at the name of Jesus every knee might bow, of beings in heaven and on earth and under the earth, [11]and every tongue confess that Jesus Christ is Lord, to the glory of God the Father. (Phil 2:9–11)

Paul's words here echo one of the central monotheistic passages of the Bible:

[22]Turn to me and be saved, all the ends of the earth! For I am God, and there is no other. [23]By myself I have sworn, the word has gone forth from my mouth in righteousness and will not turn back, that to me every knee will bow, every tongue will confess. (Isa 45:22–23)

This passage in Isaiah envisions the coming full revelation of the divine glory and name in the time of YHWH's reign. YHWH declares that, as a result of his mighty acts in Zion in the time of his coming kingdom, "to me every knee will bow, every tongue will confess" (Isa 45:23). But in Paul's stunning hymn, it is to *Jesus* that every knee will bow and every tongue confess (Phil 2:9–10). Further, in Paul's Jewish context the one who has the name that is above every name can only be the creator God of Israel. But in Paul's hymn "the name which is above every name" is the name of *Jesus* (2:9). Moreover, Paul depicts Jesus as given the glory that Isaiah declares is due YHWH alone, and all creation as giving to Jesus the worship that in Paul's Jewish context belongs to the creator alone (2:10–11). Given Paul's monotheistic context, Paul's worship of Jesus is an astonishing fact, and leads to the inescapable conclusion that he identified Jesus as the creator God of Israel, the One to whom alone worship is due.[9] And yet this worship of Jesus as Lord is not inconsistent with, but redounds to, the glory of God the Father (2:11). The "Christ hymn" of Philippians, like the confession in 1 Corinthians 8:6, thus points to a mysterious distinction within the one God between God the Father (Phil 2:11) and the Son, who is "in nature God" (Phil 2:6a) and "equal with God" (Phil 2:6b).

---

9. The worship of Jesus as striking evidence of Paul's divine Christology has been especially stressed by Larry Hurtado; see his *One God, One Lord: Early Christian Devotion and Ancient Jewish Monotheism*, 3rd ed. (London: T. & T. Clark, 2015).

Paul's Incarnational Christology

In the passages we have examined, Paul identifies Jesus Christ as the one Lord of Israel's faith (1 Cor 8:6; Phil 2:11), the creator, who was before all things (Col 1:17), the One through whom and for whom all things were made (Col 1:16), the Lord of all, whom all must confess in worship and call upon for salvation (Rom 10:9–13; Phil 2:9–11). And yet we have seen that Paul believed that Jesus Christ is fully human, born in time of a woman (Gal 4:4), from the lineage of David (Rom 1:3). The implications are startling, but unmistakable. Paul believed that the eternal creator God, the transcendent source of all reality, had become human in the person of Jesus of Nazareth. The creator had entered his creation. The central expectation of the Old Testament that, in a fashion beyond imagining, the Lord himself would come to dwell among his people in the fullness of his presence, life, and glory had been fulfilled in the embodiment of the eternal Son of God in human flesh. The human being Jesus is none other than God incarnate.

This was an astonishing claim in its Jewish context. For the Jewish people had no prior inkling of an incarnation. To be sure, they yearned for the coming of YHWH in the fullness of his presence to save his people and redeem all creation. But they had no expectation that the creator would come through being incarnate as a human being. According to Paul's gospel, the familiar and cherished hope of YHWH's coming had been fulfilled, but in an entirely unfamiliar and startling way.

The incarnation had brought with it a new revelation of the inner mystery of the one God of Israel. Within this mystery, the Father, from whom are all things, and the Son, through whom are all things, are truly distinct, yet one. The one God and Lord of Israel's faith, set in contrast to the "many gods and many lords" of pagan worship (1 Cor 8:5), is revealed as God the Father and his Son, the Lord Jesus Christ. The church's creedal confession of the Son as "true God from true God, begotten, not made, of one essence with the Father," far from being an alien imposition on Paul's writings, turns out to be not only appropriate but necessary to unpack this Pauline theology of the relation of Father and Son within the inner being of the one and only God.

The Two Streams of Expectation in Paul's Letters

In the ancient confession he places at the very forefront of his letter to the Romans, Paul writes that the apostolic message is the good news of God

> [3]concerning his Son, who was born of the seed of David in regard to his human nature, [4]who was revealed to be the Son of God in power accord-

ing to the Spirit of holiness through the resurrection of the dead, Jesus Christ our Lord, [5]through whom we have received grace and apostleship to bring about the obedience of faith among all the nations on behalf of his name. (Rom 1:3–5)

According to this early confession, through his resurrection Jesus "was revealed to be the Son of God in power" (1:4). Some interpreters argue that "Son of God" should be taken here in a merely *messianic* sense.[10] On this reading, the resurrection has marked out Jesus as the Messiah, the promised king from the lineage of David (cf. Isa 11:1–10; Mic 5:1–5; Zech 9:9–10). I believe this reading is partially correct but not fully adequate. To be sure, Jesus's messianic identity is a crucial feature of the passage—he is the Christ, that is, the Messiah (Rom 1:4), born of the seed of David (1:3). But the revelation of Jesus as the Son of God in 1:4 involves something more. The key to the passage is Paul's declaration in 1:3 that Jesus's birth from the line of David was "in regard to his human nature" (Greek: *kata sarka*). This delimitation in the confession's first clause (1:3) necessarily implies that Jesus is *more* than merely human, and prepares the reader for the full revelation of his identity in the parallel and climactic clause (1:4).[11] Therefore in 1:4 the title "Son of God" must be taken in its full *divine* sense. The resurrection reveals that the one who was born of the seed of David "in regard to his human nature" (*kata sarka*) is the divine Son of God.

As we have seen, the hopes of Israel clustered around two great streams of expectation: the hope in a coming ultimate Davidic king, the Christ, and the central hope of the Scriptures, the mysterious coming of YHWH himself to dwell forever with his people. According to Romans 1:3–4, the resurrection unveiled that Jesus had united and fulfilled both streams of expectation in himself. The resurrection revealed that, in the person of Jesus, Israel's messianic king, YHWH himself had come to Zion.

Jesus's twofold identity as both messianic king and the divine Son of God is also clear from Paul's expansion on the confession of Romans 1:3–4a in the following verses (1:4b–5). Paul here echoes the prophet Malachi's vision of the glorification of the name of YHWH, the God of Israel, among the nations in the time of his coming kingdom (Mal 1:11). Setting Malachi's prophecy alongside Paul's echoes

10. See, for example, Fredriksen, *Paul*, 141–45.

11. According to Matthew W. Bates, this implication in the first clause (1:3) of Jesus's more than human identity is strengthened by Paul's choice of the Greek verb *ginomai* (rather than *gennaō*), which connotes not merely Jesus's birth but his "'change in status' from preexistence to human existence" (Matthew W. Bates, "A Christology of Incarnation and Enthronement: Romans 1:3–4 as Unified, Nonadoptionist, and Nonconciliatory," *CBQ* 77 [2015]: 107–27 [esp. 115–17]).

of this prophecy in Romans 1:4–5 and 1 Corinthians 1:2 (with the points of verbal contact in italics) is instructive:

MALACHI 1:11	ROMANS 1:4–5	1 CORINTHIANS 1:2
For from the rising to the setting of the sun, *my name* will be great *among the nations* and *in every place* incense will be offered to *my name,* and a pure offering; for *my name* will be great *among the nations,* says the *Lord* of hosts.	Jesus Christ our *Lord,* through whom we have received grace and apostleship to bring about the obedience of faith *among* all *the nations* for the sake of *his name.*	To the church of God at Corinth, made holy in Christ Jesus, called to be saints, together with all those who call upon *the name* of our *Lord* Jesus Christ *in every place,* their Lord and ours.

Two things are clear from Paul's echoes of the Malachi passage. First, Paul regards the glorification of God's name among the peoples of the earth envisioned by Malachi as fulfilled in the spread of the good news of Christ to the gentiles. Second (just as we saw in Rom 10:12–13 and Phil 2:9–11), for Paul the name of God that is to be glorified among the nations is "Jesus Christ our Lord" (Rom 1:4–5). In the formulation "Jesus Christ our Lord," we find again Jesus's fulfillment of both streams of expectation in his own person—Jesus is both the *Christ* from the seed of David and the *Lord,* the God of Israel, whose name is to be glorified among the nations. The prophecy of Malachi 1:11 foretells a new and ultimate revelation of YHWH's name in the time of his coming kingdom and reign. In Paul's theology the kingdom has come, and that name is "Jesus Christ our Lord" (Rom 1:4–5).

We see Jesus's fulfillment of both streams of expectation also in Romans 9:5, where the climax of Israel's divine blessings is that "from them came the Christ in regard to his human nature, who is God over all, blessed forever." Paul in this text unambiguously identifies Jesus as "God over all" (cf. Rom 10:12, where Jesus is "Lord of all"). Some have argued that the words "who is God over all, blessed forever" can be taken as an independent ascription of praise to God unrelated to the previous clause (i.e., "from them came the Christ in regard to his human nature. God who is over all [be] blessed forever").[12] But recent study has shown that on syntactical and contextual grounds it is far more likely that the clause "who is God over all, blessed forever" completes the description of "the Christ"

---

12. E.g., Jerome Murphy-O'Connor, *Becoming Human Together: The Pastoral Anthropology of St. Paul,* 3rd ed. (Atlanta: Society of Biblical Literature, 2009), 59–62; Fredriksen, *Paul,* 237n13.

in the previous clause.[13] And there is a neglected feature of the passage that in my view moves this conclusion from likelihood to certainty. For in ancient Greek syntax the adverbial phrase to *kata sarka* ("in regard to his human nature") *necessarily* introduces an implied comparison or contrast with the clause that follows. The two clauses must therefore be read as coordinate and complementary (i.e., "from them came the Christ in regard to his *human* nature, who is *God* over all, blessed forever"). The thought is that Jesus, the messianic king, took his human lineage from Mary, and thus from the Jewish people ("from them came the Christ in regard to his human nature"), but that the one who did so is himself the God of all creation ("who is God over all, blessed forever"). The climax of Israel's story is the incarnation.

We have seen that in the Old Testament there is a mysterious tension between God as the only king of Israel and the central place of the human messianic king in the divine plan. Israel was to have no king but God. This mystery is resolved, in a wonderful and unexpected way, by Jesus's uniting of both streams of expectation in his own person. The messianic king is himself YHWH, the king of Israel. God's Christ is his divine Son. This explains something otherwise mysterious, that although in the Old Testament the messianic hope is not central, Jesus Christ is the center of Paul's letters. Just as in the Old Testament YHWH is the center of Israel's faith, life, and hope, so in Paul's epistles Jesus is the center of his people's faith, life, and hope.[14] He is the center because he is not only the messianic king but also the "one Lord, through whom are all things" (1 Cor 8:6), "God over all" (Rom 9:5), "the Lord of glory" (1 Cor 2:8). In his coming Jesus fulfilled the deepest promise of the kingdom, that when the kingdom came, "YHWH alone will be our king" (Isa 33:22).

In the passages we have examined thus far, Paul portrays the long-awaited coming of YHWH as fulfilled in the incarnation of the Son of God. But we have seen that in Paul's theology of the kingdom, the kingdom comes in two stages. And Paul portrays the fulfillment of this hope of YHWH's coming, inaugurated through Jesus's first advent, as fully consummated at his second coming. In 1 Thessalonians 3:13, for example, Paul's reference to "the coming of the Lord Jesus with all his holy ones" is clearly an echo of Zechariah 14:5: "Then the Lord my God will come, and all his holy ones with him!" In Zechariah 14:5, the Lord who comes is YHWH, my God; in 1 Thessalonians 3:13, the Lord who comes is the Lord Jesus. Paul identifies

---

13. The most thorough and insightful recent treatment is George Carraway, *Christ Is God over All: Romans 9:5 in the Context of Romans 9–11*, LNTS 489 (London: Bloomsbury, 2013).

14. For the striking identity of the "pattern of relation" of YHWH and Israel in the Old Testament with that of Christ and the faithful in the New Testament, see Chris Tilling, *Paul's Divine Christology* (Tübingen: Mohr Siebeck, 2012).

Jesus as YHWH in the flesh, and Jesus's coming again in glory as the final fulfill-ment of the hope of YHWH's coming. And here we find once again Jesus's fusion of the two great streams of expectation in his own person, for in Paul's theology the Old Testament expectation of "the day of the Lord" (Isa 2:10–21; Amos 5:18–20; Zeph 1:14–18) has become the hope of "the day of *Christ*" (Phil 1:6, 10; 2:16) and "the day of the *Lord* Jesus" (1 Cor 1:8; 2 Cor 1:14). It is "the blessed hope, the glo-rious appearing of our great *God* and savior, Jesus *Christ*" (Titus 2:13).

Conclusion: The Secret of Paul's Christology

In this chapter we have discovered that Paul's biblical and Jewish context, the larger biblical narrative of which he believed Jesus was the goal and fulfillment, provides the master key to his Christology. The very epicenter of ancient Israel's life was the personal presence and dwelling of the Lord among his people in his holy temple. Conversely, the inmost tragedy of the exile was the departure of God's presence from Israel. Yet the prophets also envision a time beyond the exile, when the Lord will act in power to redeem Israel and bring salvation to the nations. Uniquely in the ancient world, the people of Israel believed that history was moving toward a great climax, the kingdom and reign of God. The prophetic promises of Israel's coming redemption and renewal were united by two major streams of expectation. The first was the coming of a messianic king from the seed of David to deliver Israel and reign over all nations. The second, the central hope of the Old Testament, was the coming of YHWH himself, and his saving acts in Zion when he came. In his coming YHWH would manifest his presence in a fullness that his dwelling in the temple only foreshadowed, and bring the full revelation of his divine name to the nations.

The key to Paul's Christology is this: Paul believed that Jesus of Nazareth had united and fulfilled both streams of expectation in his own person. Paul believed that Jesus was the promised Messiah, the truly and fully human king from the line of David. But—even more crucially—Paul believed that in Jesus, Israel's messianic king, Israel's God himself had come in his own person. The central hope of the Scriptures, that the Lord would come to dwell among his people in the fullness of his presence and glory, had been fulfilled, in a fashion beyond imagination, by the coming of the eternal Son of God in human flesh. The creator had entered his creation in the person of Jesus Christ. The incarnation at one stroke resolved the mysterious and seemingly irresolvable conflict between the two streams of expectation, and brought a new revelation of the inner mystery of the one God as a communion of love between Father and Son.

In the next chapter, we will explore how Paul's proclamation of the incarnation would have struck its first hearers in the context of the ancient pagan world into which Paul's gospel came. We will also take up various questions and issues raised by Paul's incarnational Christology, including the objections of a small contingent of scholars who reject the presence of a divine Christology in Paul. In so doing, we will solidify and deepen our grasp of this centerpiece of the entire structure of Paul's theology—the incarnation.

Chapter Four

Paul's Gospel of the Incarnation

Through a fresh examination of Paul's letters within the context of Israel's Scriptures, the previous chapter sought to bring new depth and clarity to the study of Pauline Christology. In so doing, we discovered the crucial place of the incarnation in Paul's thought. In this chapter, we will deepen our understanding. We will discover how Paul's good news of the incarnation would have impacted its first hearers in the gentile world into which it came. We will explore the relation between Paul's doctrines of creation and incarnation. And this chapter will offer solutions to difficulties and problems that have been raised regarding this teaching of the apostle, including common arguments of that minority of Pauline scholars who reject the presence of a "divine" or "incarnational" Christology in Paul. The coming chapters of this book will explore the myriad ways in which the incarnation is at the center of Paul's thought. Since it is the center, it is worth our while to examine this teaching of the apostle more fully, including these challenges and objections that have been raised. When we do so, we will better understand Paul's divine Christology, and the place of the incarnation in his thought.

The Incarnation in Its Ancient Pagan Context

Paul's gospel proclaimed that the human being Jesus of Nazareth is the one Lord through whom and for whom all things were created (1 Cor 8:6; Col 1:16–17), God over all (Rom 9:5). This was a startling claim without equivalent or parallel in the ancient pagan world into which Paul's gospel came. Paul's gospel claimed for Jesus what no one had claimed for Buddha, Socrates, Plato, or the other great teachers and sages of antiquity. Even the titles of such modern books as Karl Jaspers's *Socrates, Buddha, Confucius, Jesus* and Thich Nhat Hanh's *Living Buddha, Living Christ* reflect a deep historical mistake, for neither Socrates, Buddha, nor any of the other ancient sages claimed divinity, nor did their disciples claim it about them.

Moreover, when Paul brought the good news of the incarnation, the entrance of the creator into his creation, he proclaimed a conception that would have previously never entered the minds or hearts of his hearers. To be sure, various aspects of ancient religious thought are occasionally suggested as equivalents or parallels to the Christian doctrine of the incarnation. The ancient myths of the Greco-Roman world described manifestations or visitations of the gods among human beings in various forms (Homer, *Odyssey* 17.485–87; Plato, *Republic* 2, 381d; Ovid, *Metamorphoses* 8.618–728). Moreover, these myths are filled with demigods such as Asclepius, Hercules, and Achilles, who were heroes half-divine and half-human, the offspring of sexual intercourse between the gods (conceived as physical and bodily beings) and mortal men and women (Hesiod, *Theogony* 940–55; Ps.-Homer, *Hymn to Asclepius* 1–4; Ovid, *Metamorphoses* 9–11). And the ancient Hindu sages had the concept of the avatar, the temporary manifestation of a deity in animal or human form, the most notable example being the revelation of the god Vishnu in human guise as Krishna (*Bhagavad Gita* 9–11).

However, none of this comes close to the early Christian claim of the incarnation. Among many points of contrast, five are especially crucial. First, as we saw in chapter 1, the pagan world had no notion of one transcendent creator, distinct from the cosmos, who had brought the universe into being. The many gods of the Greek and Roman pantheons, even the high gods Jupiter and Zeus, were not considered to be outside nature and the cosmos, but products of it (Ovid, *Metamorphoses* 1.1–261; Hesiod, *Theogony* 1–962). The gods portrayed in the ancient myths as interacting within the human realm were thus regarded as powerful but finite aspects of the cosmic whole. The Stoics and Hindu sages envisioned (alongside many lesser deities) a highest divinity. However, within these pantheistic systems this divinity did not transcend nature and the universe, but was identified with them (*Rigveda* 10.90; *Bhagavad Gita* 9; Marcus Aurelius, *Meditations* 8.54). In Platonic dualism, the material realm had eternally existed independently from the highest divinity, and human beings in their bodily form were the work of lesser gods (Plato, *Timaeus* 27c–69a). The pagan world addressed by Paul's gospel thus could have no prior notion of incarnation (the creator entering his creation), for it had no conception of a transcendent creator. Paul's gospel, by contrast, made the astounding claim that the one transcendent creator God, the maker of heaven and earth, had entered the creation he had made in the person of Jesus of Nazareth.

Second, in those systems of belief that came closest to the conception of a transcendent creator, this highest deity was considered incapable of manifestation on the human plane. Plato's highest divinity could have no interaction with the realm of material reality and human embodiment, the flawed work of inferior beings (Plato, *Timaeus* 29–30; 42). The Hindu sages conceived of the god Vishnu as manifesting himself through Krishna, but the unknowable highest reality Brahman, identified with the cosmic All, could itself have no avatar or manifestation (*Bhagavad Gita* 12.1). In marked contrast, Paul's gospel proclaimed a transcendent creator, who was infinitely higher than the quasi-transcendent highest divinity of Platonic and Hindu thought, but who had stooped infinitely lower—not only to be born as a little child (Rom 1:3; Gal 4:4) but also to undergo suffering, crucifixion, and death (Rom 8:3; Phil 2:6–8).

Third, the earthly manifestations of these divine and semidivine beings, whether Zeus, Athena, Asclepius, or Krishna, took place in the distant world of myth. They belonged to archaic ages and mythic kingdoms, not to the real world of the Roman Empire into which Paul's gospel came. Very differently, Paul proclaimed that the maker of all had come in the person of Jesus, a real human being, born from the lineage of David (Rom 1:3), crucified under Pontius Pilate (1 Tim 6:13), and risen from the dead according to the testimony of living eyewitnesses (1 Cor 15:1–11).

Fourth, the divine manifestations of the Greek and Roman myths, and the avatars of the Hindu sages, were *temporary* affairs, not solitary and unique but multiple and repeated. Apollo was believed to have had many manifestations (Ps.-Homer, *Hymn to Pythian Apollo* 179–546; Euripides, *Alcestis* 1–9), and Vishnu was thought to have had many avatars, both animal and human (*Bhagavad Gita* 4.7–8). Paul's gospel, by contrast, proclaimed the unique and unrepeatable embodiment of the eternal Son of God in human flesh (Rom 1:3–4; 8:3–4; 1 Tim 3:16). The incarnation was not a temporary manifestation, but permanent and everlasting. The eternal Son had become fully human, without ceasing to be the Son of God. The term for this in Christian theology is the "hypostatic union": Jesus *is* the Son of God, one person with two natures, God and man, never to be divided.

And this brings us to the fifth and final difference. The stories of divine avatars and manifestations in the world into which Paul's gospel came did not claim to announce a new event in history that had transformed the world, but to disclose in varied ways the inner truth of the world as it was, is, and always will be. They did not *change* the human condition nor *join* divinity to humanity. In an important sense, these recurring manifestations only highlighted the unbridgeable *distance* between humanity and divinity. In striking contrast, Paul's gospel brought the good news that the creator had come, in the mystery of the incarnation, to renew fallen humanity with his own presence, glory, and life (2 Cor 8:9; Col 1:19–20; 1 Tim 1:15; Titus 2:11–14). The creator had united himself with humanity, in order that (as we will explore more fully in chapter 5) humanity might be restored to union with God. He had come to renew all things (2 Cor 5:17; 2 Tim 1:9–10). And therefore in Paul's gospel the incarnation is the incomparable and unique event at the center of the cosmos and of history: "When the time was fulfilled, God sent forth his Son, born of a woman" (Gal 4:4; cf. Rom 16:25–27; 1 Cor 2:6–9; Col 1:25–27).

Paul's first hearers, then, had no prior notion of the incarnation proclaimed in Paul's gospel. And yet the gentile world's varied visions of divine manifestations, of demigods and avatars, did express a yearning—a yearning for divinity drawn near. Paul's good news of the incarnation matched this deep longing of his first hearers, but in a way beyond their wildest dreams. For we know, as a matter of history, that the story Paul brought to them was not one they had previously imagined. The incarnation, it seems, was beyond imagining.

Incarnation and Creation

We saw in chapter 1 how Paul brought to his ancient hearers the good news of the God-given and good creation. The fact that it was the direct creation out of nothing by a holy creator God endowed the world and physical existence with an essential goodness and sacredness. Paul's good news of the incarnation provided the most startling exclamation point to his doctrine of creation. Many of the ancient philosophers and sages believed the material cosmos and physical existence were illusory and evil, something to be escaped. But according to Paul's gospel, the creator himself has assumed a human body. The transcendent Lord of all has entered into physical and material existence. If Paul's doctrine of creation reveals that the body and physical existence are good, the incarnation reveals that they are good beyond the power of words or human imagination to describe. The incarnation of the creator reveals the boundless goodness of his creation. And through the incarnation, the creator has sanctified the whole physical and tangible creation in a new and ultimate way. "In the Incarnation creation is fulfilled by God's including himself in it" (Kierkegaard).[1]

The One Lord of the Old Testament in Paul's Gospel

The previous chapter touched upon many of the varied evidences that compel the great majority of Pauline scholars today to affirm a divine Christology within Paul's letters. As we saw, Paul attributes to Jesus the worship that in Paul's Jewish context

---

1. Søren Kierkegaard, *Journals and Papers*, trans. Howard V. Hong and Edna H. Hong (Bloomington: Indiana University Press, 1978), 2:1391.

is due God alone.[2] Paul ascribes eternal existence and the creation of all things to the Son, attributes which in Paul's biblical context are markers, unshared with any creature, of the God of Israel's unique identity.[3] Moreover, just as within the Old Testament YHWH is the center of Israel's faith, life, and hope, so in Paul's epistles Jesus is the center of his people's faith, life, and hope (we will see much more evidence of this in the ensuing chapters).[4] But perhaps the most striking evidence we have thus far considered is the numerous passages in Paul's letters that refer to Jesus as "Lord" (Greek: *kyrios*) in quotations and echoes of Old Testament texts in which "Lord" (*kyrios*) translates the divine name YHWH. These passages in Paul's letters are sometimes called "christological YHWH texts." The majority of Pauline scholars today would agree that these texts, as I argued in the previous chapter, are conclusive evidence of a divine Christology identifying Jesus with the God of Israel.[5]

However, a small but influential minority of scholars have sought to refute the case from the christological YHWH texts for a divine Christology in Paul. According to these scholars, in Paul's quotations and echoes of these Old Testament passages a semantic transfer takes place, in which "the Lord" no longer denotes the

2. On this aspect of the evidence, see further Larry Hurtado, *One God, One Lord: Early Christian Devotion and Ancient Jewish Monotheism*, 3rd ed. (London: T. & T. Clark, 2015).

3. This aspect of the evidence has been especially illumined by Richard Bauckham, *Jesus and the God of Israel* (Grand Rapids: Eerdmans, 2008).

4. Chris Tilling, *Paul's Divine Christology* (Tübingen: Mohr Siebeck, 2012), has shown persuasively that the "pattern of relation" between Christ and Christ followers that we find in Paul's letters corresponds to the pattern of relation between God and Israel in the Old Testament.

5. Already decades ago Lucien Cerfaux concluded that these passages apply to Christ "the same name which belonged to God in the Old Testament." Cerfaux's key studies in this regard are "'Kyrios' dans les citations pauliniennes de l'Ancien Testament," in *Recueil Lucien Cerfaux* (Gembloux: Duculot, 1954), 1:173–88, and *Christ in the Theology of St. Paul* (New York: Herder and Herder, 1959), 470–79. Later, L. Joseph Kreitzer argued that the "referential shift of 'κύριος' from God to Christ" in these texts betokens "a conceptual overlap between God and Christ in such a manner as to prepare the way for the later christological claims of the creeds" (*Jesus and God in Paul's Eschatology* [Sheffield: JSOT, 1987], esp. 93–129). N. T. Wright, in a pair of influential essays on 1 Cor 8 and Phil 2:5–11, respectively, called further attention to the christological YHWH texts, finding in them evidence for a fully incarnational Christology in Paul: see conveniently N. T. Wright, *The Climax of the Covenant: Christ and the Law in Pauline Theology* (Minneapolis: Fortress, 1991), 56–98, 120–36. David B. Capes, in the fullest study of the christological YHWH passages in the Pauline letters to date, claims that Paul in his letters "deliberately and unambiguously applies to Jesus Old Testament texts that contain the divine name" in such a way that "Paul identifies Jesus with God." See his *Old Testament Yahweh Texts in Paul's Christology*, WUNT 2.47 (Tübingen: Mohr Siebeck, 1992). An extremely thorough and insightful study of the relevant passages is provided by Gordon D. Fee, *Pauline Christology: An Exegetical Theological Study* (Peabody, MA: Hendrickson, 2007). The most valuable treatment of all in my view is found in N. T. Wright, *Paul and the Faithfulness of God*, vol. 4 of *Christian Origins and the Question of God* (Minneapolis: Fortress, 2013), 701–9.

divine *name* but is a *title* marking out Jesus as the highest of God's creatures and the chief agent of God. Moreover, they argue that the depiction of Jesus within these passages as sharing in divine attributes and prerogatives does not identify him as YHWH, but involves a merely functional participation in God's majesty and power. For these scholars, it is crucial that in these passages Paul draws upon Old Testament texts that employ the divine name "the Lord" (*kyrios*) rather than the divine title "God" (*theos*), for if it were the latter, they admit that such an intertextual association would unambiguously identify Jesus with God. They argue that Paul's use of passages employing the divine name involves a shift of reference from the divine Lord (in the Old Testament passages) to the messianic but merely human Lord Jesus (in the Pauline passages).[6]

A very long book could show how this approach fails as an adequate exegesis of *any* of the christological YHWH texts. But in this little chapter, we will take as a test case just *one* such text, 2 Thessalonians 1:6–10. In this passage, Paul seeks to encourage the Thessalonians, who are enduring suffering and persecution for the faith, by vividly describing their salvation, and the righteous judgment of the wicked, that will come about at the advent of the Lord:

> [6]Since indeed it is righteous in the sight of God to repay with affliction those who afflict you, [7]and to repay you who suffer affliction with release from suffering, together with us, at the revelation of the Lord Jesus from heaven with the angels of his power, [8]in fire of flame bringing just retribution upon those who do not know God and who do not obey the good news of our Lord Jesus. [9]Those who are such will undergo the just judgment of everlasting destruction, separated from the presence of the Lord and from the glory of his power, [10]when he comes to be glorified in his saints, and revealed as wondrous in all who believe (because our testimony to you was believed) in that day.

---

6. The major studies that have taken this line of argument are P. M. Casey, *From Jewish Prophet to Gentile God: The Origins and Development of New Testament Christology* (Cambridge: James Clarke, 1991); James D. G. Dunn, *The Theology of Paul the Apostle* (Grand Rapids: Eerdmans, 1998); "Why 'Incarnation'? A Review of Recent New Testament Scholarship," in *Christology*, vol. 1 of *The Christ and the Spirit* (Grand Rapids: Eerdmans, 1998), 405–23; Wolfgang Schrage, *Unterwegs zur Einzigkeit und Einheit Gottes: Zum "Monotheismus" des Paulus und seiner alttestamentlich-früjüdischen Tradition* (Neukirchen-Vluyn: Neukirchener Verlag, 2002); Jerome Murphy-O'Connor, *Becoming Human Together: The Pastoral Anthropology of St. Paul,* 3rd ed. (Atlanta: Society of Biblical Literature, 2009), 58–69, 235–40; J. F. McGrath, *The Only True God: Early Christian Monotheism in Its Jewish Context* (Urbana and Chicago: University of Illinois Press, 2009); and Paula Fredriksen, *Paul: The Pagans' Apostle* (New Haven: Yale University Press, 2017), 137–45.

This passage brims with multiple allusions to the Old Testament. Two of these are taken from the prophet Isaiah. In the translation below, the portions echoed in 2 Thessalonians 1 are in italics:

> [10]And now enter into the rocks and hide yourselves in the earth *from the presence* of the terror *of the Lord and from the glory of his power*, when he arises to shatter the earth. . . . [17]And every human being will be abased, and the pride of human beings will fall, and the Lord alone shall be exalted *in that day*. [18]And all the idols they will hide away, [19]bringing them into the caves and into the crevices of the rocks and into the caverns of the earth *from the presence* of the terror *of the Lord and from the glory of his power*, when he arises to shatter the earth. [20]In that day each person will cast his abominations of silver and gold, which they made to worship, to their useless things and to the bats, [21]to enter into the caverns of the strong rock and into the crevices of the rocks, *from the presence* of the terror *of the Lord and from the glory of his power*, when he arises to shatter the earth. (LXX Isa. 2:10, 17–21)

> For behold, the Lord will come as fire, and his chariots as a storm, in his wrath to *bring just retribution* and condemnation *in a flame of fire*. (LXX Isa 66:15)

Paul's use of these passages from Isaiah in 2 Thessalonians 1:6–10 powerfully reveals his incarnational Christology, and the untenability of the proposal that Paul in quoting Isaiah replaces the divine Lord of these Isaian passages with a merely human Lord who shares in divine attributes. For Isaiah 2 and Isaiah 66 are central and important passages within the book of Isaiah regarding the God of Israel and his unique, *unshared* glory. The portion of Isaiah 2 that most emphatically expresses the unique glory that belongs to God alone is the threefold refrain in 2:10, 19, and 21 ("from the presence of the terror of the Lord and from *the glory of his power*"). Remarkably, it is this threefold refrain that in 2 Thessalonians 1:9 is applied to *Jesus* ("from the presence of the Lord and from *the glory of his power*"). In attributing to Jesus the glory given in Isaiah 2 and 66 to YHWH alone, the passage identifies Jesus with YHWH, the God of Israel.

Moreover, in both Isaiah 2 and Isaiah 66, YHWH's unique glory is revealed by his *acts*. It is through his unique divine power and judgment that YHWH's sole glory is revealed. The conception of a created being who carries out these divine functions and yet is distinct from YHWH himself is in striking contradiction to the theology of the very passages of Isaiah upon which Paul reflects in 2 Thessalonians

1:6–10.[7] Paul, in his use of these passages, attributes to Jesus not only the divine name *kyrios*, but also the judgment and power that in these Isaian passages belong to God alone. The central figure in these Isaian passages is Israel's God, whose divine power manifests his unique glory. In identifying this figure with Jesus, Paul identifies Jesus as Israel's God.

Another aspect of these Isaian allusions in the 2 Thessalonians passage is even more crucial. We saw in the previous chapter that the central expectation of the Old Testament is the coming of YHWH in the fullness of his presence and glory. Both Isaiah 2 and Isaiah 66 are prophetic texts that envision the coming of YHWH: "Behold, the Lord will come" (66:15). These passages of Isaiah on which Paul draws are therefore not solely about divine *attributes* or *functions*. They are also about the divine *presence*. YHWH's presence is not an attribute, function, or prerogative of YHWH. YHWH's presence is YHWH himself. And in the Pauline passage, the presence of the Lord is the presence of Jesus: "*the presence of the Lord and the glory of his power*" (2 Thess 1:9). The reading of the christological YHWH passages in terms of a created Lord who shares in divine functions is simply impossible in 2 Thessalonians 1:6–10, for the passages on which Paul draws concern not merely divine prerogatives or functions, but the very presence and coming of YHWH himself. In applying to Jesus these passages that describe the coming of the God of Israel, 2 Thessalonians 1:6–10 identifies Jesus as Israel's God.

Paul also alludes to two Psalms texts within the passage. In the texts given below, I have italicized the portions echoed in 2 Thessalonians 1:10:

> God is *wondrous in his saints*; the God of Israel himself will give power and strength to his people. Blessed be God. (LXX Ps 67:36 [=MT 68:36; Eng 68:35])

> God is *glorified in* the council of *saints*, great and awesome above all those around him. (LXX Ps 88:8 [=MT 89:8; Eng 89:7])

These texts from the Psalms describe the glorification of God in his saints. But within 2 Thessalonians 1:10, these passages that are explicitly about *God* (LXX Ps 67:36, *theos*; LXX Ps 88:8, *theos*) are fulfilled in *Jesus*. The argument for a semantic shift, based on a claimed ambiguity of the word "Lord" (*kyrios*), is clearly falsified by 2 Thessalonians 1:10. For Paul here applies to Jesus not only passages containing

---

7. On "the fundamental Jewish correlation between divine being and divine agency," see Francis Watson, "The Triune Divine Identity: Reflections on Pauline God-Language, in Disagreement with J. D. G. Dunn," *JSNT* 80 (2000): 99–124.

the divine name ("the Lord"), but also passages containing the divine title ("God"). In all four of Paul's allusions to Old Testament passages in 2 Thessalonians 1:6–10, we find a strikingly consistent and connected pattern of interpretation. Throughout the passage, in allusions to both Isaiah and the Psalms, Paul identifies Israel's God, whether referred to as "Lord" (*kyrios*) or "God" (*theos*), with Jesus.[8] Through these intertextual echoes, Paul identifies Jesus as the Lord God, the creator God of Israel.

In this, as in the other "christological YHWH texts," proposals that seek to explain (or explain away) these passages in terms of an unspoken semantic shift in the meaning of "Lord" (*kyrios*), and a merely creaturely and functional participation in divine agency, suffer shipwreck on the evidence of the texts themselves. These passages are one crucial way in which Paul's letters express a divine and incarnational Christology.

A Divine but Not an Incarnational Christology?

Others would object to an incarnational Christology in Paul on wholly different grounds. They agree that 2 Thessalonians 1:6–10 and many other Pauline passages, through their Old Testament allusions, identify Jesus as God. But such passages, they point out, refer to the risen and exalted Christ and his coming in power and glory, not to Jesus during his ministry on earth. It is the exalted Jesus who is identified with YHWH. And therefore, the argument goes, these passages, although reflecting the belief that Jesus has been given the divine name and has been exalted to the status of God almighty, contain no hint of an incarnation. These interpreters claim that we find in Paul a *high* Christology, even a *divine* Christology, but not an incarnational Christology.[9]

This objection (it must be said) is founded upon a deep misunderstanding of Pauline theology. To these scholars, it apparently makes perfect sense to speak of

---

8. Two small but crucial details fit with and confirm this pattern of Old Testament interpretation. Through the possessive "his" in 2 Thess 1:7b, Paul describes the power of the angels, which in the Old Testament belongs to God alone, as belonging to Christ. And through the possessive "his" in the phrase "in his saints" in 1:10, the passage describes the saints, which in Jewish thought can only belong to God, as belonging to the Lord Jesus.

9. For an argument along such lines, see Bart Ehrman, *How Jesus Became God: The Exaltation of a Jewish Preacher from Galilee* (New York: HarperOne, 2014), 247–82. According to Ehrman, in Paul's theology Jesus "was an angel or an angel-like being, who only after his act of obedience to the point of death was made God's equal" (266). "Jesus has been granted the status and honor and glory of the one almighty God himself. . . . But it was not because he was God 'by nature.' . . . He was God because God made him so" (265).

Jesus as merely human in his birth, life, and death, but exalted to "divine status" at his resurrection and ascension. But not in Paul's theology. The theology of Paul is Jewish and monotheistic, thoroughly imbued with the faith of Israel. As we saw in part 1, the foundation of Paul's theology is the distinction between creator and creation. The creator God, distinct from his creation, is the fundamental conception within Paul's thought. He is the everlasting God, without beginning and without end, the transcendent creator who brought all things into being. And therefore the identification of the risen and exalted Jesus as God necessarily reveals *not only who Jesus now is, but who Jesus always was*. David Yeago writes,

> If "there was when he was not" (Arianism) or if any moment can be iden-
> tified as the beginning of his relationship with YHWH (Adoptionism),
> then his association with YHWH would amount to the enthronement of
> a "second god" alongside the Lord God of Israel. And we are forbidden
> to think *that* by the deepest logic of Israel's faith: there is only one God,
> YHWH, incomparable and unique.... Only if the exaltation manifests a
> relationship intrinsic to God's being from everlasting, does the exaltation
> not imply that there are now two gods, Jesus and YHWH, but rather
> make known that Jesus was always included in the glory of the one God,
> even before the foundations of the world were laid (John 17).[10]

The one "born of a woman" (Gal 4:4) is, together with the Father, the creator and source of all things (Col 1:16–17). He is from everlasting the "one Lord . . . through whom all things exist" (1 Cor 8:6). Within Paul's theology of the creator God, *Paul's identification of the risen and exalted Jesus as God presupposes the entire narrative of the incarnation.*

Moreover, contrary to the claims of these scholars, Paul in fact applies Old Testament YHWH passages not only to the risen and exalted Christ but also to the Son of God prior to his incarnation (1 Cor 8:6, echoing Deut 6:4), at his birth (Titus 2:11, echoing Isa 40:5), at the Last Supper (1 Cor 11:25, echoing Zech 9:11), at his crucifixion (1 Cor 2:8, echoing Ps 24:10), and at his death, burial, resurrection, and ascension (Eph 4:7–10, citing Ps 68:18). Jesus's glorification through his resurrection and ascension was not the bestowal on Jesus of a "divine status" he did not previously have. Rather (as we saw in the previous chapter), through his saving passion, death, and resurrection, Jesus had brought the new and ultimate revelation of the divine name and glory awaited in the time of YHWH's saving

10. David Yeago, "The New Testament and the Nicene Dogma: A Contribution to the Recovery of Theological Exegesis," *Pro Ecclesia* 3 (1994): 157–58.

reign (Isa 45:22–3; Zech 14:9; Mal 1:11). And in bringing the promised full reve-lation of the divine name (something only YHWH himself could do), Jesus had revealed himself as the One who bears "the name which is above every name," the very creator God of Israel (Rom 1:3–5; Eph 1:20–23; Phil 2:9–11).[11]

It is true that Paul uses Old Testament passages about the coming of YHWH *extensively* in connection with Jesus's future coming in power and glory, and *less extensively* in regard to his first coming.[12] Why is this? I propose that when he describes Jesus's first advent, Paul prefers to make the *mode* of Jesus's coming clear by using language that is specifically *incarnational*, focusing on the Son of God's advent in human flesh, especially on his sharing in the human plight of abasement and suffering:

> From whom came the Christ in regard to his human nature, who is God over all, blessed forever. (Rom 9:5)

> He emptied himself, taking the form of a slave, being made in human likeness. (Phil 2:7)

> Although he was rich, for your sake he became poor. (2 Cor 8:9)

At other times, Paul chooses to describe Jesus's fulfillment of the hope of YHWH's advent through his first coming in language that illumines *simultaneously* the incar-national mode of his coming, and that coming's revelation of the mystery of Father and Son. He does this by replacing (and thereby enriching) the prophetic language of YHWH's *coming* with the language of the Father *sending* the Son in human *flesh*:

> But when the time of fulfillment came, God *sent forth* his Son, *born of a woman*. (Gal 4:4)

> God *sent* his own Son in the likeness of sinful *flesh*. (Rom 8:3)

I would propose, then, that the reason Paul employs the Old Testament texts and language of YHWH's coming less extensively for Jesus's first advent than for his second is that, when he describes the former, Paul normally alters and enriches

11. See the insightful treatment of Richard Bauckham, *God Crucified: Monotheism and Christology in the New Testament* (Grand Rapids: Eerdmans, 1998), 56–61.

12. See Larry Hurtado, "YHWH's Return to Zion: A New Catalyst for Earliest High Christol-ogy?" in *God and the Faithfulness of Paul: A Critical Examination of the Pauline Theology of N. T. Wright*, ed. Christoph Heilig, J. Thomas Hewitt, and Michael F. Bird (Tübingen: Mohr Siebeck, 2016), 417–38.

the Old Testament language of YHWH's coming and presence, in order to more fully express the nature of the incarnation event.

God the Father and the Lord Jesus Christ

Another objection to an incarnational theology in Paul is that Paul seldom directly refers to Jesus as "God." While we have seen that Paul does apply the divine title "God" to Jesus explicitly and powerfully in Romans 9:5, in Titus 2:13, and by inter-textual allusion in 2 Thessalonians 1:10, it is true that Paul refers to Jesus as God rather seldom. Yet he refers to Jesus as Lord with great frequency. And (although this is seldom pointed out) *the reverse is also true*: Paul refers to the Father as God with great frequency but to the Father as Lord quite seldom. Why? Here again I have a proposal.

We saw above how in his reading of Deuteronomy 6:4, the core confession of Israel's belief in "one God, one Lord," Paul identified the "one God" with the Father and the "one Lord" with Jesus Christ (1 Cor 8:6). I would suggest that Paul's reading of this central confession of Israel in light of the mystery of Father and Son ("one God, the Father . . . one Lord, Jesus Christ") is the basis for his regular practice of ascribing the divine title ("God") to the Father and the divine name ("Lord") to the Son. This pattern is evident in the salutation with which Paul begins practically all his letters: "Grace to you and peace from *God* our Father, and the *Lord* Jesus Christ" (Rom 1:7; 1 Cor 1:3; 2 Cor 1:2; Gal 1:3; Eph 1:2; Phil 1:2; 1 Thess 1:1 [textual variant]; 2 Thess 1:2; 1 Tim 1:2; 2 Tim 1:2; Philem 3). In Paul's salutation Jesus Christ is identified as the coordinate and equal source with the Father of that divine grace and peace that can come only from the creator, and in this way is identified together with the Father as the Lord God of Israel. But in Paul's salutations, as in 1 Corinthians 8:6, the Father is given the divine title ("God") and the Son the divine name ("Lord"). This pattern is also a striking element of the confessional formulas and summaries of the faith in Paul (cf. Rom 1:3–4; 10:8–10; 1 Cor 12:3; Eph 4:4–6; Phil 2:9–11; 1 Thess 5:9–10; 1 Tim 6:13–16), and is a constant feature of his letters (e.g., Rom 5:1; 8:39; 15:6; 1 Cor 1:9; 6:11; 2 Cor 13:14 [Greek 13:13]; Eph 5:20; 6:23; Col 3:17; 1 Thess 3:11–13). In each of these texts in which Paul identifies the Father as "God" and the Son as "Lord," the context, either explicitly or implicitly, forbids reading the "Lord" of these passages as a mere created being alongside the one God. Rather, these Pauline texts draw upon the language and thought of Deuteronomy 6:4, Israel's core confession, to identify the "one God, one Lord" of Israel's faith as God the Father, and the Lord Jesus Christ.[13]

13. In Deut 6, verse 4 belongs together with verse 5. The Pauline passages that draw upon the

I would thus propose that Paul's christological reading of Israel's central affirmation of faith, the Shema, was fundamental in shaping Paul's way of speaking about God. This, I would argue, offers the most satisfying explanation for Paul's normal practice of ascribing the divine title ("God") to the Father and the divine name ("Lord") to the Son.

An Anachronistic Reading of Paul?

We must address one final and inevitable objection: that an incarnational reading of Paul's Christology can only be an illegitimate projection of later dogmatic categories onto New Testament texts.[14] I believe this objection fails to grasp the true relationship between Paul's letters and the church's historic Christology. For these later Trinitarian dogmas, as they were clarified and expressed in the great christological debates, creeds, hymns, and prayers of the ancient church, were themselves *the product of exegesis of the New Testament, and above all of Paul.* Historically, the theological language and categories of the church's creeds, such as the Nicene Creed, were created to flesh out the implications of the scriptural witness, especially the letters of Paul. *Nicene theology is the direct creation of Pauline incarnational theology.* The Pauline letters themselves exert a powerful theological "pressure" upon both ancient and modern interpreters that compels an incarnational interpretation. This important conception of the pressure or coercion exerted by the biblical text was first suggested by Brevard Childs and has recently been powerfully developed in an important essay by C. Kavin Rowe: "The biblical text is not inert but instead exerts a pressure ('coercion') upon its interpreters and asserts itself within theological reflection and discourse such that there is (or can be) a profound continuity, grounded in the subject matter itself, between the biblical text and traditional Christian exegesis and theological formulation."[15] Of course, the church's developed theological terms and categories (e.g., incarnation, essence,

---

language of Deut 6:4 often reflect the theological and verbal content of the larger unit Deut 6:4–5 in striking (and christologically significant) ways. For example, in Eph 6:23 "the Lord Jesus Christ" is the source, together with "God the Father," not only of peace but also of love and of faith, gifts that can only be given by the one God. Eph 6:23 thus reflects the vocabulary and thought of Deut 6:4: "The Lord our God is one Lord." The very next verse bestows grace upon "all those who love our Lord Jesus Christ" (Eph 6:24), reflecting the thought of Deut 6:5: "And you shall love the Lord your God with all your heart, with all your soul, and with all your strength."

14. For this objection, see, for example, Fredriksen, *Paul*, 137, 144.

15. C. Kavin Rowe, "Biblical Pressure and Trinitarian Hermeneutics," *Pro Ecclesia* 11 (2002): 295–312. The quote is from 308.

person) are not present in Paul's letters. However, they are not a false imposition on Paul's thought, but the logical and necessary outworking of the incarnational substance of his theology.

Conclusion: Paul's Incarnational Christology

When Paul brought the good news of the incarnation, he proclaimed a conception previously unknown to his ancient hearers—the entrance of the creator into the creation he had made. The creator had come in the person of Jesus Christ to renew fallen humanity and restore all creation. The incarnation affirmed (in the most startling way) the infinite goodness of the creation, and through the incarnation the creator sanctified the created order in a new way. "In the Incarnation creation is fulfilled by God's including himself in it" (Kierkegaard). As we have seen, Paul's Christology is divine and fully incarnational. The church's doctrine of the incarnation is not a false imposition on Paul, but the logical outworking of his theology.

In this and the previous chapter we have explored the major lines of evidence that have led the great majority of scholars today to affirm a divine Christology in Paul in continuity with the historic Christian creeds and their confession of Jesus as God incarnate. These several lines of evidence converge and, in my view, are conclusive. But (the reader may be surprised to learn) we have not yet considered the most important line of evidence. The main evidence for Paul's incarnational Christology concerns an aspect of Paul's teaching on which there is virtually unanimous scholarly agreement. However, its importance for Paul's Christology has not in my view been fully explored. This will be the focus of our next chapter. This aspect of Paul's teaching will not only confirm our results in this and the previous chapter, but will also shed a wondrous new light on the incarnation in Paul, and its place within his theology.

Chapter Five

The Epicenter of Paul's Theology

auline scholars today are agreed regarding the enormous importance of (what is called) *participation* in Paul's theology. "Participation" is the term scholars use for the Pauline teaching that through faith in Christ believers enter into a supernatural union with God, becoming the temples of the Holy Spirit. Ancient readers readily recognized this aspect of Paul's teaching. But Albert Schweitzer was the first Pauline scholar in modern times to call attention to the importance of this theme in Paul's letters.[1] In recent decades, it is E. P. Sanders who has argued most influentially for the crucial significance of this conception in Paul.[2] Sanders argues that this participatory union with God is in fact "the main theme of Paul's theology."[3] Following Sanders, the importance of "participation" in Paul's thought has become a scholarly commonplace.[4]

If the current consensus is on the right track (and I believe it is), then in the theme of participation we come close to the core of Paul's theology. In this chapter I wish to build upon this scholarly consensus concerning the importance of union with God in Paul's thought, in order to gain a better grasp of Paul's Christology, that is, his understanding of the person and identity of Jesus Christ.

---

1. Albert Schweitzer, *The Mysticism of Paul the Apostle*, trans. W. Montgomery (Baltimore: Johns Hopkins University Press, 1998 [original *Die Mystik des Apostels Paulus*, 1930]).

2. E. P. Sanders, *Paul and Palestinian Judaism* (Philadelphia: Fortress, 1977).

3. Sanders, *Paul and Palestinian Judaism*, 552. Cf. 456: "The centrality appears in what was just mentioned: *it is the theme, above all, to which Paul appeals both in parenesis and polemic.*"

4. For discussion and further literature, see Robert C. Tannehill, "Participation in Christ: A Central Theme in Pauline Soteriology," in *The Shape of the Gospel: New Testament Essays* (Eugene, OR: Wipf and Stock, 2007), 225–39; Constantine R. Campbell, *Paul and Union with Christ: An Exegetical and Theological Study* (Grand Rapids: Zondervan, 2012); Grant Macaskill, *Union with Christ in the New Testament* (Oxford: Oxford University Press, 2013); Michael J. Gorman, *Inhabiting the Cruciform God: Kenosis, Justification, and Theosis in Paul's Narrative Soteriology* (Grand Rapids: Eerdmans, 2009); and the recent volume edited by Michael J. Thate, Kevin J. Vanhoozer, and Constantine R. Campbell, *"In Christ" in Paul: Explorations in Paul's Theology of Union and Participation* (Tübingen: Mohr Siebeck, 2014).

By placing this crucial feature of Paul's thought within its Jewish context and in the context of his wider theology, we will uncover its startling implications for Paul's Christology. And we will find, I am convinced, the very epicenter of Paul's theology.

Union with the Creator God in Pauline Theology

In chapter 3 we saw how Paul believed the central hope of Israel, the coming of YHWH, had been fulfilled in the incarnation—the embodiment of the eternal Son of God in human flesh. And Paul believed that the fulfillment of this hope of YHWH's coming, which had been inaugurated at Jesus's first advent, would be fully consummated at his second coming. But Paul also believed that the promise of YHWH's coming and presence had been fulfilled in another way: in the present participatory union of God with the faithful brought about through the incarnation and saving work of Christ. This is evident in 2 Corinthians 6:16:

> And what agreement does the temple of God have with idols? For we are the temple of the living God, just as God said: "I will dwell in them and walk among them, and I will be their God, and they shall be my people."

Paul's citation is a composite quotation from two scriptural texts:

> And I will make my dwelling in your midst, and I will not abhor you. And I will walk among you, and I will be your God, and you will be my people. (Lev 26:11–12)

> My dwelling will be among them, and I will be their God, and they will be my people. And the nations will know that I am the Lord who makes Israel holy, when my holy dwelling place is in their midst forever. (Ezek 37:27–28)

Both the Leviticus and Ezekiel texts prophetically envision the abiding presence of YHWH among his people. Paul's use of these passages in 2 Corinthians 6:16 shows that he understood this promise as now fulfilled in the tabernacling presence of God among his people through their baptism into Christ. In Paul's thought, the people of God in Christ, the church, fulfills the prophetic promise of a new temple in which the creator God himself would dwell in the time of his coming reign (Isa 56:6–7; Jer 3:16–17; Ezek 37:26–28; 40–48).

Rudolf Bultmann famously sought to minimize or eliminate the concept of participation from Paul's theology, because he was uncomfortable with its obvious supernatural dimensions.[5] But this attempt was by all accounts unsuccessful. Paul truly believed that God is mysteriously united with and indwells those who believe in Jesus. This is clear from Paul's repeated declaration that the bodies of the faithful are God's *temple* (1 Cor 6:19–20; Eph 2:21)—for the one who dwells in his temple is God. It is clear from Paul's *contrast* of this participatory union with the worship of idols (1 Cor 10:14–22; 2 Cor 6:16). And it is evident in Paul's explicit, overt statements that believers are a sanctuary or dwelling place of *God* (1 Cor 3:16–17; 2 Cor 6:16; Eph 2:22). As Pauline scholars today are agreed, in Paul's theology the creator God himself is supernaturally united with and indwells the faithful.

This participatory union with God proclaimed by Paul offered a divine intimacy entirely unknown among the philosophies and religions in the ancient world into which Paul's gospel came. First, Paul's gospel offered through Christ a relationship with the transcendent creator God, maker of heaven and earth. As we saw in chapter 1, the ancient world addressed by Paul's gospel had no knowledge of a transcendent creator. The gods of ancient worship and philosophy were either identified with the cosmos, considered aspects or features of it, or regarded as but one part of a total cosmic system. Second, the conception of such an intimate union with even these lesser beings of ancient worship and philosophy would have been unknown to Paul's hearers. According to Epicurus and the Buddha, the gods were distant and remote beings without concern for humans, and humans need have no concern for the gods (Epicurus, *Letter to Menoeceus* 123; Cicero, *On the Nature of the Gods* 1.43–56; Gautama Buddha, *Anguttara Nikāya* 10.29; *Digha Nikāya* 13). For the pantheistic Stoic and Hindu sages, God and the universe were one and the same, and the human soul was itself divine by nature, rendering any conception of supernatural union with a divine being distinct from the worshiper impossible (Marcus Aurelius, *Meditations* 8.54; Seneca, *Letters* 66.12; *Bhagavad Gita* 2.12–25; 6.24–32). To be sure, in tension with these philosophic conceptions, the ancients in their religious rites and prayers regularly invoked the presence of the gods.[6] The closest ancient analogue to Paul's teaching of union with God through faith in Christ comes in the yearning expressed in ancient polytheistic worship for the presence of the divine. Paul's gospel offered the fulfillment of this yearning, but in a fullness his ancient hearers could not have previously imagined.

---

5. See Rudolf Bultmann, *Theologie des Neuen Testaments*, 9th ed. (Tübingen: Mohr Siebeck, 1984). Cf. the remarks of Sanders in *Paul and Palestinian Judaism*, 453–54.

6. For the evidence in detail, see Ramsay MacMullen, *Paganism in the Roman Empire* (New Haven: Yale University Press, 1981).

For although they invoked their presence, ancient worshipers had no notion of the gods as miraculously uniting themselves with humanity or inhabiting the human heart. Paul's gospel, by contrast, called its hearers, through faith in the incarnate Son of God, to a miraculous, transforming union with the transcendent creator, who, while remaining distinct from the worshiper, truly inhabits and unites himself with the believing soul, in a relationship of the most intimate communion.

Participation as the Key to Pauline Christology

This important theme of participation in the creator God is a neglected but crucial key to Pauline Christology. The reason is a straightforward one, but it is often overlooked in scholarly discussion of the Christology of Paul's letters. It is this: in Paul's theology this gift of the divine indwelling, the fulfillment of the promised abiding presence of YHWH, is *the presence and indwelling of Jesus Christ.*

> Put yourselves to the test whether you are in the faith, test yourselves whether you are genuine. Or do you not know this about yourselves, that Jesus Christ is in you? Unless you are not genuine. (2 Cor 13:5)

> With Christ I have been crucified. Yet I live—yet no longer I, but Christ lives in me. (Gal 2:19–20)

> To his saints God was pleased to make known what is the riches of the glory of this mystery among the gentiles—which is Christ in you, the hope of glory. (Col 1:26–27)

In Paul's theology of participation, believers have been "called to communion with his Son, Jesus Christ our Lord" (1 Cor 1:9). Through this union "all of you who have been baptized into Christ have clothed yourselves with Christ" (Gal 3:27). One of Paul's favorite ways of expressing this union is the formula "in Christ": "So then if anyone is in Christ, there is a new creation. The old things have passed away; behold, new things have come" (2 Cor 5:17). The formula "in Christ" appears with great frequency in Paul, alongside equivalent formulas such as "in the Lord" and "in the Lord Jesus."[7] Of course, the extraordinary frequency

---

7. For example, "in Christ" in Rom 6:11, 23; 8:39; 12:5; 1 Cor 1:2; 2 Cor 5:21; Gal 3:26; Eph 1:1; Phil 1:1, 13, 26; 3:8; 4:19, 21; Col 1:2; "in the Lord" in Rom 16:11; 1 Cor 7:22; 2 Cor 10:17; Gal 5:10; Eph 5:8; Phil 1:14; 2:24, 29; 4:1, 4; Col 3:18, 20; 4:7, 17; "in the Lord Jesus" in Rom 14:14; Phil 2:19; and "into

of these and other participatory formulas in Paul's letters is powerful evidence, as scholars have recognized, of the important place of participation in his thought. But the point here is that the divine union that these formulas express is union with *Christ*. Through this union believers are the *body of Christ* (Rom 12:4–5; 1 Cor 12:12–27; Eph 1:22–23; 4:11–16; 5:22–32; Col 1:18, 24; 3:15). This is not a mere metaphor in Paul's thought, but a miraculous reality (1 Cor 6:15–17; 10:16–17; 12:13; Eph 4:6; 5:31–32). It is one more way in which Paul expresses the participatory union of the faithful with Christ.

In short, the tabernacling presence of *God* within his people, so crucial to Paul's theology, is the indwelling of *Jesus Christ*. The long-awaited coming and abiding presence of YHWH are in Paul's thought fulfilled in the union of Jesus Christ with his church. Paul's doctrine of participation thus offers a hitherto neglected key to Paul's Christology.[8] The Pauline doctrine of participation reveals that in Paul's theology Jesus is not a mere creature, nor a created being exalted to divine status, but the creator God come in the flesh. Jesus's divine identity cannot be excised from Paul's doctrine of participation without unraveling the whole. It is built on the foundation that Jesus Christ is the God of Israel incarnate. If Jesus Christ is not God, Paul's doctrine of participation is simply incoherent.

The evidence from Paul's participatory theology confirms our findings in the previous two chapters regarding Paul's incarnational Christology, and does so in a striking way. Those chapters focused (as scholarly discussion of Paul's Christology generally does) on a select number of foundational passages in Paul where he sets forth this teaching. This might give the impression that the case for a divine Christology in Paul is based upon a few important passages within his letters. But our conclusions here regarding Jesus's divine identity in Paul's letters are not based on evidence culled from a few individual passages, but follow from the whole structure of Paul's doctrine of union with God. The evidence for Paul's divine Christology is far more massive than is generally realized—as massive as the evidence for Paul's participatory theology itself.

Christ" in Rom 6:3; Gal 3:27; Philem 6. See also the participatory formula "with Christ" in Rom 6:4; 2 Cor 4:14; cf. Rom 6:5–9; Gal 2:19; Eph 2:5–9; Col 2:12; 3:1–4.

8. To be sure, a number of studies have insightfully explored participation in Paul within Paul's incarnational narrative. An excellent example is Gorman, *Inhabiting the Cruciform God*. But the discussion of Paul's Christology has generally proceeded in isolation from the implications of Paul's doctrine of participation for his Christology. A welcome and encouraging exception is the recent and insightful essay by Grant Macaskill, "Incarnational Ontology and the Theology of Participation in Paul," in Thate, Vanhoozer, and Campbell, *"In Christ" in Paul*, 87–101.

Participation within the Larger Narrative of Paul's Gospel

In Paul's theology, this gift of the divine presence and indwelling within the faithful is the outworking of a prior act of God. It is the outworking of the incarnation:

> [4]But when the fullness of time had come, God sent forth his Son, born of a woman, born under the law, [5]that he might redeem those who were under the law, that we might receive adoption as God's sons. [6]And because you are sons, God has sent forth the Spirit of his Son into our hearts, crying out, "Abba, Father!" (Gal 4:4–6)

The conceptual link between verse 4 ("God sent forth his Son") and verse 6 ("God has sent forth the Spirit of his Son") brings us into the heart of Paul's theology. As we saw in chapter 2, one of the fundamental categories of Paul's thought is the binary opposition:

Union with the Creator

Separation from the Creator

In the church's participatory union with Christ, the fellowship with the creator offered to the first human beings, but forfeited in the Fall, is become a reality. And this presence and indwelling of the Son of God in the present anticipate the consummation of this union at his second coming (cf. 1 Thess 4:17, "and thus we will always be with the Lord"). But this participatory union is only made possible by a prior action of God, bridging the unbridgeable gap between fallen human beings and their creator—"God sent forth his Son, born of a woman" (Gal 4:4).

"Participation" in Paul's theology is thus but one part of a larger divine narrative of redemption. The center of this narrative is the incarnation of God in the person of Jesus Christ. Participation in Paul's thought is a miracle, but it is founded upon a more central miracle. The new birth of the Spirit (Gal 4:6) is the outworking of the birth of the Son of God (Gal 4:4), and the mighty acts of redemption he would accomplish when he came—the cross and the resurrection (Gal 4:5; cf. Rom 5:1–2; 8:3–4; 1 Cor 6:19–20; Gal 3:1–2, 13–14; Eph 2:17–18; 3:11–12; Titus 3:4–7). Human union with God is made possible by God's union with humanity through the incarnation.

In the *relationship* of Paul's doctrines of the incarnation and of participation we uncover a crucial dimension of Pauline and biblical theology. We saw in chapter 2 that, within Paul's theology, the supernatural gift of the divine image and communion with God that was given to humanity in its original creation could only be actualized through humanity's free decision to partake of this divine life (a gift that was forfeited in the Fall). Here, too, in Paul's doctrines of the incarnation and of participation in God we see the covenantal character of salvation in Christ, and the crucial place of human freedom in relation to God. The incarnation is entirely God's initiative, God's action, the creator through this mysterious union with his creation coming to renew fallen humanity with his own presence, glory, and life. But the divine presence and indwelling the Son of God came to bestow does not work automatically or magically, or override human free will. The union with God that is the purpose of the incarnation can only come about through the free response of repentance and faith:

> Participation in Christ, including the participation in Christ's death that frees people from slavery to sin, depends upon God's identification with humanity in its need, which takes place through the sending of God's Son to share the human plight, an act of self-giving by God the Father and by God's Son. This divine act of identification is primary and makes available divine transforming power. But there is an answering act of identification, which is the believer's response of faith in Christ.[9]

In other words, the condition of this miraculous divine union, a union made possible through the incarnation, is the free response of identification with Christ through faith and love. This participatory union with God thus comes "by faith" (Rom 1:17; Gal 3:14; Eph 2:8; 3:17). It is the gift of God, but a gift given only to "those who call on the name of our Lord Jesus Christ in every place, their Lord and ours" (1 Cor 1:2). "For all of you who have been baptized into Christ have clothed yourselves with Christ" (Gal 3:27). The place or locus of participation is therefore the community of Christ believers, the church (Eph 5:22–32). Paul's use of *temple* imagery (1 Cor 3:16–17; 6:19–20; 2 Cor 6:14–7:1; Eph 2:19–22) to describe this participatory union is significant. It is not simply that Christ *is* in the faithful, but that he *indwells* them as in his temple, in a covenantal relationship of friendship, love, and intimacy. The exalted and sacred character of human freedom that met us in Paul's theology of creation and fall meets us again here in his theology of the incarnation and participation. *The purpose of the unilateral act of love that is the incarnation is the reciprocal relationship of love that is participation.*

And this illumines a further aspect of Paul's theology that is often misunderstood within our contemporary context. Many people today, and some Pauline

---

9. Tannehill, "Participation in Christ," 38.

interpreters, feel that Paul's doctrine of divine judgment upon those who reject Christ is inconsistent with his gospel as the good news of the love and grace of God. John M. G. Barclay, for example, thinks that "Paul partially deconstructs his own Christological exclusivism by his pervasive appeal to the grace of God."[10] But I believe this charge misunderstands both Paul's theology of creation and his theology of the incarnation. The condition for incorporation into Christ is the free response of trust in Christ. And thus one can exclude oneself from this life-giving union through unbelief (Rom 1:18; 2:1–11; 1 Cor 9:24–10:13; 2 Cor 13:5; Gal 5:4–6; Eph 5:5–7; Col 1:21–23; 2 Thess 1:5–10). This is consistent with the sacred nature of human free will in Paul's doctrine of creation. And according to Paul's theology of the incarnation, rejection of Jesus is not the rejection of yet one more messenger or servant of God, but is self-separation from the divine Son of God, the creator and source of life. It is refusal to enter into the very communion of love with their creator for which human beings were made. Paul thus defines damnation as "the just judgment of everlasting destruction, separated from the presence of the Lord and from the glory of his power" (2 Thess 1:9). The purpose of God's grace in Paul's theology is union with the living God, not to make this union optional or irrelevant. Human beatitude apart from a freely chosen union of love with the creator would be possible only if the creator should cease to exist, or cease to be the source of all love, goodness, and beatitude (either of which is of course an impossibility). Far from being an inconsistency, the judgment of those who consciously reject the gospel of Christ is the necessary corollary of Paul's doctrines of creation and incarnation.

Participation in Father, Son, and Holy Spirit

We have seen that in Paul's thought participation involves a true miraculous union of the faithful with the creator God, fulfilling the prophetic promise of YHWH's coming and abiding presence. One of Paul's most frequent ways of describing this participation in God is in terms of the indwelling of the *Spirit of God* or of the *Holy Spirit* (Rom 5:5; 8:9–11, 15–17, 23; 1 Cor 2:10–16; 3:16–17; 6:19–20; 12:12–13; Gal 3:1–3, 13–14; 1 Thess 4:8; 2 Tim 1:7–8, 14; Titus 3:4–7). Paul also frequently describes this union of believers with God as their being "in

---

10. John M. G. Barclay, "'Neither Jew Nor Greek': Multiculturalism and the New Perspective on Paul," in *Ethnicity and the Bible*, ed. M. G. Brett (Leiden: Brill, 1996), 213. See also, following Barclay, Jouette M. Bassler, *Navigating Paul: An Introduction to Key Theological Concepts* (Louisville: Westminster John Knox, 2007), 8–9.

the Spirit" (Rom 8:9; 9:1; 14:17; 1 Cor 6:11; 12:3, 13; Eph 2:18, 22; Col 1:8; cf. Rom 7:6; 15:16; 1 Cor 12:9; 2 Cor 6:6; Eph 6:18). This feature of the Pauline concept of participation unveils another key aspect of his theology. Paul's equation of the tabernacling presence of God in his people with the presence of the Holy Spirit reveals that the Holy Spirit in Paul's thought is not a creature nor a created divine force. The Holy Spirit is God himself. The divinity of the Holy Spirit in Paul's thought is also evident from the "pneumatological YHWH texts" in which Paul applies Old Testament YHWH texts to the Holy Spirit (e.g., 1 Cor 2:16, echoing Isa 40:13; Rom 8:27, echoing Ps 139:1, 23; and Titus 3:6, echoing Joel 2:28–29 [Heb 3:1–2]). It is evident as well in Paul's ascription of unique, unshared markers of the creator's identity, such as YHWH's sole power to give life, to the Holy Spirit (e.g., Rom 8:11; 2 Cor 3:6; Gal 6:8). But Paul's participatory theology provides the most abundant and striking evidence. One of its key components, which cannot be removed without its entire structure collapsing, is that the Holy Spirit who indwells the faithful is truly God.

We saw in part 1 that the foundation of Paul's theology is belief in the one creator God, the God of Israel. And in chapter 3 we saw that the incarnation brought a new revelation of the inner mystery of the one God as a communion of Father and Son. Paul's language of participation now permits us to enrich our knowledge of that mystery. For as we have now seen, Paul describes the participatory union of believers *interchangeably* as union with God, union with the Son, and union with the Holy Spirit. Likewise, Paul applies Old Testament YHWH passages not only to the Father, but also to the Son and to the Holy Spirit. Paul thereby identifies not only the Father, but also the Son and the Holy Spirit, with the one God of Israel. And yet Paul's letters consistently *distinguish* between the Father and the Son, and between the Son and the Spirit.[11] Paul's theology of God thus has an unmistakable *Trinitarian* character, in which the one creator God is identified as a mysterious union of Father, Son, and Holy Spirit.

Moreover, this is not a minor element of Paul's theology. Paul's "God-language," his discourse about the creator God, is throughout shaped and structured as a discourse concerning the Father, the Son, and the Holy Spirit. Consider his closing prayer in 2 Corinthians 13:14 (Greek 13:13):

And may the grace of our *Lord Jesus Christ*, and the love of *God*, and the communion of the *Holy Spirit*, be with you all.

11. Rom 1:3–5; 8:3–4; 15:18–19, 30; 1 Cor 2:2–5; 6:11; 12:3–6; 2 Cor 1:21–22; 3:3–6; 4:13–15; 13:14 (Greek 13:13); Gal 4:4–6; Eph 1:17; 2:18, 20–22; 3:14–19; 4:4–6, 20–24; 5:18–20; Phil 1:27–28; 3:3; Col 1:6–8; 1 Thess 1:4–6; 5:18–19; 2 Tim 1:7–8; Titus 3:4–7.

So elsewhere Paul speaks of God, his Son, and the Spirit (Rom 1:3–5; 8:3–4; Gal 4:4–6). In many passages Paul speaks of God, the Lord, and the Spirit (1 Cor 6:11; 12:4–6; Eph 1:17; 4:4–6; 5:18–20; 1 Thess 1:4–6; 2 Tim 1:7–8). In many other passages he speaks of God, Christ, and Spirit (Rom 15:18–19, 30; 1 Cor 2:2–5; 2 Cor 1:21–22; 3:3, 4–6; Eph 2:20–22; 3:14–18; Phil 1:27–28; Col 1:6–8; Titus 3:4–7). In still others he speaks of God, Jesus, and the Spirit (Eph 4:20–24; Phil 3:3; 1 Thess 5:18–19) or Father, Christ, and Spirit (Eph 3:14–19). Paul consistently speaks of the being and activity of God as the being and activity of Father, Son, and Holy Spirit. Paul's theology has a profoundly Trinitarian structure.[12]

In sum, Paul's letters reveal a theology of God for which the only adequate language is the language of the Trinity. In its substance, Paul's Christology is both *incarnational* and *Trinitarian*. Of course, the church's later Trinitarian terminology and categories are not present in Paul's epistles. But Paul's letters express a theology of which these categories are the logical outworking. Paul's letters exert a "pressure" upon the interpreter that compels a Trinitarian interpretation.[13] The church's ancient creedal affirmation of "one divine Essence, three divine Persons" (*mia ousia, treis hypostaseis*), far from being an artificial constraint imposed upon Paul's letters from without, is in reality indispensable for their full exposition. In Paul's theology, the ultimate revelation of the incarnation is the unveiling of the inner mystery of the one God as a communion of persons: Father, Son, and Holy Spirit.

The Spirit of God's Son

Paul's participatory language raises a question that has perplexed many readers. How can Paul speak of the tabernacling divine presence in the faithful as the indwelling of Christ ("Do you not know that Jesus Christ is in you?" [2 Cor 13:5]) and also as the presence of the Holy Spirit ("Do you not know that you are the

---

12. On the Trinitarian character of Paul's thought, see the following studies: Wesley Hill, *Paul and the Trinity: Persons, Relations, and the Pauline Letters* (Grand Rapids: Eerdmans, 2015); Gordon D. Fee, *Pauline Christology: An Exegetical Theological Study* (Peabody, MA: Hendrickson, 2007), esp. 481–593; and Mehrdad Fatehi, *The Spirit's Relation to the Risen Lord in Paul: An Examination of Its Christological Implications*, WUNT 2.128 (Tübingen: Mohr Siebeck, 2000). See also Ron C. Fay, "Was Paul a Trinitarian? A Look at Romans 8," in *Paul and His Theology*, ed. Stanley E. Porter (Leiden: Brill, 2006), 327–45, and Andrew C. Gabriel, "Pauline Pneumatology and the Question of Trinitarian Presuppositions," in Porter, *Paul and His Theology*, 347–62.

13. See C. Kavin Rowe, "Biblical Pressure and Trinitarian Hermeneutics," *Pro Ecclesia* 11 (2002): 295–312.

temple of God and the Spirit of God dwells in you?" [1 Cor 3:16])? How can Paul speak interchangeably of believers as "in Christ" (Rom 8:39; 1 Cor 1:2; Gal 3:26) and as "in the Spirit" (Rom 14:17; 1 Cor 6:11; Col 1:8)? In a number of passages Paul appears to identify Christ and the Spirit (Rom 8:9–10; 1 Cor 6:17; 12:13; 15:45; 2 Cor 3:3, 17–18; Eph 3:16–17), and a few Pauline scholars have argued that Christ and the Spirit are one and the same in Paul's theology.[14] But elsewhere Paul unambiguously distinguishes the Spirit from the Son (1 Cor 6:11; 12:3; 2 Cor 11:4; 13:14 [Greek 13:13]; Gal 3:5; Eph 2:18, 22; 3:4–5; 4:4–6). How precisely is the Son related to the Spirit in Paul's theology?[15]

The answer is given in the crucial passage from Galatians quoted earlier in the chapter, in which Paul describes the new birth of the Spirit that has come about through the incarnation (Gal 4:4–6). There Paul identifies the Spirit that God has given as "the Spirit *of his Son*" (Gal 4:6). The Spirit of God is "the Spirit *of Christ*" (Rom 8:9). The indwelling Holy Spirit is "the Spirit *of Jesus Christ*" (Phil 1:19; cf. Acts 16:7). Earlier we saw the profoundly Trinitarian structure of Paul's thought. Now Paul's participatory language provides further insight. In Paul's thought the Holy Spirit is the Spirit not only of the Father (Rom 8:11; Eph 3:14–16), but also of the Son (Rom 8:9; Gal 4:6; Phil 1:19). Even as the eternal Son has his source in the eternal Father, so the Son, equally with the Father, is the source of the Holy Spirit within the eternal mystery of the triune God. Ancient interpreters of Paul sought to express this aspect of Pauline theology with various helpful images. Tertullian described the triune God as ever-flowing waters—the Father the spring, the Son the pool flowing from the spring, and the Spirit the stream flowing out of the pool (*Against Praxeas* 8). Gregory of Nyssa pictured the Trinity as an eternal fire, the flame of the Son kindled from the flame of the Father, and the flame of the Holy Spirit kindled from the flame of the Son (*Against the Macedonians* 6). Using yet another image to express the mystery, Tertullian pictured the Father as the sun, the Son as its rays, and the Holy Spirit as the light shed from the rays (*Against Praxeas* 8).

In more precise dogmatic language, the early church fathers spoke of the Spirit from all eternity *proceeding* from the Father and the Son (Cyril of Alexandria,

---

14. For example, Hermann Gunkel, *The Influence of the Holy Spirit: The Popular View of the Apostolic Age and the Teaching of the Apostle Paul* (Philadelphia: Fortress, 1979 [German original 1909]); Friedrich W. Horn, *Das Angeld des Geistes: Studien zur paulinischen Pneumatologie* (Göttingen: Vandenhoeck & Ruprecht, 1992); and I. Hermann, *Kyrios und Pneuma: Studien zur Christologie der paulinischen Hauptbriefe*, SANT 2 (Munich: Koesel, 1961). This supposed Pauline ontological identification of the Son and the Spirit is the basis for a claimed "Spirit Christology" in Paul, promoted in recent decades by some as an alternative to the divine and incarnational Christology of the church's historic creeds. But as we will see, this identification of the Spirit and the Son is mistaken.

15. For the debate, see Hill, *Paul and the Trinity*, 135–66; Fatehi, *The Spirit's Relation*, 23–45.

Thesaurus 34; *On Worship in Spirit and in Truth* 1; Epiphanius, *Ancoratus* 8, 71, 73, 75; Ambrose, *The Holy Spirit* 1.11.120; Hilary, *On the Trinity* 2:29) or from the Father through the Son (Gregory of Nyssa, *On Not Three Gods* 10; Hilary, *On the Trinity* 12.55–57; John of Damascus, *On the Orthodox Faith* 1.12). In the Western form of the Nicene Creed, the church confesses that the Holy Spirit "proceeds from the Father and the Son," and various Eastern formularies confessed the Holy Spirit's eternal procession "from the Father through the Son."[16] Many of the ancient writers, in both East and West, use both formulas interchangeably, with an equivalency of meaning (see Tertullian, *Against Praxeas* 4, 8; Hilary, *On the Trinity* 2.29; 12.55–57; Cyril of Alexandria, *Thesaurus* 34; *On Worship in Spirit and in Truth* 1).[17]

The church's ancient doctrine of the procession of the Spirit from both the Father and the Son provides a reading of the relation of Son and Spirit in Paul's theology that integrates the Pauline evidence in a striking way. That the Holy Spirit is *the Son's own Spirit* (and not only the Spirit of the Father) illumines why in participation believers become not only one body but also "one Spirit" with Christ (1 Cor 6:17). It illumines why Paul can call the Holy Spirit given to the faithful "the Spirit of *adoption*" and affirm that through the gift of the Spirit believers become *children* of God (Rom 8:15–17, 23)—because the Spirit is the Spirit of God's *Son*. It illumines how Paul can affirm that in the eucharistic cup, which "is a sharing in the blood of Christ" (1 Cor 10:16), the faithful are "given to drink of one Spirit" (1 Cor 12:13). And it illumines the question that has perplexed so many Pauline interpreters—how can Paul, without confusion or identification of the Spirit and Christ, speak interchangeably of the indwelling of the Spirit and of the Son, of being in Christ and of being in the Spirit? Paul can do so because the Spirit is the Spirit of Jesus Christ. *The mystery of the Trinity, in which the Father begets the Son, and the Holy Spirit proceeds from the Father and the Son, is the foundation that underlies Paul's participatory theology.*

Paul's theology of the Holy Spirit as the Spirit of God's Son provides, I believe, a much-needed corrective to a misapplication of the doctrine of the Trinity sometimes found in our contemporary setting. Within the teaching of the New

---

16. For the formula "from the Father through the Son," see, for instance, the restatement of the Nicene Creed by Tarasios, bishop of Constantinople, accepted at the Seventh Ecumenical Council.

17. In a much later development, which began in the ninth century, the patristic doctrine of the procession of the Spirit from the Son was eventually rejected in the East. The key figures were Photius in the ninth century, Gregory II of Cyprus in the thirteenth century, Gregory Palamas in the fourteenth century, and Mark of Ephesus in the fifteenth century. The Orthodox today embrace *monopatrism*, the doctrine that the Father alone is the hypostatic cause of the Holy Spirit. However, this reflects a departure from the unanimous patristic teaching, both East and West, through the eighth century.

Testament, Jesus is the only begotten Son of God, and therefore he alone is the way to the Father (cf. John 14:6: "I am the way, the truth, and the life: no one comes to the Father except through me"). Some contemporary theologians have made the counterclaim that, since the Spirit proceeds from the Father, the Spirit provides an alternative path to the Father apart from Christ. S. Mark Heim, for example, claims that "the Trinity teaches us that Jesus Christ cannot be an exhaustive or exclusive source for knowledge of God nor the exhaustive and exclusive act of God to save us."[18]

Paul's theology of the Spirit reveals the striking fallacy of this line of thinking. For in Paul the Spirit is the Spirit *of Christ* (Rom 8:9). The person of the Spirit from eternity proceeds from the person of the Son. The Son, together with the Father, is the source of the Holy Spirit. And therefore the Spirit is received through faith in Jesus Christ (Gal 3:1-2, 13-14; 1 Thess 1:5-6). The baptism of the Spirit is baptism into Christ (1 Cor 12:12-13). And the communion of the Spirit is communion with Jesus Christ (2 Cor 13:14 [Greek 13:13]; cf. 1 Cor 1:9). Far from providing an alternative path to the Father apart from the Son, every encounter with the Spirit is an encounter with Jesus Christ, and leads to Jesus Christ. "No one speaking by the Spirit of God says, 'Jesus is accursed!' and no one can say 'Jesus is Lord!' except by the Holy Spirit" (1 Cor 12:3). For the Holy Spirit is "the Spirit of Jesus Christ" (Phil 1:19).

The Epicenter of Paul's Theology

E. P. Sanders claims that participatory union with God is "the main theme of Paul's theology." I believe that is almost right, but not quite. For we have now seen that Paul's divine Christology is at the heart of his doctrine of participation. It is the foundation. And in uncovering the foundations of Paul's doctrine of participation, so crucial to his gospel, we discover the very epicenter of his theology. What is that epicenter? As we saw in chapter 3, the central hope of the Old Testament is the expectation of the coming and presence of YHWH. The epicenter of Paul's theology is the fulfillment of this hope in Jesus Christ, through his incarnation, the participatory union with the faithful it has brought about, and his second coming to bring the fullness of his presence. The epicenter of Paul's theology is his answer to the question, "Who do you say that I am?" (Matt 16:15). The answer Paul gives,

---

18. S. Mark Heim, *The Depth of the Riches: A Trinitarian Theology of Religious Ends* (Grand Rapids: Eerdmans, 2000), 134. Similarly the popular writer Brian D. McLaren, *Why Did Jesus, Moses, the Buddha, and Mohammed Cross the Road? Christian Identity in a Multi-Faith World* (New York: Jericho, 2012), 150-53.

as does Matthew's Gospel, is that Jesus Christ is "God with us" (Matt 1:23; cf. 28:20). *The epicenter of Paul's thought is the incarnation.* On Paul's doctrine of the incarnation, as we will see, depend the other core doctrines of his theology: the atonement and the resurrection. Only as the creator God in the flesh could Jesus offer one atoning sacrifice to reconcile all humanity, and rise again to conquer death, humanity's great enemy.

And this astounding revelation of Jesus's divine identity brought with it a new revelation of the inner mystery of the one God as a communion of persons: Father, Son, and Holy Spirit. Through the saving events of the incarnation, cross, and resurrection of his Son, the Father has revealed himself as a God of saving, redeeming love, and through the gift of the Spirit those united to the Son enter into a new relationship of intimacy and love with their creator (Rom 5:5–8; Eph 2:4–7; 5:25–32; 6:24). This saving union with the triune God through the incarnation of God's Son forms the very heart of Paul's theology.

This is evident in the majestic prayer that makes up almost the entire first half of Paul's letter to the Ephesians. In Ephesians 3:14–19, the culmination of this long, beautiful prayer begun in 1:17, Paul's climactic petition is that his readers might through this divine union know and experience the fullness of God's love:

> [14]For this reason I bow my knees to the Father, [15]from whom the whole family in heaven and earth is named, [16]that he may grant, in accordance with the riches of this glory, that you be empowered through his Spirit in your inner being, [17]that Christ may dwell in your hearts through faith, that you, rooted and founded in love, [18]may be empowered to comprehend, together with all the saints, what is the breadth and length and depth and height, [19]and to fully know the love of Christ, which surpasses all knowledge, that you may be filled with all the fullness of God.

In Paul's petition, his understanding of the incarnation as the revelation of the mystery of God as Father, Son, and Holy Spirit is strikingly evident, for this mystery is in the very heart of the structure of his prayer ("I bow my knees to the *Father* . . . that you be empowered through his *Spirit* in your inner being . . . that *Christ* may dwell in your hearts through faith"). In Paul's prayer, the Spirit is explicitly the Spirit of the Father (3:14–16), but implicitly also the Spirit of Christ, through Paul's interchange of the indwelling of Christ (3:17) and of the Spirit (3:16). And Paul's divine Christology is evident in another way. For in the very climactic petition of this prayer (3:18–19), that divine love that Paul prays his readers may know, the unsearchable love of God that surpasses all knowledge, is the love of *Christ.*

Conclusion: The Heart of Paul's Gospel

The important Pauline theme of the supernatural union of the faithful with God is a neglected but crucial key to Paul's Christology. For in Paul's epistles this indwelling of God in his people as in his temple, the fulfillment of the promised abiding presence of YHWH, is the presence and indwelling of Jesus Christ. Paul's theology of participation thus reveals that in Paul's Christology Jesus is not a mere creature, but the creator incarnate. The presence and indwelling of Christ within the faithful are in turn the outworking of a prior act of God: the incarnation of God's Son, and his saving acts of redemption when he came. In the church's participatory union with Christ, made possible by the incarnation, the union with the creator offered to Adam, but forfeited in the Fall, is brought to fulfillment. This intimate union with God that Paul's gospel offered its hearers was without equivalent or parallel in the ancient world into which Paul's gospel came. In the relation of Paul's doctrines of incarnation and participation we find once more (as in his doctrine of creation) the sacred character of human freedom of will in Paul's anthropology. For this saving participation in God, which is the goal of the incarnation, is in Paul's thought a freely chosen covenantal communion of love with the creator, a union that one enters by faith and from which one can exclude oneself by rejection of Christ.

Unveiled through the incarnation, and at the heart of Paul's theology of participation, is the mysterious identity of the one God as an eternal communion of persons: Father, Son, and Holy Spirit. This eternal mystery, in which the Father begets the Son and the Holy Spirit proceeds from both Father and Son, forms the infrastructure of Paul's entire theology of participation. The church's doctrines of the incarnation and the Trinity, far from being an anachronistic imposition upon Paul's theology, were historically the outgrowth of exegesis of his letters, and are the logical and necessary outworking of his thought.

The Pauline theme of participatory union with God, as crucial as it is, is not itself the very center of Paul's thought. Rather, the center is the prior act of God whereby God united himself with humanity, making possible humanity's union with God. *The epicenter of Paul's theology is the incarnation.* The saving mystery of Jesus as God incarnate, and the mystery of God as Father, Son, and Spirit that it reveals, is the very heart of Paul's thought.

With our discovery of the epicenter of Paul's theology, the unity of the entire scriptural narrative comes strikingly into view. The very epicenter of Israel's life in the Old Testament was the presence and dwelling of the Lord among his people in his holy temple. The central prophetic expectation of the Old Testament is the coming of YHWH in the fullness of his presence, life, and glory, a fullness of which his dwelling in the temple was only a foreshadowing. The epicenter of Paul's theology is the fulfillment of this hope in the incarnation of the Son of God, his indwelling presence among his people as in his temple, and the future consummation of this divine union at his second advent. The incarnation is crucial for every area of Paul's thought, including the cross, the atonement, and justification—the subjects of part 3 of this book.

Part Three

Covenant

Chapter Six

Paul and the Law in Full Perspective

The most important development in the contemporary study of Paul's theology is the "new perspective" on Paul introduced by E. P. Sanders.[1] Students of Paul usually come to this topic with great enthusiasm—what could be more exciting than to learn about an entirely "new perspective" on the apostle's theology? But study of Paul in light of this "new perspective" usually leaves these eager students confused and disoriented. For they learn that according to Sanders, this new perspective reveals that Paul's theology of the law is an inconsistent muddle in conflict with the Old Testament. They find that the proposed solutions to Sanders's challenge are erudite, are filled with solid insights into Paul's theology, and stoutly defend the coherence of his thought. But they also discover that these solutions are mutually contradictory, do not explain large portions of the evidence, and fail to provide a fully convincing answer to Sanders's challenge. And so an introduction to the current state of scholarly discussion on "the problem of the law in Paul," rather than preparing the reader to engage Paul's letters more insightfully, usually has a sort of reverse effect—it leaves the student of Paul more confused (and usually quite a bit less eager) than when he or she began. The fundamental reason is that the "new perspective" on Paul is at bottom a *question*—and a very important one—regarding Paul's theology of the law, but it does not provide an *answer*, nor by itself illumine Paul's theology. And none of the answers proposed to that question seem to fully satisfy.

This chapter will offer a different approach, with (it is hoped) an entirely different effect. First, the chapter will seek to identify the fundamental *question* or problem, in my view not always fully grasped, underlying the debate on Paul and the law. Second, and more importantly, by uncovering a crucial but hitherto neglected feature of Paul's theology within its Jewish and biblical context, the chapter will offer a *solution* to the seemingly irresolvable problem of the law in

---

1. This term is not Sanders's own but was coined by James D. G. Dunn to describe the effect of Sanders's work.

Paul. This is admittedly a rather bold claim! But I believe the fundamental aspect of Paul's thought we will uncover in this chapter provides the key that unlocks the unity and coherence of Paul's theology of the law, and its continuity with the rest of the Bible. And it does so in such a way that builds upon the genuine insights of previous approaches. By answering the crucial but hitherto unresolved question posed by the "new perspective," this chapter will (it is hoped) illumine and transform any reader's understanding of Paul's theology, and lead him or her back to Paul's letters, eager to dig ever more deeply into Paul's profound covenantal theology of law and grace.[2]

In this book as a whole, we are studying Paul's gospel through a double lens, as the fulfillment of Israel's Scriptures and in dialogue with the beliefs and thought systems of the ancient gentile world that Paul addressed. But in this chapter and throughout much of part 3, our focus will be on the first lens: Paul's theology in its Jewish and biblical context. Paul's Jewish context provides the fuller perspective that will enable us to solve the puzzle posed by the "new perspective" on Paul—the puzzle of Paul and the law.

The Problem of the Law in Paul: The Challenge of the "New Perspective"

The "new perspective" is a new way of looking at Paul's teaching of justification by faith, resulting from a new understanding of Paul's ancient Jewish context. According to the older view, which had dominated New Testament scholarship through most of the previous century, ancient Judaism was a religion of legalistic works righteousness, in which favor with God was earned through perfect obedience to the law of Moses. From this "old perspective," Paul's teaching of justification by faith was the antidote to the poison of Jewish merit theology, maintaining in contrast that one cannot be saved by good works but only by God's grace through faith. E. P. Sanders, in his book *Paul and Palestinian Judaism*, effectively countered this portrait, showing that in ancient Jewish thought the law functioned within the gracious framework of the covenant and its provision of mercy through repentance and sacrifice. Ancient Judaism, Sanders demonstrated, was not a religion of works righteousness, but a religion focused on God's covenantal grace, mercy, and forgiveness.[3] Sanders's work thus opened up a new angle of vision, or "new perspective," for the study of Paul.

---

2. For fuller discussion, see James Ware, "Law, Christ, and Covenant: Paul's Theology of the Law in Romans 3:19–20," *JTS* 62 (2011): 513–40.

3. E. P. Sanders, *Paul and Palestinian Judaism* (Philadelphia: Fortress, 1977), 31–428.

However, this new perspective has proven baffling and disorienting for scholars of Paul, for in key ways Paul's portrayal of the law and the covenant within ancient Judaism does not seem to square with this new understanding. For Paul *contrasts* the law of Moses with the grace of Christ (Rom 10:5–13). He portrays his Jewish brothers and sisters as seeking their own righteousness through observance of the law (Rom 9:30–10:4). Most baffling of all in light of this new perspective, he portrays the law of Moses as requiring full and perfect obedience, with no means of atonement for transgression, and thus as impossible for sinful human beings to fulfill: "by the works of the law no human being shall be justified before God" (Rom 3:20; cf. Gal 2:16; 3:10; 5:3). But in ancient Jewish thought, both within and outside the Bible, the covenantal context provided means of atonement for transgressions through expiatory sacrifices, and assurance of God's grace and forgiveness. The concept of the law as requiring perfect obedience thus seems, as Sanders noted, "extraordinarily un-Pharisaic and even un-Jewish."[4] Even prior to Sanders's work, H. J. Schoeps had argued that Paul's portrayal of the law apart from the covenant, love, and forgiveness of God was a "fundamental misapprehension" whereby Paul "wrested and isolated the law from the controlling context of God's covenant with Israel."[5] Sanders went one step further: Paul's contrast of the law and Christ involved, not a *misunderstanding* of the relationship of law and covenant, but an explicit *rejection* of the covenant: "Paul in fact explicitly denies that the Jewish covenant can be effective for salvation, thus consciously denying the basis of Judaism."[6] Paul's "real attack on Judaism," insists Sanders, "is against the idea of the covenant."[7]

Paul's claim of human inability to fulfill the law is also at the heart of a now-famous charge of Sanders that Paul's theology of the law is confused and inconsistent, not proceeding logically from plight to solution, but illogically "from solution to plight." In Sanders's view, Paul's thinking was circular, rejecting the possibility of righteousness through the law because of his prior conviction that righteousness comes not through the law but only through Christ. Sanders depicts Paul as filled with anguish and self-doubt, because his deepest Jewish and covenantal convictions about the gracious context of the law did not mesh with his convictions concerning salvation through Christ—"he could not maintain all his convictions at once without both anguish and finally a lack of logic."[8]

---

4. E. P. Sanders, *Paul, the Law, and the Jewish People* (Philadelphia: Fortress, 1983), 28.

5. H. J. Schoeps, *Paul: The Theology of the Apostle in the Light of Jewish Religious History*, trans. Harold Knight (Philadelphia: Westminster, 1961), 213 (cf. the full discussion on 175–83, 200–218, 259–93).

6. Sanders, *Paul and Palestinian Judaism*, 551–52.

7. Sanders, *Paul, the Law, and the Jewish People*, 47.

8. Sanders, *Paul, the Law, and the Jewish People*, 199 (cf. the whole discussion on 171–206).

It is thus Paul's portrayal of the law apart from God's mercy and forgiveness, and therefore as impossible to fulfill, that led Sanders to posit that at the core of Paul's theology of the law lies not only self-contradiction but also an abandonment of Jewish covenantal thought. By wresting the law from its gracious covenantal context, Sanders concluded, Paul's theology of the law is self-contradictory, in conflict with the Old Testament, fundamentally un-Jewish, and noncovenantal. Sanders's conclusions were not altogether novel, but they served to bring into sharp focus a core problem of Paul's theology of the law long recognized by scholars. Paul's portrayal of the law *apart from the covenant and its provision for mercy* is at the heart of the problem of the law in Paul.

Three Proposed Solutions to the Problem of the Law in Paul

In response to Sanders's challenge, a number of scholars have proposed fresh readings of Paul that seek to resolve the problems raised by Sanders and defend the coherence and consistency of Paul's thought regarding the law. There has been a bewildering variety of solutions proposed. But I believe they may be helpfully summarized as falling along three main lines.

The "New Perspective" Solution

The most influential proposed solution to the question raised by Sanders's "new perspective" is itself (confusingly enough) often called the "new perspective" on Paul. According to this approach (associated especially with James D. G. Dunn), the "works of the law" in Paul do not have in view the *moral* commands of Torah, but only the markers of Jewish identity (what theologians sometimes call the Old Testament "ceremonial law"): circumcision, food laws, and Sabbath keeping.[9] In teaching justification by faith apart from these "works of the law," Paul was not (as the "old perspective" claimed) opposing works righteousness (Jewish *legalism*), but was opposing the Jewish nation's boasting in its covenantal privileges and its exclusion of gentiles (Jewish *exclusivism*).[10] According to this "new perspective,"

---

9. James D. G. Dunn, *The Theology of Paul the Apostle* (Grand Rapids: Eerdmans, 1998), 354–59; Dunn, *Romans 1–8*, WBC 38 (Dallas: Word, 1988), 153–55, 158–59. See also his more recent treatment in James D. G. Dunn, "The New Perspective on Paul: Whence, What and Whither?" in *The New Perspective on Paul*, rev. ed. (Grand Rapids: Eerdmans, 2008), 23–28, 44–47. Taking an approach similar to Dunn is Richard B. Hays, "The Letter to the Galatians," *NIB* 11:238–39.

10. James D. G. Dunn, "The New Perspective on Paul," "Works of the Law and the Curse of

Paul's critique of Judaism does not involve a rejection of the covenant, as Sanders claimed, but opposes the exclusion of Christ-believing gentiles from the covenant community.

The "Two Covenants" Approach

A different solution is offered by Stanley K. Stowers.[11] Romans 1:18–3:20 is widely considered Paul's classic portrayal of sinful humanity's need for the righteousness found only in Christ. But according to Stowers, this passage does not teach universal sinfulness, nor assert that righteousness comes only through faith in Christ Jesus. Rather, Paul's argument assumes the righteousness of the Jewish people apart from faith in Christ, through the covenant and its provision of mercy through atoning sacrifice, as well as the righteousness of those pagan gentiles who apart from faith in Christ keep the moral law.[12] Paul asserts the need of faith in Christ only for sinful gentiles, who are outside the Jewish covenantal context and its means of forgiveness.[13] On this view, Paul envisions two covenants or ways of salvation: "the works of the law" for Jews and righteous gentiles, faith in Jesus Christ for sinful gentiles.

A Modified Return to the "Old Perspective"

The third proposed solution seeks to cut the Gordian knot by rejecting Sanders's portrayal of the gracious covenantal context of the law in ancient Judaism and the "new perspective" on Paul associated with it. Friedrich Avemarie, Simon J. Gathercole, Timo Laato, and Lauri Thurén have each in varied ways argued that, contrary to Sanders's claims, ancient Jewish belief (not in the Old Testament, but among Jews in Paul's day) *was* in fact characterized by a belief in works righteousness very different from Paul's gospel of grace.[14] Other scholars concede that for *many*

---

the Law (Galatians 3.10–14)," "Yet Once More—'The Works of the Law': A Response," and "Paul and the Torah: The Role and Function of the Law in the Theology of Paul the Apostle," all in Dunn, *The New Perspective on Paul*, 99–120, 121–40, 213–26, and 447–67 (see esp. 460–66), respectively. Cf. Dunn, *Theology*, 363–64.

11. Stanley K. Stowers, *A Rereading of Romans: Justice, Jews, and Gentiles* (New Haven: Yale University Press, 1994).

12. Stowers, *A Rereading of Romans*, 176–80, 187–88, 190–93, 205–6.

13. Stowers, *A Rereading of Romans*, 187–92.

14. Friedrich Avemarie, *Tora und Leben: Untersuchungen zur Heilsbedeutung der Tora in der frühen*

Jews the law functioned within the gracious context of the covenant but contend that at least *some* strands of ancient Judaism were legalistic and characterized by works righteousness. Paul's teaching of the impossibility of righteousness through "the works of the law" opposed this belief in works-based salvation held by at least some of his Jewish contemporaries.[15] Stephen Westerholm also explains Paul's denial of righteousness through the law as opposing a Jewish belief in salvation by works, but differs from the other scholars mentioned in arguing that Paul saw the works righteousness to which he objected as inherent in the law of Moses itself.[16] This third solution thus proposes a reading of Paul in which Paul's statements about the impossibility of righteousness through the law oppose a legalistic merit theology either inherent in the Old Testament itself, characteristic of postbiblical Judaism, or common among at least some of Paul's Jewish contemporaries.

The Three Proposed Solutions: Why They Do Not (Fully) Work

Some of the most wise and learned Pauline scholars in the world have contributed to the debate on Paul and the law, and many of the scholars and studies surveyed above have enriched this debate with important insights. However, none of the

---

rabbinischen Literatur (Tübingen: Mohr Siebeck, 1996); Avemarie, "Erwählung und Vergeltung. Zur Optionalen Struktur rabbinischer Soteriologie," *NTS* 45 (1999): 108–26; Simon Gathercole, *Where Is Boasting? Early Jewish Soteriology and Paul's Response in Romans 1–5* (Grand Rapids: Eerdmans, 2003); Timo Laato, *Paul and Judaism: An Anthropological Approach* (Atlanta: Scholars, 1995); Laato, "Paul's Anthropological Considerations: Two Problems," in *The Paradoxes of Paul*, vol. 2 of *Justification and Variegated Nomism*, ed. D. A. Carson, Peter T. O'Brien, and Mark A. Seifrid (Grand Rapids: Baker, 2004), 343–59; Laato, "'God's Righteousness'—Once Again," in *The Nordic Paul: Finnish Approaches to Pauline Theology*, ed. Lars Aejmelaeus and Antti Mustakallio, LNTS 374 (London: T. & T. Clark, 2008), 40–44; Lauri Thurén, *Derhetorizing Paul: A Dynamic Perspective on Pauline Theology and the Law*, WUNT 124 (Tübingen: Mohr Siebeck, 2000).

15. This approach is especially well represented by the essays collected in D. A. Carson, Peter T. O'Brien, and Mark A. Seifrid, eds., *Justification and Variegated Nomism*, 2 vols. (Grand Rapids: Baker, 2001, 2004). Similarly Thomas R. Schreiner, *The Law and Its Fulfillment: A Pauline Theology of Law* (Grand Rapids: Baker Academic, 1993), 93–121; Schreiner, *Romans*, BECNT 6 (Grand Rapids: Baker Academic, 1998), 173–74; Schreiner, "Paul's View of the Law in Romans 10:4–5," *WTJ* 55 (1993): 122–24, 133; Schreiner, "An Old Perspective on the New Perspective," *CJ* 35 (2009): 141–47; Douglas J. Moo, *The Epistle to the Romans*, NICNT (Grand Rapids: Eerdmans, 1996), 217; and Richard H. Bell, *No One Seeks for God: An Exegetical and Theological Study of Romans 1:18–3:20*, WUNT 106 (Tübingen: Mohr Siebeck, 1998).

16. Stephen Westerholm, *Perspectives Old and New on Paul: The "Lutheran" Paul and His Critics* (Grand Rapids: Eerdmans, 2004), 261–445. See also Westerholm, "Finnish Contributions to the Debate on Paul and the Law," in Aejmelaeus and Mustakallio, *The Nordic Paul*, 12–15.

approaches sketched above, I would argue, offers a true solution to the problem posed by Sanders of the disjunction of law and covenant in Paul. Let us take each of them in turn, focusing on their reading of Paul's classic portrayal of the human plight in Romans 1:18–3:20, especially Paul's climactic affirmation: "by the works of the law no human being shall be justified before God" (Rom 3:20; cf. Gal 2:16).

The "New Perspective" Solution

In this view, the "works of the law" in Paul refer, not to the moral law, but to the law's prescription of the markers of Jewish national identity: circumcision, food laws, and Sabbath keeping. This approach is in fact very insightful and helpful in calling attention to the importance of the inclusion of the gentiles apart from these markers within Paul's understanding of justification (cf. Rom 3:29–31; 4:9–17; 9:24–26; 15:7–12). However, several factors tell against this interpretation of the "works of the law" in Paul. First, Paul's affirmation in Romans 3:20 ("by the works of the law no human being shall be justified before God") functions to summarize Paul's entire argument in Romans 1:18–3:20. But Romans 1:18–3:20 is an indictment not only of Jews (2:17–29) but *also of gentiles* (1:18–32; 3:9).[17] The "works of the law" can thus hardly refer solely to the markers of Jewish national identity! Second, the indictment of both gentiles and Jews in 1:18–3:20 focuses exclusively on violations of the *moral* demands of Torah, with failure to worship, seek, and fear God at the heart of the accusation. Third, within the structure of Paul's argument, the "works of the law" in 3:20 and 3:28 correspond to the "works" of 4:1–8, and it is beyond controversy that those refer to good works generally. Within the context of 1:18–4:25, as the majority of Pauline interpreters have rightly seen, the "works of the law" has in view the *whole* law, with the focus on its *moral* demands.[18] And the plight envisioned is not Jewish boasting in the law's privileges and accompanying exclusion of gentiles, but the captivity of all people, both Jews and gentiles, under the power of sin (3:9–20).

17. Cf. Frank Thielman, *Paul and the Law: A Contextual Approach* (Downers Grove: InterVarsity, 1994), 178.

18. See, for example, Bell, *No One Seeks*, 224–35; Thielman, *Paul and the Law*, 177–78; Schreiner, *Romans*, 171–73.

The "Two Covenants" Approach

Stowers offers in my view the least convincing (and least helpful) interpretation of the passage. He claims that Paul in Romans 1:18–3:20 does not seek to describe a *universal* human need for salvation through Jesus Christ, but assumes the righteousness of Jews and morally upright gentiles apart from Christ. But this is in flat contradiction to the explicitly universal language that dominates the passage, especially the summation in 3:9–20 (e.g., 3:9, "both Jews and gentiles are all under the power of sin"; cf. 3:10, 11, 12, 19, 20). Stowers argues that Paul's universal language is "collective" (i.e., assuming many exceptions) rather than "individual." But Paul throughout the summary of his argument in 3:9–20 carefully alternates *collective* language ("all," 3:9; "all," 3:12; "all the world," 3:19; "no human being" [literally, "all flesh"], 3:20) and *individual* expressions ("not even one," 3:10; "no one," 3:11 [twice], 3:12; "not even one," 3:12; "every mouth," 3:19). The universality of the human plight, for all people and each person individually, is the main theme of the passage.

There is an important connection between the solution proposed by Stowers and the one proposed by Dunn, as different as they are. Both scholars, in different ways, seek to answer Sanders's challenge by denying that the concept of human inability to fulfill the law is present in Romans 1:18–3:20. However, Paul throughout 1:18–3:20 portrays a graphic picture of universal human sinfulness, impiety, evil, and rebellion from the creator God, culminating in 3:18 with the accusation that "there is no fear of God before their eyes." In his own summary statements of his argument in 3:9 and 3:19, Paul declares that both Jews and gentiles are all "under the power of sin" (3:9), and that the entire world is "condemned" before God (3:19). Clearly, the plight envisaged in 1:18–3:20 (as the majority of Pauline scholars agree) is universal human sinfulness and powerlessness to carry out the righteous ways of God revealed in the law.[19] Neither the "two covenants" approach of Stowers nor the "new perspective" of Dunn, each of which in its own way endeavors to exclude this concept from the text, offers a fully satisfactory solution to the problem of the seemingly un-Jewish character of Paul's understanding of the law.

19. See Schoeps, *Paul*, 284; Thielman, *Paul and the Law*, 180; Moo, *Romans*, 209–10; Westerholm, *Perspectives*, 313–21, 385–89; Laato, "Paul's Anthropological Considerations," 354–59; Schreiner, *Romans*, 170–73.

A Modified Return to the "Old Perspective"

The scholars and studies associated with this approach are very helpful and insightful in showing (contrary to Dunn's "new perspective" approach and Stowers's "two covenants" view) that the plight envisioned in Romans 1:18–3:20 is sinful humanity's need for the righteousness found only in Christ. But this third proposed explanation, which regards Paul as opposing a legalistic misinterpretation of the law among at least some Jews of his day, is not in my view a viable solution either. For the misinterpretation of the law is simply not the issue Paul addresses in Romans 1:18–3:20. Paul in Romans makes ontological assertions about *the law itself*, not the *misuse* of the law. Moreover, he portrays *all* his Jewish brethren without faith in Christ as seeking their own righteousness through the law (9:30–10:4). The argument that *some* Jews were legalistic and trusted in their works, if true, would not confirm but would *invalidate* Paul's argument, revealing it to be a distortion (as Sanders claims).

But here is perhaps the most central problem with this proposed explanation in its relation to Paul's theology. This approach claims that the malady envisioned in Romans 3:20 ("by the works of the law no human being shall be justified before God") is Jewish works righteousness. If so, the solution to that plight would be a more robust understanding of God's grace and reliance on the means of atonement and forgiveness already available within Judaism. But then, why was the sacrificial death of Christ necessary (cf. Gal 2:21)? According to Paul's gospel, as we shall see, the solution to the human plight is neither the law nor its sacrifices, but the revelation of God's righteousness through the saving work of Jesus Christ (Rom 3:21–26). But this third response to Sanders's challenge does not explain *why* this is so in Paul's theology or how Paul *grounds* this truth in his description of the human plight in Romans 1:18–3:20. Stephen Westerholm's version of this third approach, according to which in Paul's view the law of Moses itself involved the concept of trust in one's works and righteousness through the law, does not alleviate the difficulties with this third view. For Westerholm's reading of Paul posits a fundamental contradiction between Paul and the Old Testament, and fails to explain Paul's conviction that God's grace, and faith apart from works, were from the beginning the basis of Israel's relationship with God (Rom 3:3; 4:1–8; 11:1–6, 16–24; 1 Cor 10:1–5; 2 Cor. 4:13; Gal. 3:6–9). This third approach rightly seeks to defend the coherence of Paul's thought and exonerate the apostle from Sanders's charge of distorting Judaism. But in attempting to explain Paul's denial of the possibility of righteousness through the law as countering Jewish works righteousness, whether widespread or inherent in the law itself, this solution has the unintended effect of ultimately reducing Paul's theology to incoherence.

A few scholars, such as Frank Thielman, Andrew Das, Jean Noel Aletti, and N. T. Wright, have moved in a different direction than any of the three approaches sketched above. These interpreters recognize (with Sanders) the gracious covenantal context of the law within the Old Testament and in ancient Judaism, and at the same time (against Dunn and Stowers) Paul's unmistakable claim to the impossibility of righteousness through the law.[20] However, the work of these scholars only raises more acutely the problem of Paul's apparent rejection or distortion of the covenantal context of the law, without proposing an ultimate resolution of this question. In offering what I believe to be the solution to the problem, I understand my proposal here as building upon the important work of these scholars.

The Solution to the Problem of Law and Covenant in Paul

The fundamental problem of Paul's theology of the law, as brought to light above all by the work of E. P. Sanders, is Paul's separation of the law from the covenant and its promise of divine grace and mercy. Paul's portrayal of the law apart from its gracious covenantal context seems logically incoherent, radically un-Jewish, and in conflict with the Old Testament. None of the proposals thus far advanced, despite their many important insights, provides a fully satisfying answer to Sanders's challenge. I believe the reason for the intractable character of the debate is that an important factor in Paul's thought has been left out of the equation on all sides of the discussion.

Paul, we have seen, sums up his argument in Romans 1:18–3:20 in this way: "by the works of the law no human being will be justified before God" (Rom 3:20; cf. Gal 2:16). Strikingly, Paul's words are taken from an Old Testament passage, Psalm 143. It is surely curious that a formulation that in Sanders's view epitomizes the *un-Jewish* character of Paul's thought is itself an echo of the *Jewish* Scriptures! This would indicate that something went radically wrong in Sanders's attempts to think Paul's thoughts after him. Moreover, Psalm 143 is a powerful expression

---

20. See Thielman, *Paul and the Law*, esp. 100–118, 176–213, 238–45; Andrew Das, *Paul, the Law, and the Covenant* (Peabody, MA: Hendrickson, 2001); and Jean Noel Aletti, *Israël et la Loi dans la lettre aux Romains* (Paris: Cerf, 1998). Although his approach is often associated with the "new perspective" of Dunn, N. T. Wright has sought, with increasing clarity, to propose a reading of Rom 1:18–3:20 and related passages in Paul that does full justice both to the theme of gentile inclusion and to the theme of universal transgression and inability to fulfill the law; see N. T. Wright, *What Saint Paul Really Said: Was Paul of Tarsus the Real Founder of Christianity?* (Grand Rapids: Eerdmans, 1997), 95–133; Wright, "The Letter to the Romans," *NIB* 10:428–64; and Wright, *Justification: God's Plan and Paul's Vision* (Downers Grove: InterVarsity, 2009), 116–18, 200–201, 210–16.

within the Scriptures of God's *covenantal grace and mercy*. This psalm will shed light on the feature of the Bible's covenantal theology that Sanders's "new perspective" challenge rightly saw—and the crucial feature of covenant theology that Sanders failed to see.

Law and Covenant in Psalm 143

The "covenant theology" of the Old Testament focuses on the intimate union of love between YHWH and his people founded on the grace and mercy bestowed on Israel in the Abrahamic covenant. This covenantal theology is prominent throughout the Old Testament and pervades the book of Psalms. But it receives classic expression in Psalm 143, a textbook example of covenant theology within the Old Testament. The basis for the psalmist's petitions in this psalm is not his own righteousness, but his covenantal relationship with YHWH, and his trust in YHWH's mercy and faithfulness to the covenant. The poem as a whole is framed by references to YHWH's "righteousness" (Hebrew: *tsedaqah*, vv. 1, 11), that is, his covenant faithfulness that is active to save, redeem, and deliver. The psalmist repeatedly appeals to YHWH's *chesed* (vv. 8, 12), his unswerving, unconditional "covenant love." Matching the avowals of God's covenant faithfulness, the psalm is replete with expressions of the psalmist's trust in YHWH.[21] In verse 10 the psalmist invokes the covenant formula itself: "you are my God."[22] As A. A. Anderson notes, the allusion to the covenant formula here evokes "the essence of the Covenant promise."[23] Through these expressions of faith and trust, the psalmist strikingly grounds his appeal not in himself, but in YHWH's forgiving covenantal love. In Psalm 143, as throughout the Psalms (cf. Pss 1:2; 37:31; 40:8; 78:5–10; 94:12; 103:8–18; 105:45; 111; 119), the law is not considered apart from God's mercy and forgiveness, and therefore as impossible to fulfill, but within the gracious context of the covenant and its promise of mercy.

21. See v. 1, "hear my prayer, give ear to my supplications"; v. 6, "I stretch out my hands to you"; v. 8a, "I trust in you"; v. 8b, "to you I lift up my soul"; v. 9, "I take refuge in you" (following LXX, [*pros se katephugon*]; the sense of MT is disputed, but probably carries a similar meaning).

22. For the covenant formula "I will be your God, and you will be my people," see Gen 17:7–8; Exod 6:6–7; 19:5–6; Lev 11:45; 26:12, 45; 2 Sam 7:24; Jer 7:22–23; 11:4; 24:7; 30:22; 31:33; 32:38; Ezek 11:20; 14:11; 36:28; 37:23, 27; Hos 2:23 (Heb 2:25).

23. A. A. Anderson, *The Book of Psalms* (London: Oliphants, 1977), 930.

Psalm 143:2 in Covenantal Context

Puzzlingly, a seemingly contradictory thought comes to the surface in the psalmist's plea in verse 2: "do not enter into judgment with your servant, for in your presence no living being is righteous." Psalm 143:2 powerfully expresses the concept of universal sinfulness and inability to fulfill the law. Elsewhere in Psalm 143, as throughout the Psalter, the righteous (*tsadiq*) are sharply distinguished from the wicked (Ps 143:1, 11, 12; cf. Pss 1; 4; 14; 16; 32; 36; 55; 62; 63; 64; 86; 94; 97; 115; 145), and the psalmist longs for the revelation of God's righteous judgment (*mishpat*; cf. Pss 1:5; 9:4 [Heb 9:5]; 94:15; 140:12–13 [Heb 140:13–14]). But in 143:2 all such distinctions are obliterated: there is no one righteous (*tsadiq*), and God's judgment (*mishpat*) can only mean condemnation. The covenantal framework might seem to be abandoned.

But to the contrary, the psalmist's categorical denial in 143:2 of the possibility of human righteousness is not in conflict with the covenant theology found throughout the psalm. Rather, it is the point in the psalm at which this theology is given its most dramatic expression! For in the covenant theology of the Bible, the distinction between the righteous and the wicked is precisely the distinction between those who trust in YHWH and those who reject this covenantal relationship. The righteous trust in YHWH, call on his name, take refuge in him, and seek his ways (Ps 143:1, 5, 8, 9, 10; cf. Pss 31:6 [Heb 31:7]; 32:10; 37:39–40; 64:10 [Heb 64:11]; 71:1–2; 84:11–12 [Heb 84:12–13]; 86:5; 125:1–2). The wicked (including the wicked within Israel), by contrast, do not call on YHWH, but rebel against him and disregard his ways (cf. Pss 4:2 [Heb 4:3]; 5:10 [Heb 5:11]; 14:1–4; 16:4; 36:1–4 [Heb 36:2–5]; 94:4–11; 97:7; 115:2–8). The righteous in the Psalms are frequently described as sinful and in need of forgiveness (cf. Pss 32; 38; 41; 51; 85; 90; 103; 130). However, they are assured of God's mercy within the gracious context of the covenantal relationship sustained by their faith in YHWH (cf. Ps 143:1, 5, 8, 9, 10). Within the covenant theology that pervades the Psalter, the psalmist speaks of the righteous (*tsadiq*, Pss 1:5–6; 5:12 [Heb 5:13]; 14:5; 32:11; 34:15 [Heb 34:16]; 97:12; 146:8), hopes in a reward according to works (Ps 62:11–12 [Heb 62:12–13]; cf. 28:4), and longs for God's righteous judgment (*mishpat*, Pss 7:8 [Heb 7:9]; 26:1; 35:23–24; 43:1) only *within the gracious framework of the covenant.*

In Psalm 143:2 this concept is expressed in a dramatic way, as the psalmist considers the impossibility of righteousness before YHWH *apart from the covenant and its promise of mercy*. Without YHWH's grace and forgiveness, the psalmist declares, there is no one who is righteous, and God's righteous judgment can only bring condemnation. The impossibility of human righteousness on the basis of one's works in Psalm 143:2 reveals the need for God's covenantal grace, mercy, and forgiveness. The source of God's mercy is not the law, nor its sacrifices, but his "covenant love and truth" (Exod 34:6–7; Pss 25:10; 40:11; 57:3; 61:7; 85:11; 89:14), which makes those sacrifices efficacious (Exod 29:42–46; Lev 2:13; Jer 7:21–23). And the basis of the covenantal relationship is entirely the psalmist's response of heartfelt trust in this covenantal, steadfast love of YHWH (Ps 143:1, 6, 8a, 8b, 9). When he considers his own works apart from the covenant and its promise of mercy, the psalmist can only exclaim: "do not enter into judgment with your servant, for in your presence no living being is righteous."

Righteousness Apart from the Covenant in Jewish Thought

This denial of the possibility of righteousness apart from the covenant and its promise of mercy is not unique to Psalm 143, but occurs frequently throughout the Old Testament and in ancient Jewish literature outside the Bible. In ancient Jewish thought, apart from the mercy and forgiveness found within the covenantal relationship of trust in YHWH, there is no one who is righteous or who can stand before God's judgment (cf. Pss 14:1–3; 25:6–7; 32:1–2; Isa 59:1–15; Dan 9:4–19; 1QS [Rule of the Community] 11.9–14). The following passage is typical:

> If you, O YHWH, would keep a record of iniquities, O Lord, who could stand? But with you is forgiveness, that you may be feared. (Ps 130:3–4)

Most strikingly, Psalm 143:2 itself, the biblical allusion underlying Paul's key formulation in Romans 3:20 and Galatians 2:16, was a major focus of exegetical reflection within Second Temple Judaism on universal sinfulness and the need for God's grace and mercy. In the book of Enoch, for example, in an allusion to Psalm 143:2, the seven holy ones instruct Enoch to reveal to his children that "no flesh is righteous before the Lord" (1 Enoch 81.5). Within the *Hymns* at Qumran, in which assertions of the universality of human sin feature prominently, allusions to Psalm 143:2 are strikingly frequent. In 1QH (Thanksgiving Hymns) 9.13–15, for example, the psalmist declares that his sole hope is in God's forgiveness (9.13) and merciful covenant love (9.14), "for there is no one who is righteous in your judgment" (9.14–15). The same point is made in 1QH 7.28–31, again through evident allusion to Psalm 143:2: "Who is righteous before you when he enters into your judgment? . . . But you bring all the faithful into your presence through forgiveness, purifying them of their sins in your great goodness and in the abundance of your mercy."

Not only do these passages from 1 Enoch and the Qumran *Hymns* underscore the theme of universal sin and the impossibility of righteousness through the law, each of them also expresses this theme (just as Paul does) through exegetical reflection on Psalm 143:2! Moreover, these allusions to Psalm 143:2 occur in the context of passages highlighting God's *covenantal* grace and mercy (cf. 1QH 4.36–37; 5.8–9; 7.26–27; 16.14–16). These texts speak frequently of the righteous, but they are such *only* within the gracious framework of the covenant (cf. 1QH 4.29–38; 9.33–34; 13.16–17; 15.14–16; 16.11–13). These texts reinforce this concept by drawing on Psalm 143:2 to express the impossibility of righteousness *apart from the covenant and its promise of mercy.*

Romans 3:20 in Its Jewish and Covenantal Context

As Psalm 143:2 and similar passages in the Old Testament and ancient Jewish literature reveal, the denial of the possibility of human righteousness apart from God's covenantal grace, mercy, and forgiveness is a prominent strain within ancient Jewish thought. And it is this crucial feature of Jewish covenant theology, on which Paul draws through his echo of Psalm 143:2, that provides the necessary background to illumine Romans 3:20—"by the works of the law no human being shall be justified before God." When Paul here affirms the impossibility of righteousness through the law, he is not, as Sanders assumed, referring to the law within the gracious context of the covenant. Rather, the "works of the law" in Romans 3:20 refers to the observance of the law *apart from the covenant and its promise of mercy in Jesus Christ.* Whenever Paul uses the specific phrase "works of the law" (Greek: *erga nomou,* Rom 3:28; Gal 2:16; 3:2, 5, 10), this—I would suggest—is its meaning. Far from being in conflict with the covenant theology of the Old Testament and un-Jewish, as Sanders alleges, the logic of Paul's rejection of the law as a way of righteousness is thoroughly Jewish and covenantal. Indeed, to assert the impossibility of righteousness by one's works, apart from the grace and mercy of God, is (we have seen) one of the key ways in which covenant theology is given expression.

And it is the failure to grasp this key feature of Jewish covenant theology that led Sanders to a crucial misstep—the notion that Paul departs from Jewish covenantal thought, indeed, that he rejects the covenant of God with Israel. Rather, at the heart of Paul's theology is the conviction that the covenant promises of God to Abraham have reached their intended fulfillment in Jesus Christ. Thus in Romans 3:21–22 Paul announces that the righteousness of God—which in Psalm 143 and throughout the Old Testament denotes YHWH's saving activity in faithfulness to his covenant promises—has been revealed in Jesus Christ.[24] The cross of Christ

---

24. In a famous article, Richard B. Hays has argued convincingly that Paul cites Ps 143 in Rom

is both the fulfillment of God's covenant promises to Israel and the source of the covenantal grace given to Abraham and to Israel through ages past (Gal 3:6–14; cf. Rom 3:25–26; 8:32). For Paul, the true basis and foundation of the covenant and of its gracious promise of mercy and life, hidden in mystery for long ages, have now been revealed in the Son of God made flesh, his atoning death, and his life-giving resurrection.

The purpose of Paul's affirmation of the impossibility of righteousness through the law is thus *not* to deny the covenantal context in which the law was given to Israel. Sanders's famous claim that in Paul's thought the covenant "skips" from Abraham to Christ cannot be sustained. Rather, in Paul's thought the law and its sacrifices functioned for Israel in the time of promise *within the gracious framework of the covenant and its promise of mercy to come in Jesus Christ*. Apart from this assumption it is impossible to explain Paul's portrayal of God's grace and mercy operative in Israel prior to Christ (Rom 3:25–26; 4:6–8; 11:4–6, 16–24), his conviction that faith was from the beginning the basis of Israel's covenantal relationship with God (Rom 3:3; 4:1–8; 1 Cor 10:1–5; 2 Cor 4:13; Gal 3:6–9), or his theology of a faithful remnant throughout Israel's history in relationship with Israel's God through grace (Rom 11:1–6).

To be sure, in bringing about the long-awaited fulfillment of Israel's hopes, Christ Jesus has brought about a salvation-historical change involving a new covenant and a new law (Rom 7:4–6; 1 Cor 5:7–8; 9:21; 10:1–4; 11:23–25; 2 Cor 3:4–18; Gal 6:2). Through this new covenant the gentiles are included in the people of God through Christ apart from the law of Moses and the Jewish identity markers of circumcision, food laws, and Sabbath keeping (Rom 3:21–31; 4:9–17; 15:7–13; Eph 2:11–22). Yet, as we will see in ensuing chapters, the new covenant is not the abrogation of the Abrahamic covenant, but its fulfillment (Rom 4:1–25; 15:8–12; Gal 3:6–29), and the new law of Christ fulfills the true intent of the law of Moses (cf. Gal 6:2 with 5:13–14). In Paul's understanding, Israel's long history, its law and its prophets, its covenants and its promises, its sacrifices and atoning rituals, has reached its intended goal in Jesus Christ, bringing the promised blessings of the covenant to those who obey the good news within Israel and to those who turn to God among the gentiles (Rom 1:2–7; 3:21–31; 4:9–17; 8:2–4; 9:4–5; 11:16–24; 15:8–12).

Accordingly, when Paul describes his fellow Jews who reject the good news of Christ as seeking their own righteousness through the law (Rom 9:30–10:4),

---

3:20 not only for its affirmation of human inadequacy to stand before God (Ps 143:2), but also because of its witness to this gracious, covenantal righteousness of God (Ps 143:1, 11), which in Rom 3:21–22 Paul announces as now fully revealed in Christ ("Psalm 143 and the Logic of Romans 3," *JBL* 99 [1980]: 107–15).

the charge involves neither (as claimed by the "old perspective") a deficient understanding of the relationship of law and grace, nor (as claimed by the "new perspective") ethnocentric exclusion of gentiles, but rejection of the covenant and mercy of God now fully revealed in Christ (Rom 10:5–13). The core issue in Romans 9:30–10:13 (as Sanders rightly recognized) is christological (that is, focused on the person and identity of Jesus), but the thought (as Sanders failed to recognize) is Jewish and covenantal. Conversely, when Paul warns gentile believers against seeking salvation through the Jewish law (Gal 1:6–9; 5:1, 7–12), this (thoroughly Jewish and covenantal!) warning involves seeking righteousness before God apart from the covenantal grace and mercy of God received through faith in Jesus and the good news of his death and resurrection (Gal 2:15–21; 3:6–29; 4:21–31; 5:2–6; 6:16). In Paul's theology, "those who call on the name of the Lord" (Rom 10:12–13; cf. 1 Cor. 1:2), which is in the Old Testament a regular designation for the covenant people of YHWH (cf. Gen 12:8; Pss 98:6; 115:4; Joel 3:5), are all those, Jew or gentile, who confess that Jesus is Lord and believe that God raised him from the dead (Rom 10:9–10).

Thus when Paul, in Romans 3:20 and elsewhere, declares that there is no one who is righteous, who does good, or who fulfills the law, he is not referring, as Sanders, Dunn, and nearly all protagonists in the debates concerning Paul and the law have assumed, to the law "within the framework of God's covenant with Israel."[25] Rather, in Paul the "works of the law" that cannot save refer to the law *apart from the covenant and its provision of mercy in Jesus Christ*, the true and only foundation of God's saving covenantal mercy to Israel and all nations. As we will see, when Paul speaks of works *within the gracious context of the covenant founded in Christ*, he readily speaks, as does the Old Testament, of God's people as those who are righteous (Rom 2:13; 6:16–18; 1 Cor 6:1, 9; 1 Thess 2:10), who do good (Rom 2:6–7, 10; 12:9; 13:3; 2 Cor 5:10; Gal 6:10; 1 Thess 5:15), and who fulfill the law (Rom 2:13, 26–29; 3:31; 8:3–4; 9:31; 13:8–10; 1 Cor 7:19; Gal 5:13–14). The distinction between works considered *within* and works considered *apart from* the covenantal relationship of faith, which is a regular feature of Jewish thought, is the key that unlocks the coherence and profoundly Jewish character of Paul's theology of the law.

Conclusion: The Law in Paul in Covenantal Perspective

More than four decades after Sanders's famous study, the seemingly irresolvable "problem of the law in Paul" introduced by this "new perspective" remains Paul's

---

25. Dunn, "Paul and the Torah," 461.

apparent disjunction of the law from the gracious framework of the covenant and its promise of divine mercy. Paul's portrayal of the law as demanding an obedience impossible for human beings to fulfill seemed to Sanders to be incoherent, profoundly un-Jewish, and in conflict with the Old Testament, involving a fundamental misunderstanding of the covenantal context of the law, or else a rejection of the covenant altogether. This challenge of Sanders is at the heart of the problem of Paul and the law. Several solutions to the challenge have been proposed, defending the coherence and consistency of Paul's thought, and many helpful insights have been offered regarding Paul's theology of the law. However, none of the proposed solutions has provided a fully convincing resolution of this question.

I have argued in this chapter that the solution to the problem lies within a foundational feature of Jewish covenant theology. According to a widespread strain within Jewish and biblical thought, apart from the grace and forgiveness found within the covenantal relationship of trust in the God of Israel, there is no one who is righteous or who can stand before God's judgment. Within Psalm 143, a classic expression of Jewish covenant theology, this concept is expressed in a striking way, as the psalmist affirms the impossibility of righteousness before YHWH *apart from the covenant and its promise of mercy.*

Paul, through his echo of Psalm 143:2, explicitly draws on this feature of ancient Jewish thought in Romans 3:20 (cf. Gal 2:16). When Paul here denies the capacity of human beings to carry out the law, he is not, as Sanders thought, referring to the law within the gracious framework of the covenant, a covenant that in Paul's thought was operative throughout Israel's history, and had now reached its climax in Christ. Rather, the "works of the law" in Romans 3:20 refers to the observance of the law *apart from the covenant and its promise of mercy in Jesus Christ.* They are works done apart from faith in Christ and union with him, who is the foundation and source of God's saving covenantal mercy for Israel and all nations.

Paul in his letters opposes a group scholars call the "Judaizers," who taught that gentile Christ followers must be circumcised and keep the law of Moses in order to be saved (Gal 2:1–5; 5:1–12; 6:11–16; Phil 3:2–11; cf. Acts 15:1–2). We modern readers are sometimes perplexed or even disturbed by the vehemence of Paul's opposition. But that is only when we fail to grasp what was at stake. For in insisting on the necessity of circumcision and the law for those *already joined to Christ* through faith, the Judaizers proclaimed a very *un-Jewish* idea—righteousness through the law apart from the covenant, grace, and mercy of God. Paul's gospel, by contrast, proclaimed the thoroughly Jewish and biblical conception that righteousness comes only through trust in God and his covenantal mercy—the covenant and grace of God founded in and now fully revealed by the cross and resurrection of Jesus Christ.

The distinction between the law considered *within* or *apart from* the covenantal relationship of faith, which is a regular feature of biblical and ancient Jewish thought, is foundational within Paul's theology, revealing its profoundly Jewish, biblical, and christocentric character. In uncovering this distinction, we have discovered another fundamental relation or opposition essential to the structure of Paul's thought. We saw in part 1 that Paul's theology is structured by two fundamental relations or distinctions: creator/creation, and union with the creator/ separation from the creator. In part 2 we saw the distinction between the two phases of the kingdom: inaugurated/consummated. We now have discovered a fourth duality or opposition, rooted in the covenantal character of Paul's thought:

Within the Covenant

Outside the Covenant

Once this fundamental distinction within Paul's thought is grasped, the seemingly disparate strands of Paul's theology of the law fall strikingly into place, and its continuity with the rest of the Bible becomes evident.

In the following chapters of part three, we will see how the covenantal character of Paul's thought reveals the coherence of major aspects of Paul's thought sometimes considered irreconcilable: in particular, the coherence of his Jewish, covenantal convictions regarding the law with his divine, incarnational Christology, and with his conception of the participatory union of believers with Christ. We will also see how the covenantal character of Paul's thought illumines such perennial difficulties as the apparent contradiction between justification by works in Romans 2 and justification by faith in Romans 3; the relationship between grace and ethics in Pauline theology; and the meaning of key Pauline terms such as "faith," "righteousness," and "justification."

Chapter Seven

The Covenant and the Cross

W e saw in the previous chapter that the key that unlocks the solution to the much-debated "problem of the law in Paul" is the covenantal character of Paul's thought, and the distinction between the law considered *within* and the law considered *apart from* the covenantal context of faith in Christ. In Paul's theology Jesus Christ is not only the fulfillment of the Abrahamic covenant, but he is also the foundation and source of the covenantal grace and mercy of God given to Abraham long ages ago. How can Christ be both the *fulfillment* and the *source* of the gracious covenant with Abraham? To see the answer, we need to unpack Paul's rich theology of *atonement* within its Jewish covenantal context. By doing so, we will see how Paul's covenantal thought coheres with the center of his theology—the incarnation of God in the person of Jesus Christ. We will also see how in Paul's theology the love of God at the heart of the covenant could only be fully revealed in the cross of Christ, how the covenant has reached its intended fulfillment in the participatory union of believers with the Son of God, and how the covenantal relationship of trust in YHWH at the center of Israel's Scriptures finds its fullest expression in the believer's relationship with Christ through faith.[1]

---

1. The scholar who has in my view most insightfully uncovered the covenantal dimensions of Paul's thought, and the way in which the covenantal character of Paul's thought undergirds his whole theology, is N. T. Wright. See his classic chapter "Creation and Covenant" in *Paul in Fresh Perspective* (Minneapolis: Fortress, 2005), 20–39, and his most recent and full study *Paul and the Faithfulness of God*, vol. 4 of *Christian Origins and the Question of God* (Minneapolis: Fortress, 2013). I see my treatment of Paul's covenantal theology in this chapter, even where there are points of disagreement, as heavily indebted to and building upon Wright's seminal work. Another scholar whom I have found very helpful in illumining the crucial place of the covenant in Paul's theology is Frank Thielman, especially his study *Paul and the Law: A Contextual Approach* (Downers Grove: InterVarsity, 1994).

Abrahamic Covenant and New Covenant in the Old Testament

We have seen that the law of Moses functioned for Israel in the time of promise within the gracious context of the covenant and its provision for mercy. However, within the Old Testament the source of YHWH's grace and mercy to Israel is not the law in itself, but his "covenant love and truth" (Pss 25:6–11; 40:10–11; 57:1–3; 61:7; 85:9–11; 86:15; 89:14) bestowed in the covenant with Abraham. The Lord's covenant love and faithfulness, the wellspring of his mercy and forgiveness, is, on the one hand, intrinsic to his very being: "The Lord, the Lord God, gracious and merciful, slow to anger, and abounding in covenant love and truth" (Exod 34:6–7; cf. Ps 145:8; Joel 2:13; Jon 4:2). It is therefore "from everlasting to everlasting" (Ps 103:17; cf. 2 Chron 5:13; 7:3; Ps 25:6; Jer 31:3). And yet it is, on the other hand, bestowed in time on Israel through the Abrahamic covenant, YHWH's "covenant love given to Abraham" (Mic 7:20). The covenant love of God, bestowed in the foundational commitment to Abraham, provides the gracious context in which the law is given through Moses (Exod 6:2–8; 19:1–6; 29:38–46; 34:4–7).

Within this gracious context, the law provided a means of atonement and forgiveness through animal sacrifice (Exod 28–29; Lev 1–7; 16; Num 7–8; 28–29). Yet, as the unfolding of Israel's story revealed, these sacrifices were not in themselves sufficient to prevent judgment and exile, nor to bring about fallen Israel's forgiveness and restoration (2 Kings 17; 24–25; Lam 1–5; Isa 59:1–15). For this a *new* and *ultimate* divine work of atonement, forgiveness, and renewal was necessary (Isa 4:4–5; 44:22–23; Jer 33:8; 50:20; Ezek 36:22–38 [esp. vv. 25–27, 33]; Hos 2:14–23 [esp. vv. 19–20, 23]; Zech 13:1; cf. Ps 130:7–8; Isa 43:25; 54:8–10; 55:3; 59:15–21). Through this coming divine work, YHWH would "redeem Israel from all their iniquities" (Ps 130:8), "wash away" the sins of Jacob (Isa 4:4; cf. 44:22–23), and "purify them from all their iniquity" (Jer 33:8). "In that day a spring will be opened, to purify the house of David and the people of Jerusalem from sin and from impurity" (Zech 13:1).[2] This ultimate divine act would bring about a "new covenant" between God and Israel:

> [31]Behold, the days are coming, says the Lord, when I will make with the house of Israel and with the house of Judah a new covenant, [32]not like the covenant which I made with them when I grasped them by the hand to bring them out of the land of Egypt. They broke my covenant, although I was a faithful husband to them, says the Lord. [33]But this is the

---

2. On this aspect of the Old Testament expectation, see the still valuable discussion of G. F. Oehler, *Theologie des alten Testaments*, 2nd ed. (Stuttgart: Steinkopf, 1882), 710–12.

covenant which I will make with the house of Israel after those days, says the Lord: I will put my law within them, and in their heart I will write it, and I will be their God and they will be my people. [34]And they will no longer teach, each one his neighbor or his brother, saying, "Know the Lord." For they will all know me, from the least of them to the greatest of them, says the Lord, for I will forgive their iniquity, and their sin I will remember no more. (Jer 31:31–34)

The outstanding characteristics of the new covenant, as prophesied by Jeremiah, were twofold. First, this new covenant would bring about a transformed heart to know and love YHWH (Jer 31:33; cf. Ezek 36:26–27; 37:23; Hos 2:19–20). In this way the new covenant would provide the remedy not only to the malady at the root of Israel's exile (Exod 32; 2 Kings 17; Jer 7; Ezek 8–11), but also to the malady at the heart of fallen humanity's estrangement from its creator—the idolatry and wickedness of the human heart, alienated from the life of God (Gen 3; Ps 14; Isa 53:6; 59:1–15). Second, the new covenant would bring the full forgiveness and pardon that (as the exile revealed) the law and its sacrifices were unable in themselves to provide (Jer 31:34; cf. Isa 44:22–23; Jer 50:20; Ezek 36:25; Hos 2:23). In the light of this prophetic promise of a *new* covenant, it becomes clear that within the Old Testament itself the Mosaic sacrifices had only a *provisional* purpose, functioning to foreshadow this new and ultimate divine act of atonement and renewal. When the new covenant came, the old covenant given at Sinai would be no more (Jer 31:31–32). But the new covenant, and the full atonement and forgiveness it would provide, would *not* undo the Abrahamic covenant, but instead bring the covenant with Abraham, and its promise of grace and mercy to Israel, to its full realization:

Who is a God like you, who takes away iniquity, and forgives the rebellion of the remnant of his inheritance? He does not keep his anger forever, because he delights in covenant love. He will again have mercy on us, he will trample our iniquities underfoot, you will cast all their sins into the depths of the sea. You will give truth to Jacob, and covenant love to Abraham, which you promised on oath to our fathers from ancient days. (Mic 7:18–20)

The Covenant of Abraham and the Cross of Christ

It is at the heart of Paul's gospel that the new covenant foretold by the prophets has now come—in Jesus Christ, his death and his resurrection (Rom 2:28–29; 7:5–6; 1 Cor 11:23–25; 2 Cor 3:1–18). The new and ultimate atoning act promised in Israel's Scriptures, and which the sacrifices of the law only foreshadowed, has now come to pass in the cross of Christ (Rom 3:25–26). And in bringing the promised new covenant, Jesus has brought the long-awaited fulfillment of God's covenant promises to Abraham (Rom 4:1–25; Gal 3:6–29).

But in Paul's gospel Jesus Christ is not only the *fulfillment* of God's covenant promises to Abraham, he is also the *foundation* of the Abrahamic covenant, the hidden *source* of God's covenantal mercy to Israel through ages past. In Paul's thought, the cross of Christ, foreordained by God from eternity (Rom 16:25; cf. Eph 3:8–9; Col 1:26–27; 2 Tim 1:9), is the mysterious font of the grace and mercy given to Abraham (Gal 3:6–14).[3] And as Romans 3:25–26 makes clear, Paul regards the prior efficacy of Israel's atoning sacrifices as grounded proleptically in the future atoning act of Christ. The word Paul uses in Romans 3:25 to describe Christ's sacrifice, usually translated "sacrifice of atonement," is *hilastērion*. This word is regularly used in the Septuagint (the ancient Greek translation of the Hebrew Scriptures) to refer to the "mercy seat" on the ark of the covenant within the most holy place, where the blood of sacrificial animals was sprinkled to make atonement for Israel once a year on the Day of Atonement (see Exod 25:17–22; 37:6–9; Lev 16:1–15).[4] Paul thereby affirms that the cross of Christ is the true "mercy seat," the full and final means of grace and atonement, of which the mercy seat in the tabernacle under the old covenant was only a type and foreshadowing. In Romans 8:3 Paul denotes Jesus's crucifixion with the expression *peri hamartias*, the term in constant use in the Septuagint for the "sin offering" prescribed in the law of Moses (e.g., LXX Lev 5:7; 9:2; 16:3, 5; Num 8:8; Ps 39:7), in order to describe Christ as the true "sin offering" or "sacrifice for sin" to which the Old Testament sacrifices looked forward. And in Romans 8:32 Paul echoes Genesis 22:16, in order to portray the lamb provided by God to Abraham at the near sacrifice of Isaac as but a foreshadowing of the sacrifice of Christ, the true

---

3. See Thielman, *Paul and the Law*, 180–81, 240–45, to whom I am indebted for deepening my grasp of this crucial aspect of Pauline theology.

4. Scholars dispute the precise sense of *hilastērion* in Rom 3:25. For a brief summary of the debate, see Anthony C. Thiselton, *The Living Paul: An Introduction to the Apostle's Life and Thought* (Downers Grove: InterVarsity, 2009), 87–88. Whatever other nuances may be present in Paul's use of the term, *hilastērion* is normally used in the LXX to refer to the mercy seat, and therefore it is very likely that Paul intends an allusion to the mercy seat in Rom 3:25.

wellspring and source of the "covenant love and truth" given to Abraham and his seed in the Abrahamic covenant.

But why is the sin offering of *Christ* the source of the covenantal mercy of God given to Abraham? Why is *Christ's* sacrifice greater than the sacrifices under the law? The answer in Paul's theology is that in the crucifixion "God did not spare his own Son" (Rom 8:32). We saw in part 2 of this book how the center of Paul's thought is the incarnation—Jesus is YHWH, the creator God, come in the flesh. And Paul's theology of Jesus as God incarnate is at the heart of his theology of the atonement. *This* sin offering is of *infinite* atoning power, because it is the self-offering of the eternal Son of God made flesh. The blood of this offering is the blood of God incarnate. "Therefore if Christ is seen in the light of the Old Testament sin offering, there is a fundamental discontinuity in the tradition history: one is moving from an animal victim as sin offering to the pre-existent Son of God who became a human being (but who remained the Son of God). For Paul, only God could enter our place."[5] It is sometimes thought that Paul's incarnational Christology is incompatible with covenant theology. But the two belong together in Pauline thought. Paul's understanding of the cross of Christ as the foundation of the Abrahamic covenant is firmly founded in his incarnational Christology of Jesus as YHWH, Israel's God, come in the flesh.

We saw above how in the Old Testament God's covenantal mercy is depicted as grounded in his *eternal being*, but also as coming about through a *coming divine work* of atonement. This is a mystery never resolved in the Old Testament, although perhaps mysteriously foreshadowed in the *presence* of YHWH above the *mercy seat*, the place of atonement (Exod 25:22; Lev 16:2). But in the cross of Christ we see the Son of God, who is "God over all, blessed forever" (Rom 9:5), himself the eternal source of covenant love and truth, freely offering himself "for our sins" (1 Cor 15:3; cf. Rom 4:24–25; Gal 1:4) as "an offering and a sacrifice to God" (Eph 5:2; cf. Rom 3:25; 2 Cor 5:21; Col 1:22). In the cross, the *being* who is love and the *enactment* of that love are united in one atoning sacrifice, the infinite wellspring of life-giving covenantal grace and mercy. And that is why, in Paul's theology, mercy, righteousness, and life cannot be found in the law, nor in its sacrifices, but only in the atoning death and life-giving resurrection of the Son of God.

The Cross of Christ and the Love of God

Paul's gospel announced the love of God revealed in the cross of Christ: "I live by faith in the Son of God, who loved me and gave himself for me" (Gal 2:20).

5. Richard H. Bell, "Sacrifice and Christology in Paul," *JTS* 53 (2002): 1–27 (26).

This concept of the love of God has become familiar to modern persons. But for Paul's pagan hearers the conception of the sacrificial love of God would have been startling and new. And yet Paul's proclamation of the love of God would perhaps have also struck a deep, almost half-forgotten chord. The point requires some elaboration.

Within the anthropomorphic conceptions of ancient polytheism, the gods were considered subject to the full range of human-like passions and emotions: capable of lust, hatred, malice, envy, jealousy, rivalry, covetousness, and deceit—but also of love, pity, kindness, and mercy. The affectionate love or friendship of the gods for kings, heroes, and others on whom their favor rests is a staple theme of ancient mythology (e.g., Homer's *Odyssey*). The philosophers, on the other hand, tended to reject this anthropomorphic understanding and to promote a purer, higher conception of the divine untouched by frail passion. But this more remote conception of the divine, while abolishing the gods' lusts and misdeeds, also abolished the prospect of their love and friendship. Among the philosophers the Stoics came closest to a conception of divine love. They believed in a benevolent divine providence that framed the world for humanity's benefit, oversaw human affairs, and even cared for virtuous individuals (Cicero, *On the Nature of the Gods* 2.73–167; *Concerning Divination* 1.82–84; Seneca, *On Providence* 1.4–6). But even the Stoics, in their identification of the highest divinity with the material universe (Seneca, *Letters* 92.30; *On Benefits* 4.7.1; Marcus Aurelius, *Meditations* 8.54) and their belief in the human soul's own divinity and equality with God (Seneca, *Letters* 31.9–11; 48.11; 66.12), left no room for a relationship of love with a divinity outside the self. The divine friendship of the myths ultimately had no place among the philosophers. As Aristotle put it, there can be no love between gods and human beings (*Nicomachean Ethics* 8.7.4–6; *Eudemian Ethics* 7.3.3–4; *Magna moralia* 2.11.6). Cicero tells us that this philosophic view had already in his day become the view of the average person (*Concerning Divination* 2.104).

Paul's letters, by contrast, are suffused with celebration of the love of God made known in Christ (Rom 5:5–8; 8:35–39; 9:25; 15:30; 2 Cor 5:14–21; 13:14 [Greek 13:13]; Gal 2:20; Eph 2:4–7; 3:14–19; 5:1–2, 25–33; Col 3:12–13; 1 Thess 1:4–5; 2 Thess 2:13–17; Titus 3:4–7). "Friendship of God and Man, which fills the Greek mythology, was banished by philosophy's higher and remoter conception of the Divine; but is restored by Christianity."[6] But the concept is also radically transformed. Ancient philosophy's insistence, in critique of the myths, upon the moral purity of the divine is affirmed—and immeasurably heightened—in the Pauline

---

6. G. C. Armstrong, in Aristotle, *Magna Moralia* (LCL 287; Cambridge: Havard University Press, 1935), 650 (note *a*).

conception of the absolute goodness and holiness of Christ, who "knew no sin" (2 Cor 5:21) and is the source of all holiness (1 Cor 1:2, 30; Eph 5:26). Moreover, the Spirit whom believers receive is "the Spirit of *holiness*" (Rom 1:4), "the *holy* Spirit" (Rom 5:5; 9:1; 14:17; 15:13; 1 Cor 6:19; 2 Cor 13:14 [Greek 13:13]; Eph 1:13; 4:30; 1 Thess 1:5–6; 4:8; 2 Tim 1:14; Titus 3:5). In place of the friendship of unpredictable and quixotic deities is the love of a holy God. Another key difference is that in ancient pagan thought the friendship of the gods is preferential, bestowed upon a favored few, whether kings, heroes, or wise men. In Paul, God's love is "love for all humanity" (Greek: *philanthrōpia*, Titus 3:4); the love of Christ extends to every human being (2 Cor 5:14–21); and the love of God is poured out in the hearts of all the baptized (Rom 5:5). This deeper and richer conception of divine love in Paul matches the concept of the covenantal love of God for his people, as of a husband for his bride, celebrated in Israel's Scriptures, psalms, and liturgy (cf. Pss 36:5–10; 63:3–5; 136; 138; Isa 63:7–9; Jer 31:3; Hos 1–2; 11:1; Mic 7:18–20).

But there is a difference between the friendship of the gods in ancient pagan thought and the love of God in Paul that is more crucial still. In both ancient myth and ancient philosophy, the very nature of divinity precludes self-sacrifice. The friendship of the gods only goes so far. For the gods can have nothing to do with suffering, sorrow, or death. "Such is the fate the gods have spun for wretched mortals," says Achilles to Priam in the closing scene of the *Iliad*, "that we should live in sorrows, but they themselves are without cares" (Homer, *Iliad* 24.525–26)

In striking contrast, Paul's gospel is a narrative not only of the Son of God become human, but also of the Son of God become human for the purpose of suffering, crucifixion, and death—"and being found in outward form as a human being, he abased himself, becoming obedient to the point of death, even death on a cross" (Phil 2:7–8). "Christ loved us and gave himself for us, as an offering and a sacrifice to God for a sweet fragrance" (Eph 5:2). If within ancient pagan thought the friendship of the gods only goes so far, in Paul the love of God extends to the point of death, even death on a cross. The contrast is powerfully expressed in Edward Shillito's poem "Jesus of the Scars":

> The other gods were strong, but Thou wast weak;
> They rode, but Thou didst stumble to a throne;
> But to our wounds only God's wounds can speak,
> And not a god has wounds, but Thou alone.

In the pagan world into which Paul's gospel came, the philosophic divinities were incapable of love, and the gods of ancient worship bestowed friendship on a worthy few, without cost to themselves. In Paul's revolutionary gospel, by contrast, the

Son of God had given himself over to sorrow, shame, torture, physical agony, and death, in order to save the lowly and the unworthy. "God shows his love for us, in that while we were still sinners, Christ died for us" (Rom 5:8). This conception even disclosed a dimension of the love of God known by Israel and proclaimed in the Old Testament that was previously undreamed of: the *sacrificial* love of God. According to Paul's gospel, the covenantal love of God celebrated in Israel's Scriptures had now been fully revealed in the cross of Christ.

Covenant and Communion

Sanders famously insisted that because Paul's theology centers on the supernatural union of the faithful with Christ (the focus of our study in chapter 5), it cannot be covenantal. According to Sanders, Paul's doctrine of the indwelling of Christ through his Spirit is in conflict with the Old Testament and "Jewish covenantal thought."[7] But I believe this view is founded upon a deep misunderstanding of ancient Jewish covenant theology. In the Old Testament (as we saw in part 2), when God takes Israel to himself in the exodus to be his covenant people, he does so that he might *dwell* among them forever. The climax of the exodus, and of the covenant at Sinai, is the dwelling of YHWH among his people in his sanctuary (Exod 25–31; 35–40; Lev 23; Deut 16; 26; 1 Kings 6–8; 1 Chron 15–16; 2 Chron 2–7; Pss 68; 84; 87; 116; 120–34; 150). And the central expectation of the Old Testament is the coming of YHWH to dwell among his people in the fullness of his presence (Isa 35; 40:1–11; Ps 96; Ezek 37:21–28; Zech 14:1–19; Mal 3:1–5).

So too in Paul, the *indwelling* of the Son of God in the faithful, made possible by his incarnation, death, and resurrection, is the fulfillment of the *covenant*. The view that covenant and participation are contradictory seems to be based on a vague notion that this divine indwelling, because it involves a mysterious and supernatural participation in God, is incompatible with the freely chosen obedience and friendship with God that constitute the covenantal relationship. But as we saw in chapter 5, this miraculous union comes about, and is sustained and deepened, only through the free response of repentance, faith, and love (Rom 1:17; 1 Cor 1:2; Gal 3:14, 27; 5:5–6; Eph 2:8; 3:16–19; 2 Thess 1:3–4). By its very nature, then, this divine indwelling involves a covenantal relationship of dependence upon and trust in God.

Moreover, in this participatory union, it is not that Christ merely *is* in the faithful, but he *indwells* them as in his own temple, in a relationship of covenantal

---

7. E. P. Sanders, *Paul, the Law, and the Jewish People* (Philadelphia: Fortress, 1983), 208–9; Sanders, *Paul and Palestinian Judaism* (Philadelphia: Fortress, 1977), 513–15.

love, communion, friendship, and intimacy.[8] This participatory union with Christ proclaimed by Paul offered, as we explored in chapter 5, a divine intimacy unknown among the philosophies and religions in the ancient world into which Paul's gospel came—a miraculous, transforming union with the transcendent creator, who, while remaining distinct, truly unites himself with and indwells each of the faithful. In this divine indwelling, the covenant formula—"I will be your God, and you will be my people" (Gen 17:7–8; Exod 6:6–7; 19:5–6; Lev 26:12; Jer 7:22–23; Ezek 37:27)—receives its highest expression and fulfillment. For through this indwelling of God, the intimacy and friendship with God that are at the heart of the covenantal relationship are realized in a manner beyond compare.

We can now see how two fundamental distinctions or oppositions in Paul that we identified earlier belong closely together within his thought:

Within the Covenant	Union with the Creator
Outside the Covenant	Separation from the Creator

There is a deep coherence in Paul's theology between covenant and participation. The claim that Paul's doctrine of union with Christ is incompatible with covenant theology is in reality the reverse of the truth. In Paul, as throughout the Bible, *the purpose of the covenant is communion.*

Faith and the Covenant

This saving union with Christ comes about, not by works, but by faith (Rom 3:21–4:25; Gal 2:16–21; Eph 2:8–10). We discussed faith briefly in chapter 5, but here we need to consider the nature of faith more fully. For its importance within Paul's theology is evident. Faith is both the way in which one *enters* into saving communion with God (Rom 13:11; 1 Cor 15:11; Gal 2:16; 3:2; Eph 1:13) and the way in which one *grows* in it (Rom 1:12; 5:1–2; 2 Cor 1:24; Gal 2:20; 3:5; 5:5–6; Eph 3:12; Col 1:23). Having entered the kingdom by faith, the faithful then live by faith (Rom 1:17; Gal 3:11) and walk by faith (2 Cor 5:7). "The life which I now live in the flesh I live by faith in the Son of God, who loved me and gave himself for me" (Gal 2:20). This all-encompassing role of faith within the new life in Christ is the most likely meaning of Paul's assertion in Romans 1:17 that in the gospel the righteousness of

---

8. Cf. Adolphe Tanqueray, *Synopsis Theologiae Dogmaticae* (Paris: Desclée, 1938), 3:70. See also 2:672–75.

God is revealed "from faith to faith," that is, "by faith from beginning to end" (cf. Gal 3:1–5; Col 2:6–7).

The book of Acts tells us that when Paul proclaimed the good news to Lydia, "God opened her heart to give heed to the things proclaimed by Paul" (Acts 16:14). Paul in his letters likewise describes faith as a gift of God. Through the prior activity of the Holy Spirit (theologians often call this *prevenient grace*), faith is given that one may enter into saving union with God (1 Cor 12:3; 2 Thess 2:10), and through the indwelling of the Holy Spirit given in this saving union, the gift of faith is given in its fullness, enriched, and increased, together with hope and love (Eph 3:16–17; 6:23; Col 2:2, 6–7; 1 Tim 1:14; 2 Tim 1:13–14).

But what is this divinely given "faith" that receives the grace of God, and in which believers thereafter "live" and "walk"? Here it is significant that of the varied terms Paul and the earliest Christians might have chosen, their terms for "faith" (*pistis*) or "believing" (*pisteuo*) denote, not simply intellectual belief or credence, but *trust* in a person. It is "faith in Jesus Christ" (Rom 3:22; Gal 2:16; 3:22), "faith in the Son of God" (Gal 2:20), "faith in the Lord Jesus" (Eph 1:15; Col 1:4), and "faith in Christ" (Phil 3:9).[9] Here again we find Paul's unmistakably divine Christology. For in the Old Testament, to put faith or trust in anyone or anything other than the creator is idolatry (Pss 31:6; 78:7; 115:4–8; 118:8–9; 135:15–18; 146:3–6; Jer 17:5–8). But just as we saw in chapter 3 that in Paul's epistles Jesus receives the worship due to God alone, so also in Paul's letters Jesus receives the faith and trust given to God alone. Within the Jewish context of Paul's thought, Jesus can only be the object of faith because he is the divine Son of God, the One through whom and for whom all things were created (1 Cor 8:6; Col 1:16–17).

But this trust in the person of the Lord Jesus in Paul is also belief in the content of the apostolic message about him. Paul calls this variously "the gospel" (Rom 1:16), "our gospel" (1 Thess 1:5), "our testimony" (2 Thess 2:10), "the word

---

9. In my view, a red herring in the discussion of the meaning of faith in Paul is the claim that the genitive constructions *pistis Iesou Christou* (Rom 3:22; Gal 2:16; 3:22), *pistis Christou* (Gal 2:16; Phil 3:9), and *pistis Iesou* (Rom 3:26) can or must refer, not to faith in Christ (an objective genitive), but to the faith or faithfulness of Christ, that is, Jesus's own faith or faithfulness (subjective genitive). For the debate, see Jouette M. Bassler, *Navigating Paul: An Introduction to Key Theological Concepts* (Louisville: Westminster John Knox, 2007), 27–33. Space precludes discussion here, but I regard this claim as unconvincing, and as involving a forced reading of the relevant passages. The weakness of the claim is evident in the other formulations of *pistis* with a genitive in the New Testament, where by common consent the genitive must be taken as the object of the believer's faith: e.g., Mark 11:22, *pistis theou* ("faith in God"); Acts 3:16, *pistis tou onomatos autou* ("faith in his name"); Col 2:12, *pistis tes energeias tou theou* ("faith in the working of God"); and 2 Thess 2:13, *pistis alētheias* ("faith in the truth"). In my judgment, the construction *pistis Christou* in Paul likewise refers to the believer's faith in Christ.

of truth" (Eph 1:13; Col 1:5), and "the word of faith which we proclaim" (Rom 10:8). This message had a fixed, propositional content, which Paul summarizes in the various "confessional formulas" sprinkled throughout his letters (Rom 1:3–4; 4:24–25; 8:34; 1 Cor 8:6; 11:23–25; 15:1–11; 1 Thess 1:9–10; 4:14; 1 Tim 2:5–6; 3:16; 2 Tim 2:8). Paul's gospel, then, had a *propositional* character, and therefore in Paul's thought one dimension of faith is that it is an act of the *intellect*, giving assent to the truths of the gospel. It is especially in light of this aspect of faith as conviction, as belief in truths revealed by God, that Paul carefully *distinguishes* faith from hope and from love (2 Cor 8:7; Eph 1:15; Col 1:3–8; 1 Thess 1:2–10; 5:8).

We see, then, that faith, or *pistis*, in Paul, as many scholars have recognized, is multifaceted, with a primary sense of trust, alongside the conception of belief or assent.[10] But there is another crucial dimension of faith in Paul's thought that does not receive as much attention. It is the concept of *repentance*, that is, sorrow for one's sins as an offense against God, and the firm resolve to forsake sin. Although the language of "repentance" (Greek: *metanoia*) is prominent in other strands of the New Testament, it is found in Paul only rarely (Rom 2:4–5; 2 Cor 7:9–10; 12:21; 2 Tim 2:24–26). And in numerous passages Paul speaks of faith alone as sufficient for salvation, with no reference to repentance (Rom 1:16–17; 3:21–31; 1 Cor 1:18–31; Eph 2:8–10; Phil 3:9–11). One might therefore suppose that the concept of "repentance" or renunciation of sin played little role in Paul's theology. But this is mistaken, for although Paul mentions "repentance" so seldom, when he does so it is evident that in his theology it is *necessary for salvation* (Rom 2:4–5; 2 Cor 7:9–10, "repentance to salvation"). This is also the case in the speeches of Paul in the book of Acts (Acts 17:30; 20:21; 26:20).

Why, then, if in Paul's theology repentance (*metanoia*) is necessary for salvation, does he make so little mention of it in his letters? Why does he speak of faith alone as sufficient for saving relation to God? The answer is surprisingly simple: in Paul, *faith includes repentance*. Faith in Paul is thus not only an activity of the *mind* or *intellect*, it is also an activity of the *heart* and *will*. It is an orientation of the whole person, mind and heart, to God. "The love of God has been poured out in our hearts through the Holy Spirit who has been given to us" (Rom 5:5). As we will see in the following chapter, the justification that comes through faith produces true love for God (Rom 8:28; 1 Cor 2:9; 8:3; Eph 6:24; 2 Tim 4:8) and love for others, especially the family of God (Gal 5:22; Eph 1:15; Col 1:4; 1 Thess 1:3; 4:9; 1 Tim 1:5). Faith, therefore, although it is in Paul (as we saw above) *distinguished* from hope and love, is always *accompanied* by hope and love (Eph 1:15; 6:23; 1 Thess 1:2–10; 2 Thess 1:3–12; Col 1:3–8; 1 Tim 1:5), by holiness (2 Thess 2:13; 1 Tim 2:15),

---

10. For this twofold sense of *pistis* in Paul's thought, see Bassler, *Navigating Paul*, 23–24.

and by good works (Rom 3:31; 1 Cor 1:30; Eph 2:10; Phil 3:9–11; 2 Thess 3:3–5). It is "faith which operates through love" (Gal 5:6).

Paul can occasionally speak of faith as an act of the intellect only, without repentance and love (1 Cor 13:2). But he makes clear that this is a defective form of faith that does not unite its possessor to Christ (1 Cor 13:1–13; Gal 5:24). Therefore Paul's many warnings to the faithful that those who live in grave sin will not inherit the kingdom of God (1 Cor 6:9–11; 9:24–10:22; Gal 5:16–24; Eph 5:3–14; Phil 3:17–4:1; Col 3:5–7; 2 Tim 3:5–8; Titus 1:15–16). In Paul's normal usage, "faith" refers to the orientation of the whole person—mind, heart, and will—to God, and always includes repentance and love.

We now see why the word chosen by Paul to express this faith (*pistis*) highlights trust in God rather than mere intellectual assent (although we have seen it includes that as well). For this faith is a matter not only of the mind but also of the heart. And here again we see the covenantal character of Paul's thought, for this Pauline concept of faith corresponds to (and even heightens) the covenantal relationship of faith we see in the Psalms and elsewhere in the Old Testament, by which the righteous trust in YHWH, take refuge in him, and seek his holy ways.

Conclusion: Covenant, Cross, and Communion

Within the Old Testament, the source of the grace and mercy given to Israel is not the law, but YHWH's "covenant love and truth" bestowed upon Abraham. The animal sacrifices provided in the law of Moses had only a provisional purpose, functioning to foreshadow a new and ultimate divine work of atonement and forgiveness. This new covenant promised both forgiveness of sins and a transformed heart to know and love YHWH, thus bringing the Abrahamic covenant to full realization.

Paul's gospel proclaimed that the new covenant, that new and ultimate work of atonement and forgiveness promised in Israel's Scriptures, had now come in the cross of Christ. The cross of Christ is the true sin offering to which the Old Testament sacrifices looked forward, and this sacrifice of Christ is the true source and wellspring of the divine mercy and grace given to Abraham. The one offering of Christ is of infinite atoning power, because it is the self-offering of the eternal Son of God made flesh. The center of Paul's theology—the incarnation of God in the person of Jesus Christ—is at the heart of his theology of the atonement. To a pagan world in which both the philosophers and the common person believed that the nature of divinity precludes self-sacrifice, Paul brought the startling announcement of the love of God made known in the suffering, crucifixion, and death of

Christ. The cross of Christ revealed a sacrificial divine love previously unknown to Paul's gentile hearers, and brought the full revelation of the covenantal love of God celebrated in Israel's Scriptures.

As within the Old Testament YHWH took Israel to himself as his covenant people that he might dwell among them in his temple, so in Paul's letters the indwelling of Christ within the faithful is the fulfillment of the covenant. In Paul's theology, as throughout the Bible, the purpose of the covenant is communion. The faith whereby one enters this saving union is an orientation of the whole person—intellect, heart, and will—to God, and always includes repentance and love. The Old Testament conception of the covenantal relationship of trust in YHWH looked forward to its fulfillment in this intimate relationship with the Son of God through faith. In Paul's theology, Christ is the foundation of the covenant, and Christ is the fulfillment of the covenant. For Paul, the covenant is Christ.

Chapter Eight

Justification within the Covenant

One of the most debated issues in the study of Paul's letters today is the nature of "justification" in Paul's theology. What does Paul mean when he affirms that those joined to Christ are "justified" by faith (Rom 3:28; 5:1; Gal 2:16; 3:24)? As throughout Paul's theology, we will find that the Jewish and covenantal character of Paul's thought, and its foundations in the Old Testament Scriptures, are the key to grasping the meaning of justification in Paul.

Righteousness and Justification in Paul

In Romans 1:16–17, Paul introduces the central theme of his letter to the Romans, the "righteousness of God."

> [16]For I am not ashamed of the gospel, for it is the power of God for salvation for everyone who believes, to the Jew first and then to the gentile; [17]for in it the righteousness of God is revealed from faith to faith. As it is written, "The righteous will live by faith."

All Pauline interpreters agree that "the righteousness of God" is the main theme of Romans, and an important aspect of Paul's thought elsewhere in his letters as well (cf. 2 Cor 5:21; Phil 3:9). This concept is especially crucial, because our understanding of the "righteousness of God" in Paul will determine our understanding of "justification" in Paul. For, although it is lost in translation, the terms "righteousness" (*dikaiosunē*), "justify" (*dikaioō*), and "justification" (*dikaiōsis*) are in Paul's original Greek cognate terms. The terms "righteousness" and "justification" are thus (this is crucial to understand) merely *different ways in which Paul expresses the same basic theme*. Therefore our study of justification in Paul's theology must begin with the Pauline theme of "the righteousness of God."

The Righteousness of God: Belonging to God or Given to Human Beings?

Scholars are agreed on the importance of the "righteousness of God" theme in Paul, but its meaning in Paul is debated. According to one view, the "righteousness of God" in Paul refers to *God's own* righteousness.[1] But according to another view, it refers to a righteousness *given to those who believe*.[2] What is the answer?

To grasp what Paul means in Romans 1:16–17 by "the righteousness of God," it is crucial to realize that Paul is echoing a key passage from the Old Testament Scriptures, Psalm 98.[3] Scholars today are rightly in general agreement that the meaning of "the righteousness of God" in Psalm 98 (and elsewhere in the Psalms and Isaiah) provides the interpretive key to Paul's thought in Romans 1:16–17.[4] Psalm 98:1–3 (with the words echoed by Paul in italics) reads as follows:

> [1]Sing to YHWH a new song, for he has done wondrous deeds. With his right hand and his holy arm he has wrought salvation. [2]YHWH has made his salvation known, he has *revealed his righteousness* in the sight of the nations. [3]He has remembered his covenant love and his truth to the house of Israel; all the ends of the earth have seen the salvation of our God!

Psalm 98 prophetically envisions the fulfillment of the Abrahamic covenant for Israel, and an accompanying inclusion of all peoples in God's salvation.[5] Two things are evident about the "righteousness" spoken of in this psalm. First, it is clearly *God's own* righteousness (v. 2, "his righteousness"). Second, this righteousness denotes God's *covenant love* and faithfulness to his covenant promises (v. 3, "he has remembered his covenant love and his truth"). It would seem, then, that in Romans 1:16–17, which takes up Psalm 98, "the righteousness of God" is a righteousness belonging to God, and denotes his faithfulness to his covenant promises made to Abraham.

---

1. The most notable contemporary exponent of this view is N. T. Wright; see Wright, "The Letter to the Romans," *NIB* 10: 464–77; Wright, *Paul and the Faithfulness of God*, vol. 4 of *Christian Origins and the Question of God* (Minneapolis: Fortress, 2013), 841.

2. For a classic exposition of this view, see C. E. B. Cranfield, *A Critical and Exegetical Commentary on the Epistle to the Romans*, 2 vols., ICC (Edinburgh: T. & T. Clark, 1975–1979), 1:91–102.

3. On the multiple echoes of Ps 98:2–3 within Rom 1:16–17, see Richard Hays, *Echoes of Scripture in the Letters of Paul* (New Haven: Yale University Press, 1989), 36–37.

4. Paul's language of the "righteousness of God" in Romans and elsewhere "draws directly on Israel's covenant theology as expressed most clearly by the Psalmist and Second Isaiah" (James D. G. Dunn, "Did Paul Have a Covenant Theology? Reflections on Romans 9.4 and 11.27," in *The New Perspective on Paul*, rev. ed. [Grand Rapids: Eerdmans, 2008], 430).

5. On Ps 98:2–3 as envisioning the fulfillment of the covenant promises to Abraham, see A. A. Anderson, *The Book of Psalms* (London: Oliphants, 1977), 691–92.

But in Romans 3:21–24 Paul returns to the theme of the revelation of "the righteousness of God" that he introduced in 1:16–17. And here we see something different:

> ²¹But now apart from the law the righteousness of God has been revealed, to which the law and the prophets bear witness; ²²a righteousness of God through faith in Jesus Christ for all who believe. For there is no difference, ²³for all have sinned and are destitute of the glory of God. ²⁴All are justified freely by his grace through the redemption which is in Christ Jesus. (Rom 3:21–24)

Here the revelation of "the righteousness of God" in 3:21 is unpacked as believers being *given* the righteousness of God in 3:22 ("for all who believe"), and as "*justified*" (the verb *dikaioō*, cognate with the noun *dikaiosunē*, "righteousness") in 3:24. Here the "righteousness of God" is not God's own righteousness, but instead is a righteousness given to human beings. Likewise in 2 Corinthians, Paul speaks of those who are in Christ as being "made" the righteousness of God (2 Cor 5:21), and in Philippians he calls this righteousness a "righteousness from God" (*ek theou*, Phil 3:9; cf. 1 Cor 1:30). Is there a solution to the seemingly conflicting evidence concerning the meaning of the "righteousness of God" in Paul?

The answer is really quite straightforward, as has been recognized by an increasing number of scholars: in Paul's thought, the "righteousness of God" is *both* a righteousness belonging to God *and* a righteousness given to human beings.[6] But how can this be? I believe the key is the astounding nature of the righteousness of God extolled in Psalm 98. In this psalm, God's own righteousness—precisely because God is who God is—is an active, powerful, *saving* righteousness, for both Israel and the gentiles (v. 1, "he has wrought *salvation*"; v. 2, "YHWH has made his *salvation* known"; v. 3, "the *salvation* of our God"). When we now look again at Romans 1:16–17, it is clear that Paul has captured the full, astounding force of this psalm and its portrayal of God's righteousness (key points in italics):

> ¹⁶For I am not ashamed of the gospel, for it is the *power of God* for *salvation* for everyone who believes, *to the Jew first and then to the gentile;* ¹⁷for in it *the righteousness of God* is revealed from faith to faith. As it is written, "The *righteous* will live by faith."

---

6. For an excellent discussion, see David Wenham, *Paul: Follower of Jesus or Founder of Christianity?* (Grand Rapids: Eerdmans, 1995), 54–58.

In this passage God's righteousness *is* his own righteousness, but precisely because it is *God's* righteousness, it is living and active, a powerful, saving righteousness that rescues and delivers *human beings* created in his image. It is "the power of God for salvation" (Rom 1:16), the "salvation of our God" (Ps 98:3), and by it human beings are "made righteous" or "justified" (Rom 3:24). In Paul's thought, the "righteousness of God" is *God's own salvation-creating righteousness that makes human beings righteous.*

The Righteousness of God: Forgiveness or Sanctification?

But a crucial question follows: What is this righteousness of God that is given to all who believe? In what way are believers "justified" or "made righteous"? Concerning this concept of *justification* in Paul, debate has raged furiously. The key issue is this: Is this righteousness given to human beings an *imputed* righteousness, whereby their sins are not counted against them, but are forgiven for Christ's sake? Or is this an *infused* righteousness, which sanctifies and transforms human hearts, empowering them to live righteous and holy lives? The question is a crucial one for the meaning of justification in Paul's theology. Two central passages from Paul's letter to the Romans will help us find the answer. First, let us examine Romans 4:5-8 (with Paul's "righteousness" terms in italics):

> But to the one who does not work, but believes upon the One who *justifies* the ungodly, his faith is counted for *righteousness.* Just as David speaks of the person to whom God imputes *righteousness* apart from works: "Blessed are they whose iniquities are forgiven, and whose sins are atoned for. Blessed is the man whose sin the Lord does not count against him."

What kind of righteousness is this? Clearly, this is a righteousness whereby sinful human beings are forgiven and counted righteous before God. Moreover, this is not an isolated passage, but throughout Romans 4-5 Paul defines this righteousness as an *imputed* righteousness whereby sins are not counted but forgiven (see Rom 4:3, 5-8, 22-25; 5:1, 7, 16-18, 19). Those Pauline scholars who have argued that justification in Paul involves an imputed rather than an infused righteousness, that is, forgiveness rather than sanctification, appear (from Rom 4-5) to be correct.[7]

---

7. See, for example, Thomas R. Schreiner, *Paul, Apostle of God's Glory in Christ: A Pauline Theology* (Downers Grove: InterVarsity Press, 2001), 189-217; Schreiner, "Justification: The Saving Righ-

Indeed, one contemporary scholar noted for arguing that forensic imputation has no place in Paul's theology is forced, in order to maintain this argument, to claim that much of Romans 1–4 are not words of Paul, but of an opponent whom Paul quotes at length in order to refute![8] Such desperate measures only reveal how impossible it is to remove the concept of imputed righteousness, the forgiveness of sin and guilt freely for Christ's sake, from Paul's letters and theology.

But we must also look at the second passage (with Paul's "righteousness" terms in italics):

> What then? Should we sin, because we are not under law but under grace? May it never be! Are you not aware that you are slaves to whomever you present yourselves as slaves for obedience, whether obedience to sin leading to death, or obedience to God leading to *righteousness*? Thanks be to God, that although you were slaves of sin, you obeyed from the heart that pattern of teaching which was transmitted to you. And so, having been set free from slavery to sin, you became slaves of *righteousness*. (Rom 6:15–18)

What kind of righteousness is this? Clearly, this is not a righteousness whereby believers are forgiven, but a righteousness whereby they are set free from slavery to sin in order to obey God. This passage is not isolated either, but throughout Romans 6–8 Paul describes the righteousness of God as a mighty power at work in believers, freeing them from the power of sin and leading to sanctification and holiness (Rom 6:7, 13, 15–18, 19–22; 8:4). We see this also in Philippians, where Paul's possession of "the righteousness which comes from God on the basis of faith" (Phil 3:9) involves "knowing him, and the power of his resurrection, and sharing with him in his sufferings" (Phil 3:10). Likewise in Titus, being "justified by his grace" comes through the "washing of rebirth and renewal of the Holy Spirit" (3:4–7).

A moment ago I noted the exegetical contortions into which one scholar is forced in Romans 1–4 to maintain the view that justification in Paul is *solely* participatory or infused. But I believe that if we assume that justification in Paul is *solely* imputed, we are forced into similar violence against the text in Romans 6–8. The problem *in either case*, I would contend, is assuming an either/or, and holding

---

teousness of God," *JETS* 54 (2011): 20 ("it [justification] is forensic, not transformative"); Wright, *Paul and the Faithfulness of God*, 925–1032; Wright, "The Letter to the Romans," NIB 10:464–77; James D. G. Dunn, *The Theology of Paul the Apostle* (Grand Rapids: Eerdmans, 1998), 334–89.

8. See Douglas A. Campbell, *The Deliverance of God: An Apocalyptic Rereading of Justification in Paul* (Grand Rapids: Eerdmans, 2009), 519–761.

apart things that in Paul belong together. In Paul, I would argue, the "righteousness of God" whereby sinners are "made righteous" is *both* an imputed righteousness, whereby sins are forgiven, *and* an infused righteousness, whereby hearts are transformed through the power of God.[9] Paul throughout Romans structures his use of "righteousness" language in such a way as to reveal that the "righteousness of God," which he introduces in Romans 1:16–17, includes both the gift of *forgiveness* (Rom 4:3, 5–8, 22–25; 5:1, 7, 16–18, 19) and *sanctification*, the gift of transforming power for holiness and new life (6:7, 13, 15–18, 19–22; 8:4). This transforming power comes about through the presence and indwelling of Christ within the faithful (6:1–4; 7:4–6; 8:3–9), a union made possible by the incarnation—the fulfillment of the core promise of the Old Testament, the coming and abiding presence of YHWH among his people.

Justification in Paul is thus both *covenantal* and *participatory*. It moves on the twin planes we have identified earlier in this work:

Within the Covenant	Union with the Creator
Outside the Covenant	Separation from the Creator

The covenantal relationship is made possible only by the continual provision of divine forgiveness (imputed righteousness), but this same covenantal relationship involves union with God, which unleashes divine transforming power (infused righteousness). In Paul, therefore, forgiveness and sanctification are two very different things—*but they are never found apart*.

In light of the larger biblical narrative, it should hardly be surprising to us that justification in Paul involves both imputed and infused righteousness, both forgiveness and sanctification. After all, as we saw in chapter 7, the new covenant foretold by Jeremiah promised *both* forgiveness of sins *and* a transformed heart to know and love YHWH (Jer 31:31–34). Paul, especially in his great letter to the Romans, proclaims that the revelation of the righteousness of God in Jesus Christ has fulfilled both of these promised blessings of the new covenant. In fulfilling the core scriptural promise of God's coming, Jesus Christ has revealed God's active, powerful, salvation-creating righteousness, the "justification" that forgives, transforms, and gives life.

9. For two treatments of justification in Paul, one somewhat older and one more recent, which similarly argue that both elements are present in Paul's conception of justification, see John Ziesler, *The Meaning of Righteousness in Paul: A Linguistic and Theological Inquiry* (Cambridge: Cambridge University Press, 1972), and Michael J. Gorman, *Inhabiting the Cruciform God: Kenosis, Justification, and Theosis in Paul's Narrative Soteriology* (Grand Rapids: Eerdmans, 2009). See also Joseph Fitzmyer, *Pauline Theology: A Brief Sketch* (Englewood Cliffs, NJ: Prentice-Hall, 1967), 51–53, 65.

Faith and Ethics in Paul

Contemporary readers sometimes struggle to find the relationship in Paul between faith and ethics. If we are justified by grace through faith apart from works, is there any connection between faith and the moral life?[10] But such perplexity arises from what I believe are two false assumptions—that the concept of repentance had no place in Paul's theology, and that the justification that comes through faith involves in Paul's thought only imputed righteousness and the forgiveness of sins. As we saw in the previous chapter, in Paul's thought faith includes repentance. It is an orientation of the whole person, mind, heart, and will, to God, always accompanied by hope and love. And we have now seen that the justification that comes through this faith involves not only forgiveness but also sanctification—liberation from the power of sin. Paul consistently warns his readers that those who persist in unrepentant grave sin will not inherit the kingdom (1 Cor 6:9–11; 9:24–10:22; Gal 6:7–8; Eph 5:3–14; Phil 3:17–4:1; Col 3:5–7; 2 Tim 3:5–8; Titus 1:15–16). The church's traditional distinction between *venial* sins (lesser sins into which even those united to Christ by faith often fall and for which they need and receive continual divine forgiveness) and *mortal* sins (grave, persistent, and unrepentant sins incompatible with living faith in Christ and saving union with him) reflects Pauline teaching (Rom 8:12–13; 1 Cor 10:1–13; Gal 5:16–24). The former are forgiven through the covenantal grace and mercy of God in Christ (Rom 4:6–9; Eph 1:7; 4:32; Col 1:14; 3:13); the latter reveal the need for reconversion and return to the covenantal grace and mercy of God in Christ (1 Cor 5:9–13; 2 Cor 12:21; Gal 6:1).

In teaching justification by grace through faith, Paul was therefore *not* opposing grace to sanctification and good works, for these are the fruit of the justifying grace of God at work in those who believe. Rather, he was opposing grace to works done apart from union with the incarnate Son of God and the transforming power of God for righteousness that comes only through him. Once we grasp the nature of faith and justification within Paul's thought, the connection between faith and ethics in Paul becomes crystal clear.

This explains how Paul can say that we do not overturn the law through faith, but rather "we establish the law" (Rom 3:31). This leads us to another question that has long perplexed Pauline interpreters, and the final topic of this chapter.

---

10. Klyne Snodgrass notes that even for some Pauline scholars "the relation between justification and ethics in Pauline theology has been troublesome for some time" ("Justification by Faith—To the Doers: An Analysis of the Place of Romans 2 in the Theology of Paul," *NTS* 32 [1986]: 87).

The Fulfillment of the Law

As we saw in chapter 6, Paul in Romans 3 powerfully declares the reality of universal sinfulness and the impossibility of righteousness through fulfilling the law. "There is no one who does good" (Rom 3:12), Paul declares, and "by the works of the law no human being shall be justified before God" (3:20). All people, both Jews and gentiles, are in need of the mercy and grace of God found only in the cross of Christ. And yet in Romans 2 Paul appears to contradict himself, asserting that God "will render to each person according to his works" (Rom 2:6). In this chapter Paul proclaims the divine promise of glory, honor, and peace "to everyone who does good" (2:10), and affirms that "the doers of the law will be justified" (2:13). The apparent contradiction between Paul's teaching in Romans 2 and his teaching in Romans 3 has long vexed interpreters. How can the apostle declare that "the doers of the law will be justified" (2:13) and yet assert that "by the works of the law no flesh will be justified before God" (3:20)? How can Romans 2:10 promise glory, honor, and peace "to everyone who does good" while Romans 3:12 affirms that "there is no one who does good"?

The apparent contradiction between Romans 2 and Romans 3 is at the heart of E. P. Sanders's famous charge that Paul's theology of the law is confused and incoherent. Romans 2, he claims, reflects Paul's Jewish and covenantal assumption that the law is fulfillable, but Romans 3 expresses the contradictory conviction that righteousness comes not through the law but only through Christ. "Paul's case for universal sinfulness [in Rom 2–3] . . . is not convincing: it is internally inconsistent."[11]

Various solutions to the dilemma have been suggested, none of them in my view fully convincing.[12] In the apparent contradiction between Romans 2 and Romans 3 we encounter another fundamental problem in our understanding of

11. E. P. Sanders, *Paul, the Law, and the Jewish People* (Philadelphia: Fortress, 1983), 125.

12. Some scholars argue that "works" in Romans 2:6 and "law" in 2:13 refer to the whole law of Moses, whereas "the works of the law" in Romans 3:20 refers to the markers of Jewish identity that excluded gentiles: circumcision, food laws, and Sabbath keeping (so Dunn, *Theology*, 365–66). But in Romans 3, as in Romans 2, Paul addresses both Jews and gentiles (Rom 3:9), and focuses exclusively on the *moral* commands of the law (3:1–8, 10–18). Other scholars suggest that Romans 2:6–16 is only a *hypothetical* possibility, superseded by the reality of Romans 3:9–20 (e.g., John Knox, *The Epistle to the Romans* [New York: Abingdon, 1954], 409). But, as James D. G. Dunn points out, it is impossible to square a hypothetical reading of these verses with Paul's actual presentation in Rom 2:6–16, which closes in verse 16 with a solemn affirmation of coming divine judgment "in accordance with my gospel" ("The Dialogue Progresses," in *Lutherische und Neue Paulusperspektive*, ed. Michael Bachmann and Johannes Woyke, WUNT 2.182 [Tübingen: Mohr Siebeck, 2005], 405). For other proposed solutions and their difficulties, see Snodgrass, "Justification by Faith," 72–75.

Paul's theology of the law: "The ultimate challenge for an understanding of Paul is to find a center which makes it possible to understand how he could say, on the one hand, 'Not the hearers of the Law are righteous before God, but the doers of the Law will be justified' (Rom. 2.13), and, on the other, 'Through works of the Law no one will be justified before him' (Rom. 3.20)."[13]

I believe there is a solution to the dilemma, and it lies in the crucial distinction in Paul's theology, which we uncovered in chapter 6, between the fulfillment of the law considered *apart from* the covenantal relationship of faith in Jesus Christ and the fulfillment of the law considered *within* that covenantal relationship. In Romans 3:20 ("by the works of the law no human being shall be justified before God"), Paul echoes Psalm 143:2, a classic expression of Old Testament covenant theology that affirms the impossibility of righteousness before God apart from the covenant and its promise of mercy. Drawing upon this affirmation of universal sinfulness in Psalm 143:2, Paul there declares the impossibility of righteousness through observance of the law *apart from the covenant and its promise of mercy in Jesus Christ*. All human beings are in need of the righteousness that comes through Christ alone.

In Romans 2:6 (God "will render to each person according to his works"), Paul quotes Psalm 62: "covenant love is yours, O Lord, for you reward each person according to his works" (Ps 62:12). In contrast with Psalm 143:2, which declares that no one is righteous before God's judgment, Psalm 62 sharply distinguishes between the righteous and the unrighteous, and affirms a judgment according to works. But there is no contradiction between Psalm 62 and Psalm 143. For the distinction in Psalm 62 between the righteous and the ungodly is precisely the distinction between those within the covenant, who trust, hope, and take refuge in YHWH (62:1-2, 5-8), and those who reject the covenant, rebel against YHWH, and disregard his ways (62:3-4, 10). The godly are not sinless (cf. Pss 32; 38; 41; 51; 85; 90; 103; 130), but are righteous through their covenant relationship with YHWH. The psalmist hopes in a reward according to works only within the context of the covenant and its assurance of divine grace and mercy. Echoing this affirmation of Psalm 62:12 in its covenantal context, Paul speaks of the "works" (Rom 2:6) whereby "the doers of the law will be justified" (Rom 2:13) *within the gracious context of the covenant and its provision of mercy in Jesus Christ*. The "doers of the law," then, are all those in covenantal union with God through faith in Jesus Christ. They are not sinless but in continual need of God's covenantal grace, mercy, and forgiveness in Christ (Rom 4:6-8; Eph 1:7; Col 1:14). But through their living

13. Hendrikus Boers, "The Foundations of Paul's Thought: A Methodological Investigation—The Problem of the Coherent Center of Paul's Thought," *Studia theologica* 42 (1988): 61.

union with Christ they are also truly empowered to "fulfill the righteousness called for in the law" (Rom 8:4; cf. 3:31; 13:8–10; Gal 5:14).

For as we saw above, in "justification," believers in Christ are not only *counted* as righteous for Christ's sake, but they are also, through the sanctifying power of the Spirit of Christ at work in them, truly *made* righteous, and as a result lead righteous lives (Rom 6:16–18; 1 Cor 6:9–11; 1 Thess 2:10), do what is good (Rom 12:9; 13:3; 2 Cor 5:10; Gal 6:10; 1 Thess 5:15), and fulfill the law (Rom 3:31; 8:3–4; 13:8–10; 1 Cor 7:19). In Romans 2, therefore, those who "persevere in good works" (Rom 2:7), who "do good" (2:10), and who are "doers of the law" (2:13) are God's people in Christ, who through the transforming power of the indwelling Holy Spirit live out the righteousness prescribed by the law. Paul makes this explicit in Romans 2:26–29:

> [26]If therefore the one who is uncircumcised keeps the law's righteous ways, will not his uncircumcision be counted as circumcision? [27]And the one who is physically uncircumcised but fulfills the law will judge you who, despite having circumcision and the law in written form, are a transgressor of the law. [28]For the true Jew is not the one who is physically Jewish or physically circumcised, [29]but the one who is Jewish within, and the true circumcision is of the heart, by the Spirit, not by merely having the law in written form. This person's praise is not from human beings, but from God.

Here those who "keep the law's righteous ways" (2:26) and "fulfill the law" (2:27) are believers in Jesus, who through the new covenant in Christ have received "the circumcision of the heart, by the Spirit" (2:29). In bringing the promised new covenant, Jesus Christ has fulfilled its promise that "I will put my law within them, and on their heart I will write it" (Jer 31:33). The people of God in Christ, transformed from within by the Spirit, fulfill the law through faith and love (Rom 2:26–27; cf. Rom 13:8–10; Gal 5:6, 14, 22–24; 1 Thess 4:9–12; 1 Tim 1:5–7). And the one united to Christ is "the true Jew" (Rom 2:28–29), that is, a true partaker in the covenant of God with Abraham through faith in Jesus Christ. Those who belong to Christ, whether Jew or gentile, are "the Israel of God" (Gal 6:16).

Conclusion: Paul's Covenantal Theology of Justification

Paul's gospel of justification by grace fits firmly within his covenantal theology we have explored throughout part 3 of this book. In Paul the "righteousness of God" is God's own salvation-creating righteousness that makes human beings righteous, and "justification" in Paul is both covenantal and participatory, involving (as the promise of the new covenant had foretold) both the gift of forgiveness (imputed righteousness) and the gift of sanctification, that is, transforming power for holiness and new life (infused righteousness). Through this transforming union with God—that neither the law nor its sacrifices but only the cross of Christ could bring—God's people in Christ are not only counted righteous, but are truly *made* righteous, empowered by the Spirit of Christ to fulfill the law and its righteous ways. Paul's gospel affirmed a radical human sinfulness and unworthiness rendering ongoing communion with Christ possible only through the continual provision of divine forgiveness. But his gospel also affirmed a radical transformation of the human heart through this sanctifying union, and the incompatibility of unrepentant grave sin with justifying grace. Justification and ethics are thus indissolubly linked within Paul's thought.

It is sometimes thought that Paul's doctrine of the justification of the ungodly is in tension or even contradiction with the Old Testament. However, reading Paul's theology in its ancient Jewish and covenantal context, as we have sought to do in part 3 of this book, opens up a new vista before us: the unity and coherence of the entire Bible. As we saw in the previous chapter, Paul's "message of the cross" (1 Cor 1:18) proclaims the fulfillment of the ultimate divine act of atonement promised in Israel's Scriptures, and unveils the mysterious source of the divine mercy and grace given in the covenant with Abraham. The covenantal relationship of trust in YHWH at the heart of the Psalms and the entire Old Testament finds its fullest expression in the Pauline conception of faith in Christ. And the Old Testament focus on the dwelling of YHWH among his people as the purpose of the covenant finds its full realization in Paul's theology of the miraculous indwelling of Christ in the hearts of the faithful. As we have seen in this chapter, Paul's doctrine of justification by faith proclaims the fulfillment of the Old Testament's promise of the salvation-creating righteousness of God, and of its promise of a new covenant bringing both forgiveness of sins and a transformed heart to know and love the Lord. Finally, the Pauline distinction between works considered within and works considered apart from the covenantal relationship of faith, which we have explored throughout part 3, is not unique to Paul, but runs through both Old and New Testaments.

Unpacking Paul's rich covenantal theology in its ancient Jewish context not only reveals the coherence of Paul's own thought, but helps to open up for us the unity and coherence of the entire Bible.

Part Four

Kingdom

Chapter Nine

Easter in Ancient Context

P aul's favorite term for the message he proclaimed to the gentiles was the "good
news" or "joyful announcement" (*to euangelion*). Paul did not merely use
this term to describe his own understanding of his message to the gentiles, but
also explicitly described it *to them* in this way, that is, as "the good news" (1 Cor
15:1–2; 1 Thess 1:5; 2:8–9; cf. Acts 14:15). This is a striking fact. For, according to a
common understanding of Paul's theology, the good news Paul proclaimed to the
pagan world was that Jesus had opened up the prospect of a heavenly afterlife, that
is, a spiritual existence in heaven after the death of the physical body. But such a
prospect, as we will see, was a commonly held belief in antiquity, and was a staple
of ancient philosophy. To describe such a message as the "good *news*" would, in
its ancient context, make little sense. And yet it is clear, as a point of historical
fact, that in preaching to pagans Paul described his message to them as "the good
news"—and expected this to resonate with his hearers. To explain this we must
consider Paul's gospel within the context of ancient beliefs regarding the future
of human beings and of the cosmos. Examining the way in which Paul's message
would have been heard in this ancient setting will reveal that many contemporary
readers have misunderstood Paul's gospel on its most central claim. And it will illumine what Paul himself believed made his message "the good news" for his hearers.

The Everlasting Sorrow—Death and the Afterlife in Ancient Paganism

We will explore ancient beliefs regarding death and the afterlife under four head-
ings: how the philosophers viewed death and what, if anything, came afterward;
how the popular imagination and popular religion dealt with the topics; how ancient people responded to and coped with the reality of death; and the paradox
presented by the striking response in antiquity to Euripides' dramatization of the
myth of Alcestis's return from death.

Ancient Philosophy

In the world into which Paul's gospel came, the philosophers held a variety of views regarding the possibility of life after death. Socrates in the *Apology* (his student Plato's account of the philosopher's trial, which would lead to his execution) had famously posed the "Socratic alternative": death is either the soul's extinction or its journey to a new and (for the righteous) better existence (*Apology of Socrates* 40c–41c). The Epicureans chose the first alternative, believing that the soul perished together with the body (Lucretius, *On the Nature of the Universe* 3; Philodemus, *On Death* 1; 19; 20; 26; 28–32). Plato and the Middle Platonists (the philosophical successors of Plato active in Paul's day) embraced the latter alternative. They believed in the immortality of the soul—the soul, being divine and eternal, survives the death of the body. Depending on its level of virtue, the soul journeys to either painful purifications in the underworld or heavenly bliss and in either case (after a period of time) is reincarnated (Plato, *Phaedrus* 247–49). The Stoics took a sort of middle position, holding firmly to the soul's survival after the death of the body but denying both its reincarnation and its immortality (Seneca, *On Consolation to Marcia* 24–26; Diogenes Laertius, *Lives* 7.157). Thus Cicero's somewhat snarky summary of the Stoic view: "The Stoics grant us a lavish lease of life, as if we were crows; they claim our souls will continue for a long period, but deny they will do so forever" (*Tusculan Disputations* 1.77).

Amid this diversity of views, there was one point on which Stoics, Middle Platonists, and Epicureans all agreed—the iron finality and irreversibility of bodily death. The "Socratic alternative" considered whether the soul might or might not survive death, but not whether death might be reversed through the physical body's restoration to life. Disagreement existed about the possibility of soul survival, but all were agreed on the impossibility of *resurrection*—return from bodily death to an everlasting embodied life. No philosopher, regardless of school, envisioned that a human being, once dead, might live again.

To be sure, the doctrine of reincarnation or transmigration of souls was widespread in the ancient world, taught by Platonist and Pythagorean philosophers, Orphic mystics, Hindu thinkers, and Buddhist sages. This teaching conceived of a renewed embodiment of sorts, maintaining that the soul after death passes into the body of an entirely new person, and over infinite time into the bodies of numberless different persons (or animals), in an eternal cycle or wheel of death and rebirth (e.g., Plato, *Phaedrus* 247–49; *Bhagavad Gita* 2.12–22). And the Stoics taught the doctrine of "recurrence": the entire history of the universe, down to the most minute details, would repeat itself endlessly, in an infinite cycle of cosmic destruction and renewal (Zeno of Citium, in *Stoicorum Veterum Fragmenta* 1.98; Chrysippus, in *Stoicorum Veterum Fragmenta* 2.596–632; Seneca, *On Consolation to Marcia* 26.1, 6–7; *Letters* 9.16;

36:10–11; 71.11–16; 110.9; Cicero, *On the Nature of the Gods* 2.118; *Concerning Divination* 1.111). Thus, according to the Stoic teaching, the embodied life of each individual (but without conscious awareness of his or her past lives) would also be replicated in an endless cycle.

But the prospect of the soul's everlasting cyclical reembodiment through either reincarnation or recurrence is very different from the hope of resurrection. For resurrection involves the miraculous return to bodily life of the same person, involving the conscious continuation of personal and bodily identity. Neither reincarnation nor recurrence involves the concept of death's defeat or reversal—that once dead, a human being, in his or her unique individual personhood, could return to bodily life, and that life be made imperishable. Both reincarnation and the Stoic recurrence affirm death's eternal role in the cosmic scheme. They do not envision a time when bodily death will be no more.

For, in regard to the cosmos as a whole, ancient philosophers believed either that the universe would eventually self-destruct or that it would continue in its present state forever, through some form of stasis or recurrence. Stoics and Epicureans believed in a past "golden age" of cosmic and human flourishing, of righteousness, blessedness, and peace (Seneca, *Letters* 90; Lucretius, *On the Nature of the Universe* 5.925–1135). But none of the philosophers had any such hopes for the future. The future of the cosmos would bring, for the Epicureans, the destruction of the universe (Philodemus, *On Death* 36.23–26); for Plato, the continuation of the universe in its present state forever (*Timaeus* 37c–38c); for the Buddhist sages, the everlasting "mournful wheel" of death and reincarnation (*Anguttara Nikāya* 3.58–61, 103–5); and for the Stoics, the cyclical recurrence of all things to infinity (Epictetus, *Discourses* 3.13.4–7; Origen, *Against Celsus* 4.68). In each of these visions of the cosmic future, death is a permanent fixture of the cosmos, and is for every person irreversible and everlasting.

Popular Thought and Religion

Popular thought and religion agreed with the philosophers on the irreversibility of death. To be sure, the average person in antiquity (to judge from ancient literature and tomb inscriptions) believed in the soul's survival after the death of the body. A variety of beliefs and combinations of beliefs existed. The prospect of a shadowy, phantom-like existence in the underworld, the hope of a blessed afterlife in heaven, and the expectation of the soul's reincarnation following its heavenly sojourn are all well attested among everyday people (cf. Cicero, *Tusculan Disputations* 1.27–38; Virgil, *Aeneid* 6.703–51). But they did not believe in resurrection—the reversal of death through the restoration of the body to imperishable life. The common people, like the philosophers, considered this an impossibility. "It is certain," writes the poet Anacreon, "that no one who goes down to the grave will ever come up again." A typical ancient tomb inscription reads, "No one who has died rises up from here" (*Inscriptiones Graecae Urbis Romae* 3.1406).

In a few cases, the ancient stories about the gods recounted, Heracles and Asclepius (heroes half-divine and half-human) had raised people from the dead, most famously when Alcestis had been brought back to life by Heracles. But these were *resuscitations*, to live again for a time, not *resurrections*, to live eternally. Alcestis, the ancient myth tells us, later died again. As the goddess Athena explained to Telemachus in the *Odyssey*, even the gods are powerless before the invincible power of death: "A god if he wishes can easily rescue a living man, even from afar. . . . But surely not even the gods can deliver anyone, even one they love, from death, the common fate of all" (*Odyssey* 3.229–38). "When once human beings die and the dust receives their blood," the god Apollo proclaims in Aeschylus's tragedy the *Eumenides*, "there can be no resurrection. All other things his mighty power can do or undo with effortless ease, but for death alone my father Zeus has no divine enchantment" (*Eumenides* 647–49). The inescapable fate of death for all mortals was a necessity even the gods were powerless to alter.

Coping with Death in Antiquity

But it would be a mistake to think that this realism regarding death meant that people in the ancient world regarded death with indifference. On the contrary, the Epicurean poet Lucretius informs us that, for his contemporaries, the fear of death "overturns all of human life, tainting all things with the blackness of death, and allowing no pleasure to be free from care and unalloyed" (*On the Nature of the Universe* 3.37–40). The Stoic philosopher Seneca (a contemporary of Paul) writes of "the dread of death shared by every human being" (*Letters* 82). The transitory nature of life and its culmination in death fills ancient poetry and literature with an ineffable sadness. "Of all the creatures that breathe and move on the earth," writes Homer at the death of Achilles's friend Patroclus, "there is surely none that is more pitiable—than a human being" (*Iliad* 17.446–47). Evidence from funerary monuments reveals the attempt to rise from such despair to a kind of melancholy resignation to death. One frequent tomb inscription, *non fui, fui, non sum, non curo* (so common the words were often abbreviated *nf f ns nc!*), read: "I was not, I was, I am not, I care not." Others sought consolation for the death of the body in the hope of the soul's immortality, as in this typical inscription: "the ethereal regions have received my soul, the earth has received my body." Another common grave inscription sought to comfort the grieving through the reminder of death's universality: "Do not be sad; no one is immortal."

The varied philosophical movements, and the so-called "consolation literature" they produced, sought to soften death's sting by the conviction that death was part of the nature of things, and therefore neither to be feared nor lamented. The Epicureans argued that their doctrine of the soul's extinction meant that death was nothing to fear. For if death brings extinction, all fear of divine judgment is removed. And one who no longer exists, by definition, cannot sorrow or suffer (Philodemus, *On Death* 30.15–20; 32.2–15, 20–30). "Death, therefore," Epicurus famously insisted, "is nothing to us" (Epicurus, *Letter to Menoeceus* 3). The Buddha taught that the core of the human predicament was the dread of impermanence and death shared by every person, but that this fear of death could be overcome by the realization that the person or the self is in reality an illusion that does not really exist (*Saṃyutta Nikāya* 2.1.10; 3.22.59).The Middle Platonists sought to dispel the fear of death by showing the insignificance of the body within the cosmic scheme of things. Plato's account of creation, the *Timaeus*, taught that the human body was the work of inferior deities, and therefore by necessity perishable and mortal (*Timaeus* 41a–42e; 69b–d; 76e–77c). According to Plato and his followers, the body was the prison of the immortal soul, by which it is encumbered and from which it longs to be freed. Similarly in the Stoic view, human embodiment, given the inherent perishability of flesh and bone, placed limits even on the power of the very highest divinity. Suffering and death were therefore a tragic but inevitable by-product of humanity's creation (Seneca, *Letters* 107.9–10; *On Providence* 6.5–8; Epictetus, *Discourses* 1.1.10–12). The Stoics counseled noble resignation to death, a necessity that even the highest divinity was powerless to alter (Seneca, *On Providence* 6.6; *Letters* 36.11; 71.16; 94.6–8).

Thus, in each of the major philosophical views in antiquity, as in the everyday, popular understanding, suffering and death were understood as built into the fabric of the universe. Whether because the very nature of matter imposed limits on the cosmic design (Stoic pantheism, Platonist dualism) or because the cosmos had no design at all (Epicurean and Buddhist materialism), bodily death was an irreversible and everlasting feature of the cosmic order. Like the divinities of ancient worship, the powers of the philosophic gods did not extend to the realm of death.

A Powerful Yearning

There is one more component of the picture that is impossible to quantify precisely but, I believe, must be understood if we are to grasp what was going on in hearts and minds in the world into which Paul's gospel came. The myth of Alcestis's resuscitation (mentioned above) was dramatized in the fifth century BCE by the tragic poet Euripides. Of course, the many audiences and readers of Euripides's famed play through the centuries knew that Alcestis's deliverance from death belonged to the world of myth, and even in that world was only a temporary reprieve from death's cold necessity. And yet in the climactic scene of *Alcestis*, in which Alcestis, restored to life, reveals herself to her beloved husband Admetus, we see something more at work, through the power of the playwright's dramatic art. Although it is assumed, Euripides's drama does not narrate or allude to the later death of Alcestis. Rather, the play closes with a vivid celebration of life, restored in its fullness. In this final scene, unequaled for the intensity of its joy in all of ancient pagan literature, the audience envisions, if only momentarily, an order of things in which death does *not* have the last word; in which divine friendship is stronger than death; in which death is not merely postponed, but abolished altogether.

But here is the striking fact: images of the climactic scene of *Alcestis* appeared in ensuing centuries on ancient tombs, sarcophagi, and funerary monuments.[1] How are we to interpret this evidence? We should not imagine that the portrayal of Alcestis's restoration from death on these ancient monuments indicates a developed and articulate expectation of resurrection. As we have seen, the possibility of such a thing was explicitly *denied* in both pagan religion and philosophy. But clearly the portrayal of the climactic scene of Euripides's play on the tomb of a loved one expresses a longing, however undeveloped, inarticulate, and even unspoken, for the reversal of death. We discover on these ancient tombs—in their portrayal of Alcestis's return to bodily life—the expression of a longing that the widely held hopes of the soul's immortality apparently did not satisfy. We discover a longing for *resurrection from the dead*—the restoration of human life in its embodied fullness.[2]

We seem to encounter here a genuine paradox: in a world in which it was axiomatic that death was the immovable law of cosmic reality that even the gods were unable to alter, we find a yearning for resurrection. And I would suggest that it is this yearning for resurrection—the real defeat of death—that underlies not only stories of resuscitation such as *Alcestis*, but also the varied lesser visions of life after death in antiquity we have surveyed, from reincarnation to recurrence to the immortality of the soul. But this longing for the defeat of death, the ancients believed, could never be fulfilled. They yearned for a divine enchantment that would overthrow death's sting but knew (or thought they knew) that they lived in an unenchanted world. For in pagan thought, both popular and philosophical, death was an ineradicable feature of everlasting reality. Hence came what G. K. Chesterton called "that ancient sorrow that is in the heart of all heathen things."

1. For a sampling of the evidence, see Susan Wood, "Alcestis on Roman Sarcophagi," *AJA* 82 (1978): 499–510; Peter Blome, "Zur Umgestaltung griechischer Mythen in der römischen Sepulkralkunst," *MDAI/Römische Abteilung* 35 (1978): 435–57.

2. For fuller discussion of Euripides's play and its reception in antiquity, see James Ware, "Euripides' Beatific Vision," *Touchstone* 26 (2013): 27–33.

A Different Promise from a Different God

Within this ancient context, the God of the Jews was not only a different God, but a different *kind* of God altogether. As we saw in part 1, the gods of ancient worship, and the philosophical divinities of the Epicureans, the Stoics, the Hindu sages, the Buddha, and Plato, were either identified with the cosmos, considered products or aspects of it, or believed to coexist alongside an independent and eternal material realm. Both the gods of ancient worship and the philosophic divinities were accordingly limited in their powers. Evil, suffering, and death were believed to be an eternal, unchanged, and unchangeable reality of the cosmic order, unalterable even by the gods. The gods of the ancient world, whether the philosophic divinities or the gods of popular worship, were powerless before the unconquerable power of death.

In starkest contrast, the ancient Jews believed that their God, the God of Israel, was the creator God, who had brought all things into being from nothing (Isa 40:12–31; Jer 10:1–16; Amos 4:13; 5:8; Pss 33:6–9; 95:1–7; 121:2; 124:8; 134:2), and whose power was unlimited (Gen 18:14; Jer 32:17; Ps 135:5–6). The cosmos was the good creation of the good creator (Gen 1–2; Pss 104; 148). Death was not a necessary by-product of creation, but the result of the Fall and the curse (Gen 3). And, unlike their pagan neighbors, the Jews did not believe the universe's present state would continue forever. Rather, they believed that in the time of his coming kingdom the God of Israel would restore and renew all things.

As we saw in part 2, the central hope of the Old Testament was the expectation of the coming of YHWH—the promise that, in a fashion beyond imagining, the Lord himself would come to dwell among his people forever and fill all creation with his presence and glory (Isa 35; 40:1–11; Ps 96; Ezek 37:21–28; 43:1–9; 48:35; Zech 14:1–9; Mal 3:1–5). A mind-bending aspect of this expectation of YHWH's coming appears first in the later prophetic strata of the Old Testament, but looms large thereafter in the hopes of the Jewish people: when he came, the God of Israel would reveal himself as the one true God by doing what only the almighty creator God could do—he would *defeat death forever*. The book of Isaiah envisions the coming of YHWH to Mount Zion, the holy city Jerusalem, to redeem all nations:

> And on this mountain the Lord of hosts will prepare for all the peoples a feast of rich foods, a feast of aged wines, of choicest rich foods, of finest aged wines. And he will swallow up on this mountain the burial cloth which covers all the peoples, the mourning veil which veils all the nations—he will swallow up death forever! And the Lord YHWH will wipe away tears from all faces, and will remove the reproach of his people

from all the earth, for YHWH has spoken. And it will be said in that day, "Behold, here is our God! We put our hope in him, and he has saved us. Here is YHWH! We put our hope in him; let us rejoice and be glad in his salvation." (Isa 25:6–9)

In the prophetic expectation of this Isaian oracle, through his saving reign, the Lord, Israel's God, would conquer evil, remove all sorrow and suffering, and abolish death itself. According to the "salvation oracle" of Isaiah 26, and the climactic vision of the book of Daniel, this would come about through *the resurrection of the dead*:

Your dead will live, their corpses will rise. Awaken and shout for joy, you who dwell in the dust. For your dew is the dew of the light of life, and the earth will give birth to the dead. (Isa 26:19)

And many of those who sleep in the dust of the earth will awaken, some to everlasting life, others to dishonor, to everlasting disgrace. (Dan 12:2)

It is crucial to grasp what this expectation of resurrection entails. These passages from Isaiah and Daniel do not merely express the hope of a heavenly afterlife following the death of the body. Instead, they envision that, in the time of YHWH's kingdom, the death of the body will be *reversed*, and death will be no more. The Lord, in an act of unfathomable power, will give life to the physical, flesh-and-bones bodies of his people, long decayed in the earth, raising them from the dead and granting them new, indestructible, and everlasting life in the presence of the God of Abraham, Isaac, and Jacob. Daniel's vision also foresees a resurrection of the wicked to judgment, ensuring the victory of the God of justice over evil and all who cling to evil.

Moreover, the Jewish Scriptures foretell a renewal of all creation, when the wolf will lie down with the lamb, and the glory of the Lord will fill the whole earth, as the waters covering the sea (Isa 11:6–9; 65:25; 66:22–24; Amos 9:13). In contrast with pagan expectations of the destruction of the universe, or its continuation in its present state forever, the Jewish people awaited the coming reign of YHWH, when, by a new act of God, the whole created order would be restored and renewed.

This biblical hope of bodily resurrection and a renewed world to come was the mainstream and characteristic belief of the Jewish people in antiquity (despite the notable exception of the Sadducees). This hope is abundantly reflected in ancient Greek translations of the Old Testament, which emphatically express and even intensify the resurrection hope present in the original Hebrew text (e.g., LXX Dan 12:2–3; Theodotion Dan 12.2–3; LXX Isa 26:19; and LXX Job 19:25–27; 42.17), and this hope is a prominent feature of many other ancient Jewish texts (e.g., 2 Maccabees 7; 1 Enoch 22–27 [esp. 25.6]; 45.4–5; 51.1–5; Jubilees 1.29; Testament of Judah 25; and Sibylline Oracles 4.179–92). The hope of the resurrection was "the hope of Israel" (Acts 28:20).

This hope was, as we have now seen, absolutely unique in the ancient world. And yet we have also seen that ancient pagan texts and artifacts reveal an astounding paradox. For our evidence suggests that this Jewish expectation, which conflicted with the pagan world's central beliefs, converged with its deepest yearnings. Within an ancient world that yearned for the overthrow of death but believed the reign of death was everlasting, the Jewish people awaited the God of Israel's coming victory over death.

The Good News of Jesus's Resurrection

Into this world, the book of Acts tells us, Paul "brought the good news of Jesus and of his resurrection" (Acts 17:18). Strikingly, when Paul announced what had happened to Jesus after his death, he did not use the language of any of the varied expectations of the afterlife within the pagan world (soul survival, recurrence, reincarnation, immortality of the soul). Instead, Paul employed a very different vocabulary, the Jewish language of *resurrection*. He proclaimed that "Christ has been raised from the dead" (1 Cor 15:12; cf. Rom 1:3–4; 10:9–10; 1 Cor 6:14; 15:20; 2 Cor 4:14; Gal 1:1; Eph 1:20; Col 2:12; 1 Thess 1:9–10). Paul used a different *language* than the pagan expectations because he was referring to a very different *reality*. For in claiming that Jesus had been raised from the dead, Paul was not merely claiming that Jesus's death had been followed by some form of afterlife. Instead, Jesus's death had been *reversed* through his restoration, three days after his death and burial, to full bodily life (1 Cor 15:3–5). The tomb was empty. Jesus's once-dead body, the body of flesh and bones laid in the tomb, had been restored to life and made imperishable. Paul's gospel announced *the restoration to life of Jesus's crucified body*, an event within the space-time universe, verified by eyewitness testimony:

> For I transmitted to you from the first, which I also received, that Christ died for our sins in fulfillment of the Scriptures, and that he was buried, and that he was raised on the third day in fulfillment of the Scriptures, and that he was seen by Cephas [=Peter], then by the twelve apostles; then he was seen by more than five hundred brothers and sisters at the

same time, of whom the majority remain until now, but some have fallen asleep; then he was seen by James, then by all the apostles; and last of all, as to one born out of due time, he was seen by me as well. (1 Cor 15:3–8)

Moreover, Jesus's resurrection was not a mere resuscitation, a temporary postponement of death, but a permanent reversal of death and the overthrow of its power: "Christ having been raised from the dead can never die again; death no longer has mastery over him" (Rom 6:9). After showing himself alive to chosen apostles and eyewitnesses over a limited period of time (forty days, according to Acts 1:3), Jesus ascended bodily into the heavens (Eph 1:20–23; 4:8–10; cf. 1 Tim 3:16), is now at the right hand of God (Rom 8:34; Col 3:1), and will come again in glory and power (1 Cor 1:7–8; Phil 3:20–21; Col 3:3–4; 1 Thess 1:9–10; 2 Thess 1:5–10).

This brings us to the center of Paul's understanding of Jesus's resurrection and the heart of Paul's gospel. As we saw in part 3, according to Paul's preaching Jesus suffered and died "for us" (1 Thess 5:10; cf. Titus 2:14), in our place, as humanity's representative. And therefore *when he rose from the dead, Jesus conquered death on behalf of all humanity.* He had done what the prophets promised the God of Israel would do in the time of his coming kingdom and reign. He had undone the ancient curse. The curse of death, which had come upon all humanity through the rebellion of Adam, had been abolished by Jesus's resurrection from the dead (Rom 5:12–21; 1 Cor 15:21–22). Jesus had "abolished death, and brought to us the light of life and incorruptibility, through the good news" (2 Tim 1:10). Paul's gospel announced that *in Jesus's resurrection, death itself, humanity's great enemy, had been conquered by the creator God* (Rom 1:3–4; 8:9–11; 1 Thess 4:14–17).

The fulfillment of the scriptural promise of death's conquest, Paul proclaimed, has now come in Jesus's resurrection, but in a way involving two distinct phases or stages. The first stage is Jesus's own resurrection. Jesus is the "*firstfruits*" of the harvest, anticipating the full harvest to come (1 Cor 15:20). He is "the *firstborn* from the dead" (Col 1:18). And as we will see in chapter 11, the power of Christ's resurrection life is already at work in those who believe, freeing them from the power of sin and from demonic enslavement (Rom 6:1–4; Col 1:13). But the full outworking and consummation of Christ Jesus's life-giving resurrection await his future coming in glory, when all those who belong to Christ will be raised to imperishable bodily life. This is the second stage, when death, the baneful distortion of God's good creation, already vanquished through Jesus's life-creating resurrection, will be abolished at his coming in glory:

But now Christ is risen from the dead, the firstfruits of those who sleep. For since death came through a human being, the resurrection of the dead came through a human being. For just as in Adam all die, so in Christ all will be made alive. But each in his own order; Christ the first-fruits, then those who belong to Christ at his coming. Then comes the consummation, when he delivers over the kingdom to his God and Father, when he abolishes all opposing rule, and all authority and power. For Jesus must reign as king until the Father puts all things under his feet. The last enemy that will be abolished is death. (1 Cor 15:20–26)

Paul's gospel thus announced Jesus's resurrection as the fulfillment of the promise in Israel's Scriptures of the creator God's victory over death, and looked forward in hope to the day when he would bring that victory to full consummation, giving imperishable life to the mortal bodies of his people, raising their bodies of flesh and bones from the dust of death to a new, embodied, and indestructible life:

Behold, I tell you a mystery: we shall not all sleep, but we shall all be changed. In a moment of time, in the twinkling of an eye, at the final trumpet: for the trumpet will sound, and the dead will be raised imperishable, and we shall be changed. For this perishable body must clothe itself with imperishability, and this mortal body must clothe itself with immortality. And when this perishable body clothes itself with imperishability, and this mortal body clothes itself with immortality, then will come to pass the word which stands written: "Death has been swallowed up in victory." (1 Cor 15:51–54)

Paul's final words in the passage above, "Death has been swallowed up in victory," are taken from Isaiah 25:8, and function to evoke the entire prophetic oracle in Isaiah 25:6–9, which as we saw envisions the coming of YHWH to swallow up death and wipe away the tears from all faces. In evoking this Isaianic vision, Paul makes clear that the resurrection will not only destroy death but also bring about a new world order in which evil will be vanquished and suffering and sorrow will be no more. Through the resurrection, the covenant's ancient promise of *life* to the people of God (Deut 30:15–20; 32:47; Ezek 18; Amos 5:4–7; Zech 14:8) will come to pass in an unimagined fullness.

The Interim State

What is the state of those who have died in Christ prior to the coming resurrection? Paul's letters speak warmly of an interim or intermediate state between death and renewed embodiment, in which the faithful are "away from the body but present with the Lord" (2 Cor 5:6–8). Their bodies "sleep" in the grave (1 Cor 15:18, 20; 1 Thess 4:13; cf. Dan 12:2), to be awakened on the day of Christ, but in the interim their spirits or souls are in heaven with Christ (cf. Luke 23:43; Acts 7:59). Paul writes from prison that, if he should be executed by Nero, he will "depart and be with Christ, which is far, far better" (Phil 1:20–24). But within Paul's thought this intermediate state, although blessed, is incomplete, awaiting the fullness of salvation to come in the resurrection of the body on the day of the Lord Jesus. For this reason Paul speaks of this heavenly interim astonishingly rarely. In Paul's letters it is the coming resurrection, which will bring about the destruction of death and the fullness of bodily life, that is the focus of eager and expectant hope.

Cosmic Judgment and Cosmic Renewal

This Pauline expectation of newly embodied life involved not only the resurrection to life of those who belong to Christ (1 Cor 15:23), but also a resurrection to judgment of the wicked who oppose God and disobey the good news (Rom 2:1–11, 16; 14:9–12; 2 Thess 1:5–10; cf. 2 Tim 4:1–2; Acts 17:30–31; 24:14–16, 24–25). This expectation of a coming judgment is a crucial component of Paul's proclamation of the fullness of salvation to come, confirming the creator God's victory over all evil, and the just and righteous character of his coming reign: "For we must all appear before the judgment seat of Christ, that each person may receive the things done in the body, whether good or evil" (2 Cor 5:10).

Moreover, according to Paul's gospel, the full outworking of Christ's resurrection would bring to pass the fulfillment of the scriptural promises of the creator God's *renewal of the entire created order* (Rom 8:18–25; Eph 1:9–12; Phil 3:20–21). And in this way the covenant's ancient promise of an *inheritance* for the people of God would find an astonishing fulfillment. The original promise to Abraham, fulfilled in the exodus and conquest, involved the nation's inheritance of the land of Canaan (Gen 12:7; 13:14–17; 15:18–21; 17:7–8). In the prophetic literature and in the Psalms, the promise is widened, through the covenant promises to David, to embrace the entire earth (Pss 2:7–8; 22:27–28; 47:9; 67; 72:8–11; Isa 11:10; Mic 5:2–5; Zech 14:9–10). Reflecting this wider canonical framework, Paul in Romans describes the inheritance promised to Abraham, and to all who follow in the steps of Abraham's faith, as *the world*, that is, the entire creation (Rom 4:13). Later in the same letter, Paul explains that this will come about at the time of the resurrection, when the whole creation, in its physicality and materiality, will be radically remade and transformed by the glory of the Lord:

But if we are God's children, we are also heirs; heirs of God, and fellow heirs with Christ, if indeed we suffer with him that we may also be glorified with him. For I consider that the sufferings of this present age are not worthy to be compared with the glory which will be revealed to us. For the longing expectation of the creation eagerly awaits the revelation of the children of God. For the created order was subjected to futility, not of its own accord but because of the will of God who subjected it, in the hope that *the creation itself will be set free from its slavery to decay, to share in the freedom of the glory of the children of God.* (Rom 8:17–21)

In this passage we see that within Paul's theology the full outworking of Jesus's life-creating resurrection will bring about the creator God's redemptive liberation of all creation. In the coming consummation, Paul's gospel proclaimed, all things will be made new, death will be swallowed up in victory, and the entire creation will be filled with the glory of the Lord.

The "Good News" of the Resurrection in Ancient Context

The hope for the future of humanity and of the cosmos that Paul proclaimed was thus very different from the pagan expectations of life beyond death. To be sure, ancient literary and philosophical texts consider a great variety of possibilities regarding life after death, ranging from the denial of any postmortem survival to firm belief in the immortality of the soul. What is *not* envisioned in these texts, however, is the possibility of the defeat of death through the resurrection of the physical, earthly body. The pagan expectations, however varied, assumed that physical, bodily death was invincible, and that its place in the cosmos was everlasting.

Paul's gospel, by contrast, proclaimed that, three days after his crucifixion, death, and burial, Jesus had risen bodily from the dead, fulfilling the prophetic promises of the God of Israel's victory over death. And when he came again in glory, he would raise the flesh-and-bones bodies of his people, abolish death forever, and renew the entire physical creation. Paul's gospel proclaimed a coming renewal of all things, and the fulfillment of human, embodied life, in an unimagined fullness. And thus, strikingly, in Paul's letters the ancient vocabulary of resignation and acquiescence with regard to death is entirely lacking; in its place we find an astonishingly pervasive vocabulary of *hope, expectancy, joy,* and *thanksgiving,* centered on the new and living hope brought by Jesus's resurrection (Rom 5:2–5; 8:20–25; 12:12; 15:13; 1 Cor 1:7–8; 1 Thess 5:8).

We are now in a position to answer the question posed at the beginning of the chapter as to why Paul called his message, and described it *to his pagan hearers* as, "the good news" (*to euangelion*). In light of the ancient world's sorrowful resignation to the inexorable power of death, the remarkable fact that Paul called his message the "gospel" or "good news"—and expected this to resonate with his gentile hearers—becomes lucidly comprehensible. To an ancient world that longed for the defeat of death but believed this longing could never be fulfilled, Paul's gospel announced that Jesus had conquered death. Through Jesus's resurrection, death itself, humanity's great enemy, had been overcome by the creator God. This was "the good news of Jesus and of his resurrection" (Acts 17:18).

The God Who Gives Life to the Dead

Paul thus proclaimed good news, but it was good news that was at the same time a summons. In a world of many gods and goddesses, Paul's gospel claimed to be the revelation of the one true God. And therefore this good news demanded a decision and a response. Paul's gospel called upon its hearers to "turn from idols to a living and true God" (1 Thess 1:9). It called for "the obedience of faith" (Rom 1:5; 16:26; Gal 3:2). It was therefore "the power of God for salvation *to everyone who believes*" (Rom 1:16). But those who reject the good news, Paul proclaimed, forfeit a share in the life it promises (2 Thess 1:6-10). Paul's gospel was thus both an announcement of *good news* and a summons to *conversion* from false gods to the one true God.

This exclusive claim of Paul's good news is often considered offensive in our contemporary world. Many today would argue: since Paul's "good news" offered the same or similar prospect of a heavenly life after death as offered by the deities of ancient worship and the divinities of the philosophers, is it not illogical and intolerant on Paul's part to privilege his own gospel as the message of the true God, and deny that these other gods and goddesses offer equally valid paths of salvation? But this common argument is founded upon a misconception: that Paul's gospel offered yet one more promise of afterlife following the death of the body, alongside those already on offer in pagan religion and philosophy. As we have seen, this is mistaken. The good news Paul proclaimed was not the prospect of life after bodily death, but Jesus's triumph over physical, bodily death through his resurrection from the dead.

And therefore in Paul's proclamation, *Jesus's resurrection was not only the content of the good news, it was also the grounds of the summons to conversion.* For in the world into which Paul's gospel came, as we have seen, none of the pagan gods claimed the power to bring the dead to life. Both the gods of ancient worship and the philosophic divinities of Plato, Epicurus, and the Buddha were considered by their devotees to be powerless before the almighty power of death. The creator God of the Jews was a different kind of God, who promised that in the time of his coming reign he would conquer even death. And Paul's gospel proclaimed that in Jesus's resurrection this promised victory of the God of Israel over death had come true. In conquering death through Jesus's resurrection, the God of the Jews had done what he had promised, and what none of the other so-called gods could do, or even claimed to do. And thus *through Jesus's resurrection the God of Israel had revealed himself in power as the only true God.*

This understanding of Jesus's resurrection as fully revealing the identity of the true God, although often missed by modern interpreters, is a foundational feature of Paul's theology. Because of it Paul creates a *new way of speaking about God.* In the Jewish Scriptures, the God of Israel's identity as the true God and the author of life was expressed in the description of Israel's God as "the living God," in contrast with dead idols (2 Kings 19:4; Jer 10:10; 23:36; Dan 5:23 [LXX]; 6:20, 26; 12:7 [LXX]; Bel and the Dragon 5, 25 [Theodotion]; Hos 1:10; 2 Maccabees 7.33). In Jewish synagogue worship in Paul's day, the unique power of the God of Israel to raise the dead was expressed in the prayer "Blessed are you, O Lord, who gives life to the dead" (Berakhot 18.2). These are *timeless* expressions, referring to the creator's essential life, and life-giving power over death, a power to be exercised in the time of his kingdom. Paul can also describe the unique identity of the creator God in these ways. He calls God the "living God" (Rom 9:26; 2 Cor 3:3; 6:16; 1 Thess 1:9; cf. 1 Tim 3:15; 4:10; Acts 14:15) and "the God who gives life to the dead" (Rom 4:17; cf. 2 Cor 1:9).

But according to Paul's "good news," God had now taken that life-creating divine power, the unique property of the living creator God, and *actualized it by raising Jesus from the dead.* And therefore he describes God in a *new* way, reflecting this new and ultimate act in salvation history, the creator God's conquest of death, *which has now happened.* The God of Abraham, Isaac, and Jacob is now "the One who raised Jesus our Lord from the dead" (Rom 4:24). The importance of this new way of naming God within Paul's theology is evident from the frequency with which it occurs in his letters:

"The One who raised Jesus our Lord from the dead" (Rom 4:24)
"The One who raised Jesus from the dead" (Rom 8:11)
"The One who raised Christ Jesus from the dead" (Rom 8:11)
"The One who raised the Lord Jesus" (2 Cor 4:14)

"God the Father, who raised him [Jesus Christ] from the dead" (Gal 1:1)
"The God who raised him [Jesus Christ] from the dead" (Col 2:12)[3]

Within the Old Testament narrative, it is in the exodus event that the God of creation and covenant first revealed himself also as a saving, rescuing, delivering God. Thereafter in the Old Testament, the God of Israel would be identified by this mighty act in salvation history: "The Lord, who brought Israel out of the land of Egypt" (Lev 26:13; Deut 6:12; 8:14; 13:5, 10; 20:1; Judg 2:12; 1 Kings 9:9; 2 Kings 17:17, 36; Ps 81:10; Jer 16:14). Paul's new predication similarly identifies God on the basis of a mighty act in salvation history. But Paul's name is different, for it names God by means of that *ultimate* act of life-creating power that the Jewish people expected to come in the time of God's kingdom and reign. What God always was ("the God who gives life to the dead"), he had now, through Jesus's resurrection, proved himself to be. He had shown himself to be the God who raises the dead, in contrast to the false gods of the nations who are powerless before death. The creator had reclaimed his creation. Through Jesus's resurrection, the God of Israel had revealed himself, as he promised he would do in the time of his kingdom, as the one true living God.

Jesus's Resurrection and the Mystery of God

And this brings us face-to-face with the ultimate revelation of the resurrection. Jesus's resurrection, as we have seen, fulfilled YHWH's promise of the conquest of death. But in defeating death, Jesus had done what the prophets had foretold *YHWH himself* would do in the time of his kingdom. He had done what only the living creator God could do. And thus in conquering death, Jesus had revealed himself as none other than YHWH, the creator God, come in the flesh. We see this in the "Christ hymn" of Philippians 2, where through his resurrection and exaltation Jesus is given *"the name which is above every name*, that at the name of Jesus every knee might bow" (Phil 2:9), and in Ephesians 1, where through his resurrection and ascension Christ is enthroned far above *"every name that is named*, not only in this age, but also in the age to come" (Eph 1:21). Within Paul's Jewish context, the One who has the name above every name that is named can only be the creator God of Israel. But in both the Ephesians and Philippians passages, the resurrection reveals that this divine name, the name that is above every name, is the name of *Jesus*.

---

3. See Wesley Hill, *Paul and the Trinity: Persons, Relations, and the Pauline Letters* (Grand Rapids: Eerdmans, 2015), 49–75, on this crucial Pauline formulation.

Likewise in the ancient confession at the forefront of Paul's letter to the Romans, Jesus has been "revealed to be the Son of God in power according to the Spirit of holiness through the resurrection of the dead" (Rom 1:4). Strikingly, this ancient formula refers to the event of Jesus's resurrection on the third day as "the resurrection *of the dead*," employing the *plural* form of "the dead" (Rom 1:4; cf. 1 Cor 15:21; Acts 26:23). When Jesus rose, the confession affirms, he brought about the resurrection of *all* the dead! Here we see once again that Paul understood Jesus's resurrection as the fulfillment of the God of Israel's promised conquest of death.[4] Jesus's life-creating resurrection is the source and first installment of the resurrection of all the dead, when he comes again to earth in glory to raise the bodies of his people to everlasting life and renew all things. And according to this ancient confession, through the resurrection event Jesus "was revealed to be the Son of God in power" (Rom 1:4). As we saw in chapter 3, the title "Son of God" must be taken here in its full *divine* sense. The resurrection has therefore powerfully revealed Jesus's true identity. The one "born of the seed of David" (1:3) is the incarnate Son of God (1:4). We saw in part 2 of this book that the incarnation of God in Christ is the very heart of Paul's thought. The resurrection of Jesus, Paul believed, was the full revelation of that reality.

"My Lord and my God!" the apostle Thomas exclaims in John's Gospel after seeing and touching the risen Lord (John 20:28). Paul shared this same theology of the resurrection as the revelation of Jesus as God incarnate. Paul's theology here agrees with that of the angel at the empty tomb in Luke's Gospel, whose question to the women, "Why do you seek the Living One among the dead?" (Luke 24:5), employs a title for the risen Jesus ("the Living One") reserved in the Old Testament for the living God (Dan 4:34 [Theodotion]; 12:7; cf. Gen 41:45; Ps 93:2; Dan 6:26). The oath "As YHWH lives!" or (when spoken by God) "As I live!" pervades the Old Testament.[5] Through the resurrection, the oath "As YHWH lives!" had come true in a new, startling, and salvation-creating way (Rom 14:9–11).[6]

---

4. Paula Fredriksen also notes Paul's reference in Rom 1:4 to the general resurrection of the dead (*Paul: The Pagans' Apostle* [New Haven: Yale University Press, 2017], 141–43), although her interpretation of this fact differs from that proposed here.

5. See, for example, Judg 8:19; Ruth 3:13; 1 Sam 14:39, 45; 19:6; 20:3, 21; 25:26, 34; 26:10, 16; 28:10; 29:6; 2 Sam 2:27; 4:9; 12:5; 14:11; 15:21; 1 Kings 1:29; 2:24; 17:1, 12; 18:10, 15; 22:14; 2 Kings 2:2, 4, 6; 3:14; 4:30; 5:16, 20; 2 Chron 18:13; Isa 49:18; Jer 12:16; 16:14–15; 23:7–8; 38:16; 44:26; 46:18; Ezek 5:11; 14:16, 18, 20; 16:48; 17:16, 19; 18:3; 20:3, 31, 33; 33:11, 27; 34:8; 35:6, 11; Hos 4:15; Zech 2:9.

6. On Rom 14:9–11, see J. Ross Wagner, *Heralds of the Good News: Isaiah and Paul "in Concert" in the Letter to the Romans*, NovTSup 101 (Leiden: Brill, 2002), 336–38, and N. T. Wright, *Paul and the Faithfulness of God*, vol. 4 of *Christian Origins and the Question of God* (Minneapolis: Fortress, 2013), 702.

And, as we saw in part 2, the astounding revelation of Jesus's divine identity brought with it a new revelation of the inner mystery of the one God as a communion of persons: Father, Son, and Holy Spirit. We saw there how Paul read the central monotheistic confession of the Old Testament (Deut 6:4, "The Lord is our God, the Lord is one") in light of the mystery of Father and Son, and that this underlies Paul's regular practice of ascribing the divine title ("God") to the Father and the divine name ("Lord") to the Son, for example, "Grace to you and peace from *God* our Father, and the *Lord* Jesus Christ" (Rom 1:7 and parallels). And so it is fitting that this mystery, now revealed through Jesus's resurrection, is in the heart of the new way of naming God that we have seen was opened up by the resurrection event: "*God* the Father, who raised Jesus our *Lord* from the dead" (cf. Rom 4:24; 2 Cor 4:14; Gal 1:1; Col 2:12). The resurrection is the full revelation of the incarnation, and of the mystery of God as Father, Son, and Holy Spirit.

Conclusion: The Good News of a Different God and His Victory

In the wider ancient world into which Paul's gospel came, death was believed to be an eternal and unchangeable reality of the cosmic order, unalterable even by the gods. Although a variety of beliefs existed regarding soul survival, heavenly afterlife, and reincarnation, neither the common person nor the philosophers believed that a human being, once dead, might live again. All agreed on the impossibility of resurrection—the return from bodily death to an everlasting embodied life. We also discovered a longing for the reversal of death that the widely held beliefs in the soul's immortality apparently could not satisfy. But the ancients believed this was a longing that could never be fulfilled. As Apollo explained in the *Eumenides*, "for death alone my father Zeus has no divine enchantment." Both the gods of ancient polytheistic worship and the philosophical deities of Plato, Epicurus, and the Buddha were considered powerless before the invincible power of death. Death was the everlasting sorrow.

The God of the Jews was not only a different God, but a different kind of God altogether, who had made a very different promise. The prophets envisioned that in the time of his coming kingdom and reign the God of Israel would vanquish evil, do away with suffering and sorrow, and *abolish death forever*. In a world of gods powerless before death, the Jewish people awaited their God's saving reign, when he would reveal himself as the one true God by defeating even death, raising his people bodily from the dead, and renewing the entire creation.

Paul brought to this world "the good news of Jesus and of his resurrection" (Acts 17:18). Paul's gospel proclaimed the restoration to life, three days after his crucifixion and burial, of Jesus's crucified body of flesh and bones. And in rising from the dead, Jesus had fulfilled the prophetic promise of the God of Israel's victory over death. He had conquered death on behalf of all humanity. His resurrection was the "firstfruits" (1 Cor 15:20) of the full harvest to come, when the risen and exalted Jesus would come again in glory to raise the bodies of his people to everlasting life and renew the entire physical cosmos. To an ancient world that believed that death was invincible and everlasting, Paul's gospel proclaimed the victory of life over death, life in an unimagined fullness. Paul's gospel replaced the everlasting sorrow of the world into which it came with the joyous good news of the resurrection.

But the good news of the resurrection was also a summons to conversion from false gods to the one true God. Neither the gods of ancient worship nor the philosophical deities claimed the power to give life to the dead. Through Jesus's resurrection, the God of Israel had done what none of the other so-called gods even claimed to do, thus revealing himself in power as the one true living God. Paul therefore describes God in a new way, reflecting this new and ultimate act within salvation history: "the One who raised Jesus our Lord from the dead" (Rom 4:24). And in rising from death, Jesus himself had been "revealed as the Son of God in power" (Rom 1:4). For in conquering death, he had done what the prophets promised *the Lord* would do in the time of his kingdom and reign. He had done what only the living God could do. The resurrection was the full revelation of the incarnation. In revealing Jesus's identity as the divine Son of God, the resurrection also brought the revelation of the mystery of God as Father, Son, and Holy Spirit, reflected in Paul's full formulation: "God the *Father*, who raised Jesus our *Lord* from the dead." Jesus's resurrection was the ultimate revelation of the identity of the creator God.

Chapter Ten

The Resurrection of the Body in Paul's Gospel

Have you ever wondered why the Gospels are so emphatic that Jesus rose from the dead in the same body in which he was crucified, leaving behind him an empty tomb? In Luke's Gospel, for example, the resurrection narrative begins with the disciples' discovery that Jesus was no longer in the tomb (Luke 24:1–12; cf. 24:23–24). At the climax of the narrative, Jesus shows himself alive to the Eleven and the other disciples, inviting them to "touch me and see, because a spirit does not have flesh and bones as you see that I have" (Luke 24:39). In John's Gospel, Jesus invites doubting Thomas to probe the scars in his hands and side (John 20:24–29). The speeches of the apostles in Acts similarly stress that the flesh of Jesus was raised without undergoing decay (Acts 2:25–31; 13:34–37), and that the risen Jesus ate and drank with his disciples (10:40–42; cf. 1:3–4; Luke 24:41–43). Why do both the Gospels and Acts emphasize so strongly that Jesus's resurrection was a concrete, physical event involving his body of flesh and bones? The answer is at the heart of the message of all four Gospels: by rising physically and bodily from the dead, Jesus has fulfilled the creator God's promised conquest of death, bringing the hope of bodily resurrection for all who believe (John 5:24–29; 6:39, 40, 44, 54; Acts 4:1–2; 23:7–10; 24:14–15; 26:6–8, 22–23; cf. Matt 27:52–53). That is why each of the Gospels calls the story it tells, culminating in Jesus's resurrection, the "gospel" or "good news." And that is why, as we saw in the previous chapter, Paul likewise calls his message to the gentile world the "good news." For to a pagan world in which death was the eternal sorrow, invincible and everlasting, Paul brought the startling announcement of Jesus's victory over death through his resurrection from the dead.

Paul's great "resurrection chapter," 1 Corinthians 15, is by far the fullest treatment of this hope of resurrection in the entire Bible. Ironically, some modern readers, both on a popular and on a scholarly level, believe they find something less in this chapter than the announcement that Jesus has conquered physical, bodily death for all who believe in him. Some think they discover here an understanding of Jesus's "resurrection" that involved neither his crucified body nor an empty tomb. Others believe they find in this chapter a conception of the resurrection hope of the faithful that excludes the earthly, physical body from final salvation. In the chapter that follows we will explore why some read 1 Corinthians 15 in these ways—and why this is a radical misreading of Paul's theology.

The Good News of the Resurrection: The Church's Historic Reading of 1 Corinthians 15

Throughout the history of the church, the future resurrection hope of the faithful expounded in 1 Corinthians 15 was understood in terms of a resurrection of the physical body, identifying the resurrected body of this passage with the earthly, fleshly body raised to life and transformed to be imperishable.[1] To be sure, "Gnostic" interpreters such as the Valentinians and Ophites, who believed that the material world and the physical body were inherently evil, read this chapter in ways that excluded a literal resurrection of the body (Gospel of Philip 56.26–57.22; Irenaeus, *Against Heresies* 1.30.13).[2] And the Alexandrian exegete Origen, influenced by Gnostic thought, interpreted 1 Corinthians 15 as involving a resurrection of a heavenly or spiritual body composed of ethereal matter, distinct from the earthly body of flesh (*Selections on the Psalms* 11.384 [on Ps 1:5]; *Commentary on Matthew* 17.29–30; *First Principles* 2.10–11; *Against Celsus* 5.18–23).[3] However, these Gnostic views were rejected within the ancient church, and Origen's teaching on the resurrection was condemned as heretical by the Fifth Ecumenical Council (II Constantinople). The church's "classical theologians," such as Irenaeus, Tertullian, Jerome, and Augustine, unanimously interpreted 1 Corinthians 15 in terms of a physical resurrection of the body of flesh and bones (see Irenaeus, *Against Heresies* 5.7–14; Tertullian, *The Resurrection of the Flesh* 48–57; Methodius, *On Resurrection* 1.13–14; 3.5–6; Rufinus, *Commentary on the Apostles' Creed* 41–47; Jerome, *Epistles* 108.23–24; and Augustine, *The City of God* 20.20; 22.21–24). This reading was in agreement with the generally received ancient Christian doc-

---

1. The fullest discussion is found in Francois Altermath, *Du corps psychique au corps spirituel: Interprétation de 1 Cor. 15,35–49 par les auteurs chrétiens des quatre premièrs siècles*, BGBE 18 (Tübingen: Mohr Siebeck, 1977).

2. See further Elaine E. Pagels, "'The Mystery of the Resurrection': A Gnostic Reading of 1 Corinthians 15," *JBL* 93 (1974): 276–88.

3. See Henry Chadwick, "Origen, Celsus, and the Resurrection of the Body," *HTR* 41 (1948): 83–102, and Henri Crouzel, "La doctrine origenienne du corps réssuscité," *BLE* 31 (1980): 175–200, 241–66. Crouzel's article is widely considered the authoritative study of the subject.

trine of resurrection as the reconstitution and glorious transformation of the present mortal body, a transformation involving "enhancement of what is, not metamorphosis into what is not."[4] M. E. Dahl described this orthodox conception as involving the claim that "the resurrection body is *this* body restored and improved in a miraculous manner."[5] The church's ancient creeds gave expression to this hope in the most striking way by affirming "the resurrection of the *flesh*."[6] Throughout the centuries, exegesis of 1 Corinthians 15 was carried out in the context of this conviction, shared alike by Catholic, Orthodox, and Protestant interpreters, that the resurrection hope of the faithful that Paul expounds in this chapter is a resurrection of the flesh.

Less Than Good News:
Contemporary Misreadings of 1 Corinthians 15

However, the average person today, reading 1 Corinthians 15 in isolation from this theological and ecclesial context, sometimes gains a very different impression. This is also true of some New Testament scholars. To be sure, many modern interpreters, including such eminent scholars as N. T. Wright, Richard Hays, and Anthony Thiselton, read this chapter, in continuity with the Gospels and the church's historic teaching, in terms of the resurrection (and glorious transformation to imperishability) of the once-dead body of flesh and bones from the tomb.[7] But another stream of contemporary New Testament scholarship

4. Caroline Walker Bynum, *The Resurrection of the Body in Western Christianity, 200–1336* (New York: Columbia University Press, 1999), 8.

5. M. E. Dahl, *The Resurrection of the Body: A Study of 1 Corinthians 15*, SBT 36 (London: SCM, 1962), 7.

6. Cf. the Old Roman Creed (c. 175 CE): *pisteuo eis . . . sarkos anastasin* ("I believe in . . . the resurrection of the flesh"); Creed of Jerusalem (c. 350): *pisteuomen eis . . . sarkos anastasin* ("we believe in . . . the resurrection of the flesh"); *Apostolic Constitutions* 7.41 (fourth century): *baptizomai kai . . . eis sarkos anastasin* ("I am baptized also . . . into the resurrection of the flesh"); Creed of the First Council of Toledo (400): *resurrectionem vero humanae credimus carnis* ("we believe indeed in the resurrection of our human flesh"); Apostles' Creed (sixth century): *credo in . . . carnis resurrectionem* ("I believe in . . . the resurrection of the flesh"); Symbol of Faith of Leo IX (1053): *credo etiam veram resurrectionem eiusdem carnis, quam nunc gesto* ("I believe also in the true resurrection of the same flesh which I now have").

7. See N. T. Wright, *The Resurrection of the Son of God*, vol. 3 of *Christian Origins and the Question of God* (Minneapolis: Fortress, 2003), 340–61; Richard B. Hays, *First Corinthians* (Louisville: Westminster John Knox, 1997), 270–75; and Anthony Thiselton, *The First Epistle to the Corinthians: A Commentary on the Greek Text*, NIGTC (Grand Rapids: Eerdmans, 2000), 1257–306. Cf. Earle Ellis, "*Soma* in 1 Corinthians," *Int* 44 (1990): 132–44, and Martin Hengel, "Das Begräbnis Jesu bei Paulus

is represented by scholars such as Dale Martin, Troels Engberg-Pedersen, and Paula Fredriksen, who argue that Paul in 1 Corinthians 15 envisions an ethereal or "spiritual" body that excludes participation of the earthly body in the life of the world to come.[8]

This latter reading of 1 Corinthians 15 is the basis for a view of Christian origins in which belief in the resurrection of Jesus's crucified body from the tomb, such as we see reflected in the gospel accounts, was a later development, unknown to Paul and the earliest Christ followers. As Rudolf Bultmann (an exponent of this view) famously remarked, "The [Gospels'] accounts of an empty tomb are legends, of which Paul as yet knew nothing."[9] From this perspective, the good news of the resurrection proclaimed in 1 Corinthians 15 is a different gospel from the good news narrated by Matthew, Mark, Luke, and John; they are fundamentally at variance regarding the meaning of the affirmation that Jesus has been raised from the dead on the third day, and the nature of the hope Jesus's resurrection offers those who believe. According to this view, 1 Corinthians 15 does not announce the good news of Jesus's victory over physical death, but the not-so-good news that Jesus left his crucified body in the tomb and was only "alive" in some ethereal or celestial form. On this reading, 1 Corinthians 15 does not offer the good news of the redemption of this world and this body, but the less than good news of a heavenly or spiritual existence apart from this world and this body. This is the way some scholars read Paul's great "resurrection chapter" today. Lay interpreters often read the chapter in a mixed way, understanding Jesus's resurrection (1 Cor 15:1–11) as physical and bodily, but the future resurrection of believers in Christ (1 Cor 15:35–58) in a "spiritual" or ethereal sense.

But such readings are in direct conflict with the resurrection hope in Paul's theology we explored in the previous chapter. They are in flat contradiction to the four Gospels and Acts. And such a "gospel" would merely offer yet one more expectation of spiritual afterlife among many in the ancient pagan world—rendering it simply incomprehensible that Paul should describe such

---

und die leibliche Auferstehung aus dem Grabe," in *Auferstehung—Resurrection*, ed. Friedrich Avemarie and Hermann Lichtenberger, WUNT 135 (Tübingen: Mohr Siebeck, 2001), 119–83.

8. See Fredriksen, *Paul*, 4, 183n8; Fredriksen, "Vile Bodies: Paul and Augustine on the Resurrection of the Flesh," in *Biblical Hermeneutics in Historical Perspective*, ed. Mark S. Burrows and Paul Rorem (Grand Rapids: Eerdmans, 1991), 75–87; Dale Martin, *The Corinthian Body* (New Haven: Yale University Press, 1995), 108–32; and Troels Engberg-Pedersen, *Cosmology and Self in the Apostle Paul: The Material Spirit* (Oxford: Oxford University Press, 2010), 8–38.

9. Rudolf Bultmann, *Theologie des Neuen Testaments*, 9th ed. (Tübingen: Mohr Siebeck, 1984), 48.

a message to his pagan hearers as the good *news*. For in such a case, it would be anything but new.

Why do contemporary readers sometimes interpret 1 Corinthians 15 in this way today? Three reasons are usually given. First, Paul in this chapter sharply contrasts the present mortal body with the risen body to come (15:42–44). This seems to imply that the present body is done away with. What is placed in the tomb is x, what is raised to life is y. Second, Paul speaks of this risen body as a "spiritual body" (15:44). Therefore, readers suppose, Paul conceived of the risen body as composed of spirit, not flesh. Third, Paul asserts that "flesh and blood cannot inherit the kingdom of God" (15:50). To many readers, this seems proof positive that Paul envisioned a "resurrection" (whether of Jesus at Easter, or of the faithful at his coming, or both) that does not involve the body of flesh and bones.

The purpose of this chapter is twofold. First, we will show that this understanding of 1 Corinthians 15 is based on a mistaken reading of the passage. We will take the arguments for this view one by one, and show how each of them is founded upon a failure to read 1 Corinthians 15 in its literary and historical context. In making this case, we will be writing in agreement with such scholars as Thiselton, Wright, and Hays, but we will also be seeking to add to our understanding of Paul's great "resurrection chapter" with fresh analysis, arguments, and evidence. Second, we will mine the riches of this tremendous passage to shed further light on the resurrection hope in Paul's theology that we began to explore in chapter 9. As we will see, the resurrection Paul proclaims in this chapter is a resurrection of the physical body. It is a resurrection of the *flesh*. And this is of central importance to his theology.

The Structure of Paul's Argument in 1 Corinthians 15:36–54

I believe the exegetical key to Paul's understanding of the resurrection in 1 Corinthians 15 is the structure of Paul's own argument in that chapter's central portion, 15:36–54.[10] The structure of 15:36–54 may be set out as follows:

10. For full discussion, see James Ware, "Paul's Understanding of the Resurrection in 1 Corinthians 15:36–54," *JBL* 133 (2014): 809–35.

SUBJECT	VERB	PREDICATE COMPLEMENT
[36] that which you sow	dies	—
	is made alive	—
[42] (the body)	is sown	in decay
	is raised	in incorruption
[43]	is sown	in dishonor
	is raised	in glory
	is sown	in weakness
	is raised	in power
[44]	is sown	a body given life by the soul
	is raised	a body given life by the Spirit
[49] we	were clothed with	the image of the man of dust
	will be clothed with	the image of the Man from heaven
[51] we all	will be changed	—
[52] the dead	will be raised	imperishable
we	will be changed	—
[53] this perishable body	must be clothed with	imperishability
this mortal body	must be clothed with	immortality
[54] this perishable body	is clothed with	imperishability
this mortal body	is clothed with	immortality

For some readers, Paul's series of contrasts between the present and risen body, with their reference to what is sown being x and what is raised being y (15:42–44; cf. 15:52–54), point to a radical discontinuity between the mortal body and the risen body in Paul's thought, precluding the possibility that Paul conceived of resurrection in straightforward bodily terms. However, if we examine the actual function of this series of contrasts within the structure of Paul's exposition, we see that Paul's point is quite different. Four observations are crucial (and the reader will want to refer to the diagram as we explore each one).

First, within 15:36–49, which is structured by twelve antithetically paired verbs (that is, six pairs of verbs) denoting death (or the mortal state) and resurrection (or the risen state), the *subject* of these antithetical verbal pairs is *one and the same* both for verbs denoting death and for verbs denoting resurrection (see the diagram). The subject throughout is the perishable body, which "dies" but "is made alive" again by God (15:36), which is "sown" (Greek: *speiretai*) in mortality and death but "raised" (Greek: *egeiretai*) to imperishable life (15:42–44). This simple observation has profound implications. Paul does not describe resurrection as an event in which *x* (the present body) is sown but *y* (a body distinct from the present body) is raised, but as an event in which a single *x* (the present body), having been sown a perishable *x*, is raised an imperishable *x*. Paul's sequence of paired verbs in 15:36–49 shows that in Paul's thought it is precisely that which perishes—the mortal body—that in the resurrection is given new, imperishable life.

Second, in 15:50–54—which is structured by seven verbs denoting resurrection or transformation (see the diagram)—it is again the *present perishable body* that is the subject of this resurrection and transformation (15:51, 52, 53–54). In 15:53–54, the subject that clothes itself with imperishability is explicitly "this perishable body" (*to pharton touto*) and "this mortal body" (*to thnēton touto*). Paul's fourfold repetition of "this" (*touto*) emphasizes that it is *this* mortal, perishable body—corruptible human flesh—that is the subject of the transformation.

Third, in addition to the verb *egeirō*, or "raise" (which will be discussed below), Paul in this chapter employs a variety of verbs to denote the resurrection event: "make alive" (*zōopoieō*, 15:36, 45; cf. 15:22), "be clothed" (*phoreō*, 15:49), "change" (*allassō*, 15:51, 52), and "clothe" (*enduō*, 15:53, 54). These additional verbs are significant, for they each express, in different ways, not the annihilation or replacement of the fleshly body, but its revival (*zōopoieō*), investiture (*phoreō*, *enduō*), and transformation (*allassō*). Paul's affirmation that the present body will be "changed" (15:51, 52) and "clothed" (15:53, 54) of necessity implies its revivification and enhancement.

Fourth, as the diagram above reveals, the series of contrasts within 15:36–54 between the mortal and risen body do not occur in the *subjects* of these sentences but in their *predicates* (verbs and verbal complements). These predicate complements invariably describe a change of *quality* rather than of *substance*, in which what was once perishable, dishonored, weak, and mortal is endowed with imperishability, glory, power, and immortality (15:42–43, 52–54). Paul's series of oppositions do not describe two different bodies, distinct in substance, but two contrasting modes of existence of the same body, one *prior* to and the other *subsequent* to the resurrection. Many modern readers assume that the point of Paul's range of contrasts between the present body and the resurrection body is to show that the mortal, perishable body is excluded from participation in final salvation. But Paul's point is in fact the opposite: to show how the perishable body, through resurrection, will partake of imperishable life.

The Analogy of the Seed in 1 Corinthians 15:36–41

As is evident from the repetition throughout 1 Corinthians 15:36–54 of the language of "sowing" (*speirō*, 15:42–44; cf. *ho speireis*, 15:36) and of "clothing" (*phoreō*, 15:49; *enduō*, 15:53–54; cf. *gumnos kokkos*, 15:37), Paul's analogy of the seed in 15:36–41 is foundational for the argument of the entire chapter. The analogy points to both the *material continuity* of the mortal and risen body and the *transformation* of the mortal body that takes place in the resurrection event. The structure of the analogy in its three phases may be set out as follows: *seed* is to *plant* (15:36) as (1) the *present body* is to the *transformed body* (15:37–38), as (2) the *present flesh* is to the *transformed flesh* (15:39), and as (3) the *present glory* of the body is to the *transformed glory* of the risen body (15:40–41).

What is often missed is the critical significance of verse 39 (phase two of the analogy) for our understanding of resurrection in Paul. For the juxtaposition of 15:39 with 15:37 and 15:40–41 shows that here, reflecting the normal usage of Paul's Greek-speaking audience, "flesh" (*sarx*) and "body" (*sōma*) function as synonymous terms for the human body. Paul's analogy in 15:36–41 assumes both that the risen body will be a *body* (15:37–38, 40–41) and that it will be composed of *flesh* (15:39). Paul's reminder of the various kinds of flesh (15:39), bodies (15:40), and bodily splendor (15:41) functions to prepare the reader for the depiction of transformed embodiment to follow in 15:42–54, in which the risen body of flesh is differentiated from its mortal counterpart not by change of substance, but by its freedom from weakness, mortality, and decay.

The "Spiritual Body" in 1 Corinthians 15:44

Central to the belief that 1 Corinthians 15 excludes the resurrection of the flesh is the assumption that the "spiritual body" (*sōma pneumatikon*) in 15:44 refers to a body composed of spirit, distinct from the body of flesh laid in the tomb.[11] How-

---

11. So Engberg-Pedersen, *Cosmology and Self*, 26–34; Martin, *The Corinthian Body*, 117, 120, 126; Fredriksen, *Paul*, 4, 183n8.

ever, this assumption is based on a misunderstanding of the actual lexical meaning of the key terms in question.[12] The adjective Paul contrasts with *pneumatikos* (spiritual) is not *sarkinos* (fleshly), cognate with *sarx* (flesh), and thus referring to the *flesh*, but *psychikos* (literally "soulish"), cognate with *psyche* (soul), thus referring to the *soul*. This adjective is used in ancient Greek, without exception, with reference to the properties or activities of the soul (e.g., 4 Maccabees 1.32; Aristotle, *Nicomachean Ethics* 3.10.2; Epictetus, *Discourses* 3.7.5–7; Ps.-Plutarch, *On the Opinions of the Philosophers* 1.8). Modifying "body" (*sōma*), as here, with reference to the present body, the adjective describes this body as *given life or activity by the soul*. The adjective has nothing to do with the body's composition, but denotes the source of the body's life and activity.

The meaning of the adjective *psychikos* in 15:44 is extremely significant, for it reveals that the understanding of Paul's term "spiritual body" as denoting a body composed of spirit involves a misreading of the passage. For if the *sōma pneumatikon* ("spiritual body") in this context describes the *composition* of the future body, as a body *composed solely of spirit*, its correlate, *sōma psychikon*, would necessarily describe the composition of the present body, as a body *composed only of soul*. Paul would assert the absence of flesh and bones, not only from the risen body, but also from the present mortal body! The impossibility that *psychikos* here refers to the body's composition rules out the notion that its correlated adjective *pneumatikos* refers to the body's composition. Contrasted with *psychikos*, the adjective *pneumatikos* (spiritual) must similarly refer to the source of the body's life and activity, describing the risen body as *given life by the Spirit*. The mode of existence here described by the adjective "spiritual" (*pneumatikos*) is further clarified by the larger context of the letter. For elsewhere in 1 Corinthians this adjective is uniformly used with reference to *physical* persons or *material* things enlivened, empowered, or transformed by the Spirit of God: flesh and blood human beings (2:15; 3:1; 14:37), palpable manna and water (10:3–4), and a very tangible rock (10:4). Used with "body" (*sōma*) in 15:44, the adjective *pneumatikos* (spiritual) indicates that the risen body will be given life and will be empowered by God's Spirit.

Both contextual evidence and lexical evidence thus indicate that the phrase *sōma pneumatikon*, or "spiritual body," in 1 Corinthians 15:44 does not refer to a body composed of spirit, but to the fleshly body endowed with imperishable life by the power of the Spirit. Although the expression "spiritual body" (*sōma pneumatikon*) is unique here in Paul, the concept of *the Spirit as the giver of resurrection life* is a major theme within Paul's theology (Rom 8:9–11, 23; 2 Cor 5:4–5; Gal 5:25; 6:7–8). Within this theology, the work of the Spirit in those who

---

12. For fuller analysis, see Ware, "Paul's Understanding," 831–34.

belong to Christ will culminate in the resurrection, when "the One who raised Christ from the dead will also *give life to your mortal bodies through his Spirit* who indwells you" (Rom 8:11). This theme forms a common thread uniting Romans 8, 2 Corinthians 5, Galatians 5–6, and 1 Corinthians 15. The "spiritual body" of 1 Corinthians 15 is the body of flesh and bones given imperishable life by the power of the Spirit.

Does 1 Corinthians 15:50 Preclude the Resurrection of the Flesh?

First Corinthians 15:50 is often assumed to be obvious evidence of Paul's exclusion from the resurrection of all that is fleshly, physical, and material. Adela Yarbro Collins, for instance, writes: "The remark in verse 50, 'flesh and blood cannot inherit the kingdom of God, nor does the perishable inherit the imperishable,' implies that the resurrection 'body' is not material in the same way that the earthly body is."[13] According to Fredriksen, Christ arose "in a spiritual body, Paul insists, and definitely *not* in a body of flesh and blood (1 Cor 15:44, 50)."[14] But as we have now seen, Paul's larger argument in the chapter precludes such a reading of this verse. What, then, is Paul's specific point here in 15:50, in the context of that larger argument?

The answer lies in the relation of 15:50 to the revelation of the mystery ("Behold, I tell you a mystery") that follows in 15:51–54. As we saw above, this is a hinge point within the structure of Paul's argument. Within this structure, 15:50 expresses the *dilemma*, to which Paul's exposition of the mystery in 15:51–54 functions as the *solution*. This dilemma is expressed by means of two parallel clauses:

> *flesh and blood* (*sarx kai haima*) cannot inherit the kingdom of God
> *what is corruptible* (*phora*) does not inherit what is incorruptible (*apharsia*)

In correlating "flesh and blood" (*sarx kai haima*) and "what is corruptible" (*phora*), Paul's synonymous parallelism (in which each clause serves to define and delimit the other) functions to identify a single subject of the two clauses: the perishable, mortal body. "Flesh and blood" in this context therefore does not refer to humanity's material makeup, the substance of flesh, but rather refers to the frail, transitory nature of the mortal body in its perishability and corruptibility.

13. Adela Yarbro Collins, "The Empty Tomb in the Gospel according to Mark," in *Hermes and Athena: Biblical Exegesis and Philosophical Theology*, ed. Eleonore Stump and Thomas P. Flint (Notre Dame: University of Notre Dame Press, 1993), 113. See in the same vein Martin, *The Corinthian Body*, 126; Fredriksen, "Vile Bodies," 81–82.

14. Fredriksen, *Paul*, 4.

This is also evident in the contrasting function in antiquity of the phrases "flesh and bones" and "flesh and blood." In ancient usage, the phrase "flesh and bones" connotes the body's *materiality* (e.g., Luke 24:39, "Touch me and see, because a spirit does not have flesh and bones, as you see that I have"). The phrase "flesh and blood," by contrast, focuses not on the body's materiality but on its *weakness* and *perishability* (e.g., Sirach 14.18, "So is the generation of flesh and blood, one dies and another is born"). In 1 Corinthians 15:50, Paul chooses the term "flesh and blood," not the term "flesh and bones." The plight envisioned in 15:50 is therefore *not* humanity's embodiment in flesh, but that flesh's need of redemption from its bondage to corruption.

To grasp the dilemma precisely, it is important to note that Paul in 15:50 does *not* affirm that the corruptible body cannot be *raised*, but that it cannot *inherit the kingdom of God*. As the foregoing verses have stressed, it is precisely the mortal, corruptible body that will be *made alive* (15:36, 45) and *raised* by God (15:42–44). But to inherit the imperishable kingdom, the perishable body must not be raised merely to die again, but must also be *transformed* so as to share Christ's indestructible life. And this transformation is precisely the divine solution to the dilemma Paul now unveils through the revelation of the mystery: "we will not all sleep, but we will all be changed" (15:51). Whether the faithful are living or dead at the time of Christ's second coming, their bodies must be transformed so as to be made incorruptible (15:52–54). The sequence of thought is as follows:

Human Dilemma	(50) *perishable* flesh cannot inherit the *imperishable* kingdom
Divine Answer	(51) we shall all be *changed*
	(52) the dead will be raised *imperishable*
	(53) this *perishable* body must be clothed with *imperishability* (cf. 54)
	(cf. 42) the body is sown in *decay*, it is raised in *imperishability*

Clearly, the plight envisioned in 15:50, as made evident by the solution provided in 15:51–54, is not the physical or fleshly nature of the body, but the mortal body's perishability and slavery to decay. Flesh and blood *in its present perishable state* cannot inherit the kingdom of God. And the answer provided in the revelation of the mystery (15:51) is not the destruction of the mortal flesh, but its transformation to imperishability (15:51–58). Mortal flesh, far from being excluded from this divine, saving action, is the *object* of that action. Flesh and blood are not annihilated, but "raised" (15:52), "transformed" (15:51–52), and "clothed" with imperishability and immortality (15:53–54), and thus fitted to inherit the imperishable kingdom.

The Central Verb for the Resurrection Event in 1 Corinthians 15

The main verb Paul employs for the resurrection event in 1 Corinthians 15 (both the resurrection of Jesus at Easter and the resurrection of the faithful at his coming) is *egeirō*, or "raise" (1 Cor 15:4, 12–17, 20, 29, 32, 35, 42–44, 52). Some scholars hold that the verb *egeirō* is an elastic one, denoting some form of ascension to heavenly life after death, but not necessarily a revival of the earthly, mortal body. Scholars who take this approach generally interpret Paul's affirmation in the chapter that Jesus has been "raised" (15:4, 12–17, 20) to mean that Jesus has been *taken up* into heaven in a celestial form or body discontinuous with his earthly, flesh-and-bones body. On this understanding of the verb, Paul's affirmation that Jesus is "raised" is entirely consistent with the crucified body of Jesus either (on one view) moldering in the grave or (on another view) ceasing to exist, being replaced by a body of ethereal substance.[15] And on this view, Paul's assertion that the faithful in Christ will be "raised" (15:16, 29, 32, 35, 42–44, 52) likewise involves a spiritual *elevation* into heaven that leaves the corpse in the grave.

Surprisingly, given its central place in early Christian language for the resurrection, the verb *egeirō* has received little detailed study. I have recently undertaken such a detailed study, and I will summarize the results of that study here.[16] The verb was a common term of everyday ancient life, and its specialized function as resurrection language grew out of that wider usage. That wider nonresurrection usage provides the key to understanding the meaning of *egeirō* when used to denote resurrection. The significance of this ancient evidence is explosive.

Although it is usually translated by the English verbs "raise" or "rise," the semantic range of *egeirō* is crucially different. Like *egeirō*, these English verbs can be used of "rising to stand" from a reclining position or from the posture of sleep. However, the English verbs also frequently express the wider concept of ascen-

15. Cf. Martin, *The Corinthian Body*, 135; Collins, "Empty Tomb," 111; Engberg-Pedersen, *Cosmology and Self*, 27–28, 37–38.

16. James Ware, "The Resurrection of Jesus in the Pre-Pauline Formula of 1 Cor 15.3–5," *NTS* 60 (2014): 475–98. In that study I provide evidence from the entire range of ancient Greek literature; in this chapter I will confine myself largely to evidence from the New Testament texts, which are accessible to and can be cross-checked by the average reader.

sion or elevation. We speak, for instance, of a spark that "rises" from the flames, of the moon "rising" into the night sky, or of a balloon that "rises" into the air. The Greek verb *egeirō*, however, has a more restricted semantic range, and cannot mean "raise" or "rise" in this wider sense of elevation or ascension. Rather, the Greek verb means to "get up" or "stand up," that is, to raise from a supine to a standing position. Thus the verb is regularly used to denote the raising or rising up of one who has fallen (Matt 12:11; Mark 9:27; Acts 9:8), or of one kneeling or prostrate being raised back to a standing position (Matt 17:7; Luke 11:8; Acts 10:26), or of one sitting who rises to stand (Matt 26:46; Mark 3:3; 10:49; 14:42; Luke 6:8; John 11:29; 13:4; 14:31). The verb is also frequently used of one lying down, very often of one lying sick, who is restored to a standing posture (Matt 8:15; 9:5, 6, 7; Mark 1:31; 2:9, 11, 12; Luke 5:23–24; John 5:8; Acts 3:6–7; James 5:15). In no instance within ancient Greek literature does *egeirō* denote the concept of ascension, elevation, or assumption. Rather, it denotes the action whereby one who is prone, sitting, prostrate, or lying down is *restored to a standing position.*

The use of *egeirō* as resurrection language grows out of the semantic map of the verb sketched above. In resurrection contexts, the verb therefore does not denote that the dead *ascend* or are *assumed* somewhere; rather, the verb signifies that the corpse, lying supine in the grave, *arises to stand* from the tomb. An inscription from ancient Rome (*Inscriptiones Graecae Urbis Romae* 3.1406) provides striking confirmatory evidence of this. The final line of this burial inscription reads *enteuthen outhis apothanein eg[e]iret[ai]* ("no one who has died gets back up from here"). In this inscription, the use of the verb *egeirō* together with the adverb *enteuthen* ("from here") unambiguously indicates the concept of getting up or arising to stand *from the tomb.*

In view of the evidence discussed above, the assumption that *egeirō* can mean "raise" in the sense of elevation or assumption into heaven is excluded. *The very semantics of this ancient Greek verb involves the concept of the mortal body's restoration to life.* Within 1 Corinthians 15, this restoration to life is accompanied by a glorious transformation, from weakness and mortality to glory, power, and imperishability (15:42–44, 52–54; cf. Rom 6:9; Phil 3:21; Col 3:4). But, as our brief synopsis of the semantics of *egeirō* has shown, the subject of this glorious transformation is the once-dead body, which in being "raised" does not *ascend* to heaven, but *arises to stand* from the tomb.

The Resurrection of the Body Elsewhere in Paul

The understanding of resurrection as the reconstitution and transformation of the fleshly body, which we have seen is integral to the structure of Paul's argument in 1 Corinthians 15, is powerfully evident elsewhere in his letters. In Philippians 3:21 it is specifically the present, mortal "body of our lowly state" that is to be transformed to be like Christ's "glorious body." In Romans 8:23 Paul describes eschatological resurrection as "the redemption of our body"—the mortal, fleshly body is not shed or abandoned, but redeemed by God. As Nikolaus Walter notes, the conception in Romans 8:23 involves "not a redemption *from* the body or out of the body, but the salvific *transformation* of bodies."[17] In Romans 8:11, Paul's declaration is unambiguous that the subject that in resurrection is transformed and given imperishable life is the mortal body of flesh and bones: "But if the Spirit of the One who raised Jesus from the dead dwells within you, the One who raised Christ from the dead *will also give life to your mortal bodies* through his Spirit which dwells within you."

The Importance of the Resurrection of the Flesh in Paul's Theology

As we saw in the very beginning of this book, Paul's gospel brought to the ancient world into which it came a new and radically different understanding of the body, physical existence, and the cosmos. The physical body and material existence were not illusory or evil, things to be escaped, as in ancient Hinduism, Buddhism, and Platonic dualism. They were good and God-given, the holy creation of a good creator God. Jesus's bodily resurrection was the ultimate affirmation of creation and its goodness. In contrast with the message of Plato, of Buddha, and of the Hindu sages, which was *world-negating*, Paul's good news of Jesus's resurrection was *world-affirming*. For it affirmed the transcendent value and goodness of *this* world and of *this* body. "The body . . . is for the Lord, and the Lord is for the body. And God both raised up the Lord, and will raise us up by his power" (1 Cor 6:13–14).

And to an ancient world for which death was the everlasting sorrow, unconquerable even by the gods, the resurrection of Jesus's crucified body from the tomb brought the good news of the creator God's victory over death. In Paul's theology, death is the last and great enemy (1 Cor 15:26), an intruder into the good cosmos

---

17. Nikolaus Walter, "Leibliche Auferstehung? Zur Frage der Hellenisierung der Auferweckungshoffnung bei Paulus," in *Paulus, Apostel Jesu Christi*, ed. Michael Trowitzsch (Tübingen: Mohr Siebeck, 1998), 120.

(Rom 5:12), and the negation of creation (1 Cor 15:21–22). But death has now been vanquished by the bodily resurrection of Jesus Christ from the dead (1 Cor 15:54, "Death has been swallowed up in victory!"). In Paul's theology the full outworking and consummation of Christ's resurrection will bring about the renewal of the entire created order (Rom 8:18–25; 1 Cor 15:23–28; Phil 3:20–21). Jesus's resurrection reveals that *the kingdom is the restoration and fulfillment of creation.*

The resurrection is also the fulfillment of the covenant. For in the resurrection of the faithful to the fullness of bodily life, the covenant's promise of *life* to the people of God (Deut 30:15–20; 32:47; Ezek 18; Amos 5:4–7; Zech 14:8) will receive its ultimate fulfillment. And as we saw in chapter 9, in Paul's thought Jesus's resurrection was also the full revelation of the incarnation. For in conquering physical, bodily death, Jesus had done what only the living God could do, revealing himself as "the Son of God in power" (Rom 1:3–4). There is thus a wonderful symmetry in Paul's gospel. The One through whom all things were created (1 Cor 8:6; Col 1:16–17) is the One through whom all things have been renewed in the resurrection. In Jesus's resurrection the creator has reclaimed his creation.

"In the Incarnation creation is fulfilled by God's including himself in it" (Kierkegaard).[18] And Jesus's bodily resurrection *completes* the story of the incarnation, and thus brings creation to its fulfillment. In the resurrection Jesus does not *divest* himself of his human body, born of the Virgin Mary (Rom 1:3–4; Gal 4:4). No, in the resurrection Jesus's body of flesh and bones is *glorified* (Rom 6:4; 2 Cor 3:18; Phil 3:21), and the full outworking of his resurrection will bring about the glorification of the whole creation (Rom 8:21). "The union between God and Nature in the Person of Christ admits no divorce. He will not *go out* of Nature again and she must be glorified in all ways which this miraculous union demands."[19] *The resurrection, in completing the story of the incarnation, fulfills the story of creation.* The resurrection of Jesus's flesh-and-bones body is therefore central to Paul's theology of creation, incarnation, covenant, and kingdom. Consequently, readings of resurrection in Paul as mere transferal to an ethereal or spiritual state fail to comprehend, not a minor detail of Paul's thought, but *the entire narrative of God and creation* that is at the heart of his theology. At the heart of Paul's gospel is the resurrection of the flesh.

---

18. Søren Kierkegaard, *Journals and Papers*, trans. Howard V. Hong and Edna H. Hong (Bloomington: Indiana University Press, 1978), 2:1391.

19. C. S. Lewis, *Miracles: A Preliminary Study* (New York: Macmillan, 1947), 128.

Conclusion: The Easter Gospel of 1 Corinthians 15

Some today believe they find in 1 Corinthians 15 a conception of the resurrection that excludes the earthly, physical body from final salvation. However, close study of Paul's "resurrection chapter" reveals that Paul's gospel proclaimed a bodily resurrection in continuity with the Easter faith evident in the Gospels, the book of Acts, and the historic Christian creeds. The specific way Paul shapes his argument, the structure of the syntax in which his thought is given expression, and the lexical meaning of his key terms reveal that he conceived of resurrection as a tangible, physical event involving the body of flesh and bones. Resurrection in Paul is not an event in which x (the present body) is sown and y (a different body) is raised, but an event in which a single x, which has been sown a perishable x, is raised an imperishable x. Paul in his seed analogy in 15:36–41 uses "flesh" (15:39) and "body" (15:35, 37–38, 40–41) interchangeably to refer to the material body of flesh that will be made alive (15:36) and raised up (15:42–44) by God. The "spiritual body" of 15:44 does not, as so many English readers assume, refer to a body composed of spirit, but to the body of flesh and bones given imperishable life by the Spirit of God. Paul's affirmation that flesh and blood cannot inherit the kingdom of God (15:50), so commonly used as a "proof text" of Paul's denial of the resurrection of the flesh, affirms that the present perishable body must be transformed (15:51) in order to share in Christ's indestructible life (15:52–54). Finally, the very verb that Paul employs for the resurrection event (*egeirō*, or "raise," 15:4, 12–17, 20, 29, 32, 35, 42–44, 52) necessarily involves the conception of the mortal body's restoration to life. In affirming that Jesus has been "raised" (15:4), Paul affirmed the resurrection of Jesus's crucified body from the tomb. And in affirming that the faithful will be "raised" (15:42–44, 52), Paul affirmed that our present perishable bodies will be endowed, through the power of Jesus's resurrection, with imperishable life. In 1 Corinthians 15, as in the four Gospels and Acts, the resurrection is understood as the miraculous revivification of the mortal body of flesh and bones, and its transformation so as to be imperishable.

That Jesus's resurrection, and the future resurrection of those who belong to him, is a resurrection of the *flesh* is of crucial importance in Paul's thought. As we saw in chapter 9, both the gods of ancient pagan worship and the philosophical divinities were regarded by their devotees as powerless before the unconquerable power of death. By rising physically and bodily from the tomb, Jesus had conquered death, the last and great enemy (1 Cor 15:26); revealed himself as the true living God; and replaced the everlasting sorrow of the pagan world into which Paul's gospel came with the joyous hope of the resurrection. Moreover, Jesus's resurrection is in Paul's theology the ultimate affirmation of creation and its goodness. In the resurrection Jesus did not abandon his body, assumed in the incarnation, but rose again gloriously in the same body in which he was crucified, in order to conquer physical death and restore the whole material creation. The glorification of Jesus's body in his resurrection is the firstfruits of the glorification and final perfection of the whole created order (1 Cor 15:20–28). *The resurrection, in completing the story of the incarnation, fulfills the story of creation.* The resurrection of the body is at the heart of Paul's gospel, for at the heart of Paul's gospel is the restoration of creation.

Chapter Eleven

The New Life

I n the previous two chapters, we have seen that Paul understood Jesus's resurrection as the new and ultimate act of the creator God to conquer death and renew the created order. *The kingdom is the restoration and fulfillment of creation.* But we have also seen that the promise of the kingdom of God is fulfilled through Jesus's conquest of death in a way that involves two distinct phases or stages. The kingdom of God that will come in its fullness on the day of the Lord is already present now through the power of Jesus's resurrection. This distinction between the two stages of the kingdom is, we saw in part 2, one of the four fundamental relations that structure Paul's thought:

Inaugurated Kingdom

Consummated Kingdom

In the two prior chapters we focused on the consummation of the kingdom; in this and the following chapter we focus on the inaugurated kingdom. For Paul believed that the life-creating and creation-renewing power of Jesus's resurrection, although it would receive its full outworking at Jesus's advent in the day of Christ, was *already* at work in those who believe. Through his mighty, saving resurrection Christ Jesus has bestowed a new life, transforming the heart and liberating from the power of sin, and in his teaching he has given a new law to guide that new life. In chapters 7 and 8 we saw how Paul understood the work of Christ as the fulfillment of the Old Testament's covenantal promises of a new and ultimate work of divine atonement, of a heart-renewing new covenant, and of the salvation-creating righteousness of God, empowering the faithful in Christ to live out the law's righteous ways. But Paul also understood this saving and justifying work of Christ within the faithful as the outworking of a supernatural new life unleashed by his resurrection. This new life bestowed by Christ is the subject of this chapter.

Creation's Renewal Now Come in Christ

The understanding of Jesus's resurrection as the work of the creator God to restore and renew the creation is at the heart of Paul's majestic prayer for his readers in Ephesians 1:

> [17]I pray that the God of our Lord Jesus Christ, the Father of glory, may give to you a spirit of wisdom and revelation in your knowledge of him, [18]the eyes of your heart illumined, that you may know what is the hope of his calling, what are the riches of the glory of his inheritance among the saints, [19]and what is the immeasurable greatness of his power toward us who believe, in conformity with the outworking of the might of his power, [20]which he worked in Christ, when he raised him from the dead and enthroned him at his right hand in the heavens, [21]far above all rule and authority and power and dominion, and every name that is named, not only in this age, but also in the age to come. (Eph 1:17–21)

Within this prayer for the illumination of his readers, the first of Paul's three petitions focuses on the coming *resurrection of their bodies* (1:18, "the hope of his calling"), and the second on the *renewed cosmos* they are to inherit (1:18, "the riches of the glory of his inheritance among the saints"). The third petition is a prayer that they may grasp the immeasurable greatness of God's life-creating power "in conformity with the outworking of the might of his power, which he worked in Christ, when he raised him from the dead" (1:19–20). Paul's petition employs the precise phrase "the might of his power," found elsewhere only in Isaiah 40:26, in order to recall that prophet's celebrated description of the one creator God in Isaiah 40. Paul's point is that the resurrection of Jesus was a new outworking of the same unique divine energy that created all things. Jesus's resurrection on the third day was an act of *new creation*.

This conception of Jesus's resurrection as the beginning of the new creation is also evident in Paul's practice (which he shared with the other apostles) of worship on "the first day of the week," that is, Sunday (1 Cor 16:2; cf. Acts 20:7–12; Rev 1:10). This astounding change of the chief day of worship from the Sabbath (Saturday), the Jewish celebration of God's work of creation, to Sunday, the day on which Jesus rose from the dead, reflected an astounding theological claim: the true creator God had now acted *in a work of life-creating divine power transcending the original act of creation.* For in Jesus's resurrection, the creator's glorious restoration of creation has begun.

This third petition of Paul's prayer, that his readers may know the power of Jesus's resurrection (Eph 1:19–20), has a *present* as well as a future dimension. For in Paul's theology, the life-creating power of Christ's resurrection, the same divine energy that brought all things into being out of nothing, is already at work in those united with Christ in baptism, leading to an inner transformation of mind and heart in the present through the power of the Holy Spirit: "you were buried with him in baptism, through which you were raised to life with him, through your faith in the work of God who raised him from the dead" (Col 2:12). This is the reason for Paul's massive use elsewhere of the language of *new creation* in his description of present life in Christ. "If anyone is in Christ, there is a new creation. The old things have passed away; behold, all things have been made new!" (2 Cor 5:17). This is why Paul uses the word *poiēma*, used in ancient Christian literature only of divine creation, to describe those united to Christ as "God's *work of creation*, created in Christ Jesus for good works" (Eph 2:10). In them the *divine image*, given in creation (Gen 1) but effaced through the Fall (Gen 3), is in process of being restored (Rom 8:29; 2 Cor 3:17–18; Eph 4:20–24; Col 3:9–11). In this renewal the division between Jew and gentile has been abolished, that God "might *create* in him one *new humanity*" (Eph 2:15). "Circumcision does not matter, nor does uncircumcision matter—it is a *new creation!*" (Gal 6:15). According to Paul's third petition, the life-creating energy of Christ's resurrection ("the immeasurable greatness of his power toward us who believe") is *already* at work in power in those united to him by faith.

Paul's powerful prayer in Ephesians 1:17–21 goes on to assert that, through his resurrection and subsequent ascension, Jesus has been exalted far above all "rule and authority and power and dominion" (1:21), that is, demonic powers who oppose God and enslave humanity (cf. Rom 8:38–39; 1 Cor 2:6–8; 15:24–28; 2 Cor 4:4). Through the cross and resurrection of his Son, God has trampled down the power of Satan and freed those united to Christ from his enslavement, "rescuing us from the power of darkness, and bringing us into the kingdom of his beloved Son" (Col 1:13). "Where Satan is bound, humanity is set free" (Irenaeus, *Against Heresies* 5.21.3). By adding "and every name that is named" (Eph 1:21), Paul identifies these satanic powers with the varied gods and goddesses within the gentile world, behind whose worship, Paul asserts, lay the power of these malevolent demonic beings, leading human beings into falsehood, evil, and destruction (cf. 1 Cor 10:19–21). Through the resurrection, the God of Israel has triumphed over these false gods, and the demonic powers that enslave humanity through their worship.

It is precisely at this point in Paul's prayer that one more crucial dimension of his theology of Jesus's resurrection opens clearly into view. According to Paul's prayer, the name of Jesus is above "every name that is named" (Eph 1:21). Within Paul's Jewish context, the one who has the name above every name that is named can only be the creator God of Israel. But in Paul's prayer, the one to whom the name that is above every name belongs is *Jesus*. Jesus is the creator God come in the flesh. His incarnation is the fulfillment of the promised coming and abiding presence of YHWH, and his cross and resurrection the fulfillment of YHWH's promised mighty acts in Zion at his coming. This startling incarnational Christology gives Paul's entire prayer its power and coherence. Only as One who is not a mere creature, but the author of creation, could Jesus perform the divine work of *new creation* in those who believe (1:19–20). Only the creator can renew the creation. And only as One who is not a mere servant or emissary of God, but the divine Son of God in the flesh, could Jesus triumph over the creaturely demonic powers that enslave humanity through the false gods of the nations and their worship (1:21).

This promise of restoration and renewal was unique in the ancient world. The philosophers and sages we have discussed throughout this book offered their disciples a *new self-understanding*, leading to a transformed conception of the world and of one's own identity. Come to the true understanding, they said, to discover *who you really are*. Paul's gospel, by contrast, offered not only a change in self-understanding but also a *miraculous new identity* through supernatural union with the living God. Come to Jesus Christ, Paul said, to become a *new creation in Christ* (2 Cor 5:17). Paul's gospel addressed a deep and mysterious human need the philosophers and sages could not satisfy—the need for liberation and transformation. In Paul's theology, the need is not to discover the person you are, marred by the Fall and sin, but to become the person you were created to be, by being made new and set free in Christ. According to Paul's gospel, paradoxically the self "arrives at his own identity through the mystical union with the Spirit of Christ: 'I live, yet no longer I, but Christ lives in me' (Gal 2:20)."[1]

As we saw in chapter 8, Paul uses the key term "justification" when speaking of this renewal. *Justification* involves the process whereby, through the gift of God's own life-giving and salvation-creating righteousness, believers are both forgiven of their sins (*imputed* righteousness) and set free from the power and dominion of sin (*infused* righteousness). But Paul employs another key term as well, "sanctification." Unlike justification, which embraces both forgiveness of sin and liberation from the power of sin, the closely related term "sanctification" focuses entirely on this latter element of moral formation and renewal. It is thus a subset of justification. It involves the process whereby believers are transformed through the indwelling Holy Spirit into the image of Christ, that they may share in and reflect the holiness of God (Rom 6:19–22; 1 Cor 1:30; 1 Thess 4:3–8; 2 Thess 2:13–14; 1 Tim 2:15).

---

1. Adriana Destro and Mauro Pesce, "Self, Identity and Body in Paul and John," in *Self, Soul, and Body in Religious Experience*, ed. Albert I. Baumgarten, J. Assmann, and G. G. Stroumsa (Leiden: Brill, 1998), 191.

The true significance of the Pauline term "sanctification" comes out with especial clarity when we consider it in light of the word it *replaced*. The ubiquitous term for ethical and character formation in the ancient moral philosophers was *aretē*, that is, "moral excellence" or "virtue." Paul (with one exception) avoids this word like the plague. In its place he substitutes "sanctification." This is a word first found in this ethical sense in Paul's letters, and this usage may in fact have been coined by Paul himself. This word, normally translated "sanctification" or "holiness," is the Greek word *hagiasmos*, which means etymologically "the process of being made holy (by God)." In contrast with *aretē*, Paul's term envisions a different *goal* of the process of moral formation—not merely human virtue but a sharing in God's holiness. Even more crucially, Paul's term envisions an entirely different *means* of moral transformation—the power of the living God, at work in those who believe through supernatural union with the risen Christ.

A Sacramental New Life

In Paul's theology (and practice), persons enter into this new life through baptism, a onetime initiatory immersion in water (Rom 6:1–11; 1 Cor 6:9–11; 10:1–4; 12:12–13; Gal 3:26–29; 4:4–6; 5:25–27; Col 2:11–12; Titus 3:4–7). This baptismal washing was followed by an anointing with oil (2 Cor 1:21–22; 2:14–16; Eph 1:13–14; 4:30; cf. 1 John 2:20; 2:27).[2] On the first day of the week (Sunday) Christ followers gathered to partake in the Eucharist or "Lord's Supper" (1 Cor 11:17–34; cf. Acts 20:7–12). Water, oil, bread, wine, bodily immersion, bodily anointing, physical eating and drinking—some find it surprising that this new life should be conveyed by physical elements and actions such as these. But as we have seen, Paul's gospel is the good news of the creator, and of the God-given and good cosmos. The center of that gospel is the incarnation, whereby the Son of God took on our flesh, and rose in that flesh from the dead, sanctifying the entire physical creation in a new and ultimate way. And his gospel proclaimed the good news of the coming resurrection of our bodies, and a future transformation of the entire physical cosmos. This incorporation of the cosmos, matter, and the body into the new life in Christ through the bodily acts of baptism, anointing, and Eucharist is in striking coherence with Paul's gospel.

2. Cf. Wayne A. Meeks, *The First Urban Christians*, 2nd ed. (New Haven: Yale University Press, 2003), 151, who argues convincingly that these Pauline passages presuppose an actual physical anointing with oil. For this practice in the early church, see Tertullian, *Baptism* 7–8; *The Resurrection of the Flesh* 8; *Against Marcion* 1.14; Hippolytus, *The Apostolic Tradition* 21; Cyprian, *Letters* 70.2. This practice is continued by Catholic and Orthodox Christians today. Orthodox Christians refer to this anointing as the sacrament of *chrismation*, Catholic Christians as the sacrament of *confirmation*.

These sacramental acts provided a point of connection with the religious rites of the pagan world into which Paul's gospel came, for these rites also incorporated physical elements and actions. Paul points to this connection in 1 Corinthians 10:21 when he contrasts "the *table* of the Lord" (i.e., the Eucharist) with "the *table* of demons" (i.e., the sacrifices made to the varied pagan gods).[3] But the striking difference between the sacraments of the early church and these pagan rituals is that the material actions of the first Christ followers were grounded in *historical events*—Jesus's passion, death, and resurrection from the dead—and linked the worshiper to those events.[4] Moreover, in Paul's theology the church's sacramental actions do more than simply commemorate these saving events. Through baptism those who believe enter into a saving participatory union with Jesus Christ and his death and resurrection, leading to a transformation of life: "Or are you unaware that whosoever of us were baptized into Christ Jesus were baptized into his death? Therefore we were buried with him through baptism into death, in order that, just as Christ was raised from the dead through the glory of the Father, we too might walk in newness of life" (Rom 6:3–4). The Lord's Supper is in Paul's thought a miraculous communion in the body and blood of Christ: "The cup of blessing which we bless, is it not a sharing in the blood of Christ? The bread which we break, is it not a sharing in the body of Christ?" (1 Cor 10:16). For Paul this sharing in the cup and loaf is "a real 'participation' in Christ's body and blood and thereby in Christ, who died for us and is present in the Lord's Supper."[5] In their union, through these sacramental actions of baptism and Eucharist, with the incarnate and risen Son of God, the people of God in Christ fulfill the prophetic promise of a new temple in which YHWH himself would dwell in the time of his kingdom (1 Cor 3:16–17; 2 Cor 6:16; Eph 2:21–22; cf. Isa 56:6–7; Jer 3:16–17; Ezek 37:26–28; 40–48).

3. Because of these connections, some scholars in the past have claimed that the practices of baptism and the Eucharist were derived from the pagan mystery religions. But this false trail has now been almost universally abandoned; see Leander E. Keck, *Paul and His Letters*, 2nd ed. (Philadelphia: Fortress, 1988), 10–11; Frank J. Matera, *God's Saving Grace: A Pauline Theology* (Grand Rapids: Eerdmans, 2012), 171–72n14; and Anthony C. Thiselton, *The Living Paul: An Introduction to the Apostle's Life and Thought* (Downers Grove: InterVarsity, 2009), 120.

4. Cf. Bernard J. Cooke, *Christian Sacraments and Christian Personality* (New York: Doubleday, 1968), 224.

5. Gunther Bornkamm, "Lord's Supper and Church in Paul," in *Early Christian Experience* (London: SCM, 1969), 146. Cf. Joseph Fitzmyer, *Pauline Theology: A Brief Sketch* (Englewood Cliffs, NJ: Prentice-Hall, 1967), 74: "One cannot argue away the realism of the identity of Christ with this Eucharistic food in Paul's teaching, even if Paul does not explain how this identity is achieved."

The Transformation of the Intellect

According to Paul, idolatry and disconnection from God darken the intellect: "you must not walk as the gentiles walk, in the futility of their *intellect* (Greek: *nous*), darkened in their *understanding* (*dianoia*), alienated from the life of God because of the *lack of knowledge* (*agnoia*) within them" (Eph 4:17–18; cf. Rom 1:28). Therefore, in the new life of sanctification not only the heart but also the mind must be transformed: "do not be conformed to this age, but be transformed by the renewal of your *intellect* (*nous*)" (Rom 12:2). "Be renewed in the spirit of your *intellect* (*nous*)" (Eph 4:23). "This I pray, that your love may abound yet more and more in full *knowledge* and all *intellectual perception*" (Phil 1:9). Clearly the moral transformation to which Paul calls his readers has a strongly cognitive, intellectual dimension. For Paul, comprehension is an essential part of Christian discipleship.[6]

Moreover, Paul envisages his own letters as having a *performative* role in this process. It is striking that Paul in his letters not only gives commands but also normally tells *why* the commands should be followed. He weaves intricate theological arguments and expects his readers to follow along. In the hortatory section of Romans, where Paul emphasizes the renewal of the intellect (Rom 12:1–2), he explicitly envisages his own letter to the Romans as playing a role in this renewal (15:14–15). We are here in touch with a core element of Paul's own understanding of the function of his epistles, which should guide our own reading of his letters: their role in *the transformation of the intellect within the new life of Christian discipleship*. As we will see in the next chapter, one way in which Paul's letters perform this function is through the transmission, interpretation, and application of the "law of Christ," the new way of living given by Jesus corresponding to the new life he has bestowed.

Conclusion: The Creation-Renewing Power of Easter

According to Paul's gospel, Jesus's resurrection was a new work of life-creating divine power transcending even the original act of creation. Moreover, the life-creating power of Jesus's resurrection, although it will receive its full outworking in the bodily resurrection of the faithful at Christ's second advent, is already at work in the present in those united to Christ in baptism, freeing them from demonic enslavement and the dominion of sin. Paul's language of new creation to describe

---

6. See Gunther Bornkamm, "Faith and Reason in Paul," in *Early Christian Experience*, 29–46 (esp. 35–42).

this renewal reflects the conception that the power at work in the faithful through Jesus's resurrection is the same divine energy that brought all things into being out of nothing. The kingdom is the restoration and fulfillment of creation.

In contrast with the ancient philosophers and sages, Paul's gospel offered not only a new self-understanding but also a miraculous new identity through union with Christ. Paul's gospel addressed a deep need of the human heart that the philosophers did not even pretend to satisfy—the longing of the heart to be forgiven, transformed, and set free. The communication of this new life through the bodily acts of baptism and Eucharist reflects the God-given character of all creation, and the sanctification of matter and the cosmos through the incarnation of the Son of God and through his bodily resurrection from the dead. The moral transformation brought by this new life had a strongly cognitive dimension, requiring not only a new heart but also a renewed intellect, and Paul understood his own letters as having a key role in this process. In bestowing this new life, the Son of God reveals his divine glory—for only the creator could renew the creation.

Chapter Twelve

The New Law

We saw in the previous chapter that the new life in Christ, the outworking of the creation-renewing power of his resurrection, brings about a moral renewal, whereby those who belong to Christ are set free from slavery to sin. And in chapter 8 we saw how Paul described the faithful as empowered to fulfill the righteous ways of God at the heart of the law of Moses (Rom 3:31; 8:4). But although Christ followers *fulfill* the righteous requirements of the law of Moses, they do not *follow* the law of Moses. They follow the new law of Christ.

The Law of Christ

Paul in his epistles gives commands (Greek: *parangellō*, 1 Thess 4:11; 2 Thess 3:4; *parangelia*, 1 Thess 4:2; *entolē*, 1 Cor 7:19; 14:37) and instructions (*diatassō*, 1 Cor 7:17; 9:14; *diatagē*, Rom 13:2; *thelēma tou theou*, Rom 12:2; Eph 6:6; 1 Thess 4:3; *thelēma tou kuriou*, Eph 5:17) for how the new life in Christ is to be lived out. But in so doing, Paul does not understand himself as transmitting the old law, the law of Moses, which has been abolished: "[Christ] having abolished the law of commandments with its decrees" (Eph 2:15; cf. Rom 7:2, 6; 2 Cor 2:14; 3:11, 13, 14). Rather, Paul teaches and transmits a new law, "the law of Christ" (Gal 6:2). To be sure, the interpretation of this phrase in Galatians 6:2 is controversial.[1] But the most natural reading of the genitive "of Christ" (*tou Christou*) here is as a genitive of source or origin—it is the law *given by Christ*.[2] This is confirmed by 1 Corinthians 9:20–21, where Paul's contrast of "under the law [of Moses]" (9:20, *hypo nomon*) with "under the law of Christ" (9:21, *ennomos Christou*) indicates

1. For discussion, see John M. G. Barclay, *Obeying the Truth: A Study of Paul's Ethics in Galatians* (Edinburgh: T. & T. Clark , 1988), 125–35; Femi Adeyemi, "The New Covenant Law and the Law of Christ," *BSac* 163 (2006): 438–52; Frank Thielman, *Paul and the Law: A Contextual Approach* (Downers Grove: InterVarsity, 1994), 140–44.

2. Rightly Adeyemi, "New Covenant Law," 439–44; Thielman, *Paul and the Law*, 141.

that "the law of Christ" is the law given by Christ. In Paul's theology, no less than in Matthew's Gospel, the Teacher and Lawgiver for the new life in Christ is Christ himself.

That believers follow the new law of Christ, and not the law of Moses, is evident in another way. When Paul speaks of the faithful (see chapter 8 above) as fulfilling the law of Moses through the transforming power of the new life in Christ, he regularly uses qualifying circumlocutions that do not refer to the law itself, but refer to the *substance* and *intent* of the law (Rom 2:14, *ta tou nomou*, "the things of the law"; 2:15, *to ergon tou nomou*, "the work required by the law"; 2:26, *ta dikaiōmata tou nomou*, "the law's righteous ways"; 8:4, *to dikaiōma tou nomou*, "the righteousness called for in the law"). In this way Paul carefully distinguishes between the law of Moses, from which his converts are free but fulfill in its essence, and the law of Christ, which his converts are to follow as their norm and guide. In one sense the law is not "abolished" (*katargeō*) but "confirmed" by Christ (Rom 3:31). For in obeying the law of Christ, the faithful fulfill the true intent of the law of Moses (Rom 2:13–16, 26–27; 13:8–10; Gal 5:14). But in another sense the law is "abolished" (*katargeō*) for the followers of Christ (Rom 7:2, 6; 2 Cor 3:7, 11, 13; Eph 2:15). For they are not subject to the law of Moses, but to the law of Christ.

Paul models this Christian life under the law of Christ for his followers when he describes himself as "not under the law" (1 Cor 9:20), that is, the law of Moses, yet "not without the law of God, but under the law of Christ" (9:21). Here "the law of Christ has become God's law in place of the law of Moses."[3] Paul can therefore in one magnificent formulation describe the Christian life as free from the law of Moses, but guided by the commands of God: "Circumcision is nothing, and uncircumcision is nothing, but the keeping of the commands of God" (1 Cor 7:19). The "commands of God" are the law of Christ.

Here again Paul's divine Christology is evident, for the only one who could replace the old law is the One who gave it. When he gives the new law for the new covenant, Jesus's role does not correspond to the role of Moses under the old covenant, but to the role of YHWH. And therefore the law of Christ is infinitely superior to the law of Moses, for it has not been given by God through a mediator, but by the incarnate Son of God himself (see Gal 3:19–20; 2 Cor 3:4–18). The new law of Christ brings to fulfillment the promise in Isaiah 33:22 regarding the coming kingdom of God: "YHWH is our deliverer, YHWH is our lawgiver, YHWH is our King, he will save us."

The law of Christ is transmitted through the apostolic teaching. Therefore Paul can describe his moral instruction as "the commands we gave you through the Lord

---

3. Thielman, *Paul and the Law*, 141.

Jesus" (1 Thess 4:2). The words "through the Lord Jesus" (*dia tou kuriou Iesou*) are not equivalent to "in the Lord Jesus," and can hardly mean that the Lord is Paul's intermediary. Rather, they must be understood as commands given *by the direction and authority of the Lord Jesus*. These commands are the law of Christ (1 Cor 7:19; 9:21; Gal 6:2). Paul's apostolic role in his moral exhortation is therefore to *transmit*, *interpret*, and *apply* the "law of Christ," the new way of life taught by Jesus.

A full analysis of Paul's ethical teaching is far beyond the scope of this little book. We will focus here on just two major areas of Paul's moral teaching: the Pauline ethic of love, and Paul's teaching regarding marriage and sexual morality. I have chosen to focus on these two areas because of the importance of both in Paul's moral instruction, and the keen interest in (and frequent misunderstandings of) the latter aspect of Paul's ethical teaching among contemporary readers of Paul.

A Revolution of Love

The command to love is at the heart of Paul's ethics (e.g., Rom 13:8–10; Gal 5:13–14). The source of this teaching of Paul is the teaching of Jesus. Matthew's Gospel narrates the encounter between Jesus and an expert in the law of Moses:

> And one of them, an expert in the law, questioned him, putting him to the test: "Teacher, what is the greatest commandment in the law?" And he said to him, "'You shall love the Lord your God with all your heart and with all your soul and with all your intellect.' This is the great and first commandment. And the second is like it: 'You shall love your neighbor as yourself.' On these two commands all the law and the prophets depend." (Matt 22:35–40)

Scholars refer to Jesus's response as "the twofold love command." It was indeed new in one sense: no one prior to this had brought together the command to love God (Deut 6:5) and the command to love one's neighbor (Lev 19:18) in this way. But in another sense it was not new, for the twin themes of love of God (Deut 6:5; Josh 22:5; Ps 31:33) and love of neighbor (Lev 19:18; Jer 7:5–7; Amos 5:15) fill the Jewish Scriptures. Jesus's twofold love command therefore did not offer a new teaching so much as a sort of copingstone on the teaching of the whole Old Testament. As we will see, Jesus's twofold love command was at the heart of the law of Christ that Paul proclaimed to the gentile world—and here it would be new and startling indeed.

Love for God

It is interesting that 1 Corinthians, the letter of Paul that contains the densest concentration of references to love for God (1 Cor 2:9; 8:3; 16:22), also contains Paul's "love chapter" (1 Cor 13)—Paul's fullest exposition of love to neighbor. The letter as a whole thus transmits and illustrates Jesus's *twofold* love command.

But how would the command to love God have impacted Paul's ancient gentile readers? The conception of love for the gods was generally rejected by the philosophers. As Aristotle put it, "It would be inappropriate for anyone to say he loves Zeus" (*Magna moralia* 2.11.6; cf. *Nicomachean Ethics* 8.7.4–6). But the conception was not altogether unknown in the wider ancient world. What would have surprised Paul's gentile readers was not so much the language of love as something even larger that framed that language and made it distinctive. It involves a crucial aspect of Paul's moral exhortation that is sometimes left out of discussion of Pauline ethics but would have immediately struck any ancient hearer as startling and unique.

In the ancient world into which Paul's gospel came, the philosophers included one's duties to the gods, which they called *eusebeia* ("worship" or "piety"), as part of their moral instruction. But they classed this among the *subordinate* virtues rather than as a major element of the moral life. The Platonists defined *eusebeia*, or "piety," as "just activity in regard to the gods" (*dikaiosunē peri theous*, Ps.-Plato, *Definitions* 412c) and classed it among the many forms of the cardinal virtue "justice." The Stoics defined it as "knowledge of how to worship the gods" (*episteme theon therapeias*, Sextus Empiricus, *Against the Mathematicians* 9.123) and classed it as one of many forms of the cardinal virtue "knowledge." Both for the philosopher and the common person, one's relationship to the gods was but one subordinate concern of the moral life.

The centrality of God in Paul's ethical teaching is in striking contrast. Paul's focus in his moral teaching on the love of God (Rom 5:5–8; 8:35–39; 2 Cor 5:14–21; Eph 2:4–7; 2 Thess 2:16–17), communion with God (1 Cor 6:12–20; Gal 2:19–20; Phil 3:8–11), hope in God (1 Cor 15:1–58; Gal 5:5–6; Eph 1:15–20), and imitation of God (1 Cor 11:1; Eph 5:1–2; Phil 2:5–11; 1 Thess 1:6) is so pervasive and central that citing all the relevant passages in his letters would be impossible. In addition, Paul's ethical exhortation is filled with a striking effusion of the language of praise, prayer, thanksgiving, and worship (only a few examples—Rom 1:18–25; 4:17–25; 12:1–2; 15:7–13, 30–33; Phil 1:9–11; 3:2–3; 4:6–7; 1 Thess 3:9–13; 5:16–18). And in Paul the goal of the whole moral life is "to please God" (1 Thess 4:1; cf. Rom 12:1–2; 2 Cor 5:9). For the moral philosophers, the gods were on the periphery of the moral life. In Paul's letters, God is "all in all" (Col 3:11). This centrality of God within morality, this centrality of the divine-human relationship within human life, is nothing short of a revolution in ethics. Love for God is now at the center of all of life. In Paul's teaching, love for God is indeed, as Jesus taught, "the *great* and *first* commandment" (Matt 22:38).

In the pagan world the very word *eusebeia* ("worship" or "piety") carried with it the concept discussed above of the "compartmentalization" of the divine-human relationship to one subordinate area of human life and ethics. This readily explains the striking fact that Paul in his undisputed letters never uses the word *eusebeia*. For Paul's purpose was to replace the former understanding of his converts with a new way of life focused on God. However, in Paul's Pastoral Epistles (1 Timothy, 2 Timothy, and Titus) we see a very different strategy. There *eusebeia* (piety) and its cognates are frequent, and play an important role in the theological vocabulary of these letters (1 Tim 2:2, 10; 3:16; 4:7–8; 5:4; 6:3–6; 2 Tim 2:16; 3:5, 12; Titus 1:1; 2:12). This difference in theological vocabulary between the Pastoral Epistles and Paul's other letters is one of the major reasons why many scholars reject Pauline authorship of these letters. The Pastorals, they say, by taking up the term *eusebeia*, compromise Paul's radical gospel, reducing it to the prosaic outlines of ancient conventional wisdom.

But in the Pastoral Letters the word *eusebeia* is in fact used in a radical and revolutionary way. For in the Pastoral Epistles *eusebeia*, or "piety," is not a human virtue, but is a supernatural gift bestowed through *union with Christ* (1 Tim 3:16; 2 Tim 3:5, 12; Titus 2:11–14). Moreover, it is not compartmentalized, but *embraces all of life* (1 Tim 2:2, 10; 3:16; 4:7–8; 2 Tim 3:12; Titus 1:1; 2:11–12). It is "the distinctive title for the sum of Christian behavior."[4] In their use of *eusebeia*, the Pastoral Letters are not doing something prosaic, safe, or conformist, but are doing something radical, subversive, and countercultural—co-opting ancient ethical vocabulary into a Christian framework. The Pastorals transform, "baptize," "Christianize" the word *eusebeia* so that it now expresses the conception of the centrality of God in the human moral life. The ancient Greek term for "worship" now embraces all of ethics and all of life! The theological *vocabulary* is very different from Paul's other letters, but the *thought* is strikingly and unmistakably Pauline. This is one of many reasons why, as I mentioned in the introduction, I see a collaboration of theological minds at work in the Pastoral Letters—that of Paul, and that of a Pauline coworker authorized by Paul to write and imbued with his theology.

There is one more aspect of love toward God in Paul's letters that opens up another crucial dimension of his thought. The letter to the Ephesians closes like

---

4. Hermann Cremer, *Biblico-Theological Lexicon of New Testament Greek*, 4th ed. (Edinburgh: T. & T. Clark, 1895), 525.

this: "May grace be with all those who love our Lord Jesus Christ with an imperishable love" (Eph 6:24). We see here once again the ancient Jewish context of Paul's gospel, in the absolutely central place of God and love for God in the lives of his people. We are reminded of many other passages in ancient Jewish literature, such as the conclusion of one of the Psalms of Solomon: "May your mercy, Lord, be upon all those who love you" (4.25). But in the Pauline passage there is a striking difference. For in Ephesians 6:24, this love is directed toward "*our Lord Jesus Christ.*" We meet here the conception that is at the very heart of Paul's theology—the incarnation. "Hear, O Israel! The Lord our God is one Lord. And you shall love the Lord your God with all your heart, with all your soul, and with all your strength" (Deut 6:4–5). The one Lord (cf. Deut 6:4) whom the Christians at Ephesus are to love with all their heart, soul, and strength (cf. Deut 6:5) is the Lord Jesus Christ.

Love of Neighbor

Following Jesus's teaching in the twofold love command, Paul teaches that love for one's neighbor fulfills the whole law: "for the whole law has been fulfilled in one word, in the command 'you shall love your neighbor as yourself'" (Gal 5:14). This *command* of love, as an act of the will and not personal inclination, would have been new to Paul's gentile converts.[5] But what would have been most startling was the way Paul grounded this exhortation to human love in *God's* love revealed in the cross of Christ: "Be imitators of God, as his beloved children, and walk in love, as Christ loved us and gave himself for us, as an offering and a sacrifice to God for a sweet fragrance" (Eph 5:1–2).[6] As we saw in chapter 7, in both ancient myth and ancient philosophy the gods could have nothing to do with suffering and death, and the very nature of divinity precluded self-sacrifice. To this world Paul's gospel brought the astounding news that the Son of God had become human in order to undergo suffering, crucifixion, and death for our salvation. Within Paul's thought, this *divine* love becomes in turn the pattern or model for *human* love. It is striking that in the Old Testament the concept of *imitation of God* has little or no place, but in Paul's letters it plays an important role. The reason is simple but profound: the divine model has now come in the incarnate Son of God. Thus in Paul's letters, imitation of God is always imitation of *Christ* (1 Cor 11:1; 1 Thess 1:6), and of his

---

5. See the classic discussion in Cremer, *Biblico-Theological Lexicon*, 14–17.

6. See the helpful discussion in Frank J. Matera, *God's Saving Grace: A Pauline Theology* (Grand Rapids: Eerdmans, 2012), 176–77.

self-giving to the point of death on a cross (Rom 15:1–7; Eph 5:1–2, 25–33; Phil 2:5–11).[7] In Paul, *the cross is the foundation of the command to love.*

As a result, the self-sacrificial virtue of love assumes within Paul's ethics a central place that the virtue of love or friendship (which the ancients called *philia*) never had in ancient philosophy. So revolutionary is the conception that, to express it, the first Christians, Paul among them, generally eschewed the time-honored word *philia* as inadequate. Instead, they adopted a previously little-used word, *agapē*. They made this word central to their proclamation—*all* the New Testament passages cited in this chapter (except one) use the word *agapē* or its cognates rather than *philia*. And they invested the word *agapē* with this new significance: an unconditional, sacrificial love that comes from God, was revealed in the cross of Christ, and is henceforth to be the way of life for all Christians.

Marriage and Sexuality

In Paul's moral exhortation to his churches, sexual morality is regularly on the "front burner" (e.g., 1 Cor 5:1–13; 6:9–11, 12–20; Eph 4:17–19; 5:3–7; Col 3:5–7; 1 Thess 4:1–8). It is an important—and frequently misunderstood—element of his moral teaching. The thousand and one contemporary misunderstandings of this aspect of Paul's ethical teaching depend upon two false assumptions. The first is that Paul emphasized such things because of a negative view of the physical world, human embodiment, and sexuality. As the reader of this book already knows, this claim is far wide of the mark. As we saw in part 1, the foundation of Paul's theology is the creator God, and the God-given and good creation. The human body, including its sexual differentiation as male and female, is the direct creative work of a holy creator, and thus endowed with an intrinsic goodness and sacredness. In contrast with ancient philosophical teachings that located human personhood within the soul and regarded the body as a mere instrument, in Pauline anthropology the body is an integral aspect of the fullness of the human being. Moreover, it is at the heart of Paul's gospel that the creator himself has assumed a human body, sanctifying human embodiment in a new and ultimate way (cf. Eph 5:23, "he himself is the savior of the body"). Paul's prohibitions of certain kinds of sexual conduct are therefore not given because the body is *bad*, but because the body is so *good*. "The body is not for sexual immorality but for the Lord, and the Lord is for the body" (1 Cor 6:13).

---

7. See Stephen E. Fowl, *The Story of Christ in the Ethics of Paul*, JSNTSup 36 (Sheffield: Sheffield Academic Press, 1990).

The second false assumption is an understandable one, but is equally misleading. Readers naturally assume that Paul and his first hearers shared a common conception of marriage, and that this was the foundation for Paul's moral instructions to them regarding sexual morality. But in reality Paul's gospel brought to its ancient hearers a new and revolutionary conception of marriage, of human sexuality, and of the human person. It was a crucial aspect of the "good news" Paul had for them.

The source of Paul's startling new teaching on marriage was the teaching of Jesus. The Gospel of Mark narrates Jesus's encounter with certain Pharisees:

> [2]And Pharisees came to him and were asking him if it is permissible for a man to divorce his wife, putting him to the test. [3]And he answered and said to them, "What did Moses command you?" [4]And they said, "Moses permitted a man to write a certificate of divorce and divorce his wife." [5]But Jesus said to them, "Because of the hardness of your hearts he wrote you this command. [6]But from the beginning of creation 'God made them male and female.' [7]'For this reason a man shall leave his father and his mother and be joined to his wife, [8]and the two shall become one flesh.' So then they are no longer two, but one flesh. [9]Therefore what God has yoked together, a human being must not separate." [10]And in the house the disciples were asking him again about this. [11]And he said to them, "Whoever divorces his wife and marries another is committing adultery against her, [12]and if she herself divorces her husband and marries another, she is committing adultery." (Mark 10:2–12)

Jesus's marital ethic was revolutionary in the ancient world. In the pagan context, even the strictest moralists and philosophers had few qualms about divorce and remarriage. In the Jewish context, the possible grounds for divorce were debated. The disciples of Shammai argued that the only sufficient ground was sexual immorality, while the disciples of Hillel maintained that a man could divorce his wife for any reason whatsoever. But all sides agreed that divorce and remarriage was permissible (m. Gittin 9.10). After all, the law of Moses in Scripture permitted divorce (Deut 24:1–4). Jesus, by contrast, strictly forbade divorce and remarriage for his followers (Mark 10:11–12; cf. Matt 5:31–32; 19:3–9; Luke 16:18). He taught the *indissolubility* of marriage. As a supernatural bond created by God himself, marriage is a sacred covenant binding a man and a woman together as long as they both should live (Mark 10:6–9). Divorce followed by remarriage violates this sacred bond and is a form of adultery

(10:11-12). By this teaching, Jesus "sanctified the family more than his [Jewish] tradition did."[8]

Matthew's version of Jesus's saying prohibiting divorce and remarriage includes an exception clause that permits divorce in the case of sexual immorality: "And I tell you that whosoever divorces his wife (except for sexual immorality) and marries another is committing adultery" (Matt 19:9; cf. 5:32). Some scholars have seen this "Matthean exception clause" as Matthew's own invention, compromising Jesus's radical teaching of the absolute indissolubility of marriage. But Matthew's account is not in conflict with Mark and Luke, for in ancient Greek syntax the exception clause qualifies the divorce, but not the remarriage.[9] Jesus's teaching in Matthew permits divorce (without remarriage) only in the case of unrepentant marital unfaithfulness, and forbids remarriage after divorce altogether. This is confirmed by the astonished reaction in Matthew of both the Pharisees (Matt 19:7) and the disciples (19:10) to Jesus's radical marital ethic, going beyond the alternatives of Shammai and Hillel. Moreover, this is the virtually universal understanding of Jesus's teaching and Matthew's exception clause in the early church within the first three centuries.[10] In prohibiting divorce and remarriage, which Jesus tells the Pharisees had been permitted under the law of Moses "because of the hardness of your hearts" (Mark 10:5; cf. Matt 19:8), Jesus made an implicit claim to be the bearer of the long-awaited new covenant, which would transform the human heart to do God's will (Mark 14:22-25; cf. Rom 2:28-29; 7:5-6; 1 Cor 11:23-25; 2 Cor 3:1-18).[11] Jesus's new law restored matrimony to its original indissolubility as intended by the creator (Mark 10:6, "from the beginning of creation"). "Jesus's ethical vision was of a return to the perfection of creation."[12]

Jesus's startling new teaching on marriage was part of the new "law of Christ" that Paul entrusted to his churches. In 1 Corinthians 7 we see Paul not only trans-

---

8. Marcus Borg, *Jesus: A New Vision* (San Francisco: HarperCollins, 1987), 114.

9. Rightly David Wenham, *Paul: Follower of Jesus or Founder of Christianity?* (Grand Rapids: Eerdmans, 1995), 242-45. On the structure of the ancient Greek sentence, see Raphael Kühner and Bernhard Gerth, *Ausführliche Grammatik der griechischen Sprache* (Hannover: Hansche, 1992), II, 2, 558-604; Friedrich Blass, Albert Debrunner, and Friedrich Rehkopf, *Grammatik des neutestamentlichen Griechisch*, 18th ed. (Göttingen: Vandenhoeck & Ruprecht, 2001), 388-414.

10. See Hermas, *Mandate* 4.1; Justin, *First Apology* 14-15; Athenagoras, *Embassy for the Christians* 33; Clement of Alexandria, *Miscellanies* 2.24; Tertullian, *Against Marcion* 5.7; cf. Jerome, *Commentary on Matthew* 3.19; Augustine, *Sermon on the Mount* 1.14-16; Council of Elvira (c. 300), canons 8-11; Council of Arles (314), canon 10.

11. See the insightful discussion in N. T. Wright, *Jesus and the Victory of God*, vol. 2 of *Christian Origins and the Question of God* (Minneapolis: Fortress, 1996), 282-87.

12. Wenham, *Paul*, 222.

mitting this teaching but also authoritatively interpreting and applying Jesus's teaching for his converts:

> [10]And to the married I command—not I but the Lord—that a woman must not separate from her husband [11](but if she does separate, she must remain unmarried or be reconciled with her husband), and that a man must not divorce his wife. [12]But to the rest I say (I not the Lord), that if a brother has an unbelieving wife and she is happy to dwell with him, he must not divorce her. [13]And if a woman has an unbelieving husband and he is happy to dwell with her, she must not divorce her husband. [14]For the unbelieving husband has been sanctified by his wife, and the unbelieving wife has been sanctified by the brother. Otherwise your children would be unclean—but they are holy. [15]But if the unbelieving partner departs, let him depart; the brother or sister has not been bound in such cases, but God has called us in peace. (1 Cor 7:10–15)

Paul here transmits Jesus's revolutionary teaching (1 Cor 7:10, "not I but the Lord") regarding the indissolubility of matrimony and the impermissibility of divorce and remarriage for followers of Christ (7:10, "a woman must not separate from her husband"; 7:11, "a man must not divorce his wife"). As in Matthew's exception clause, Paul allows divorce in some cases, but not a second union (7:11, "if she does separate, she must remain unmarried or be reconciled with her husband"). We also see Paul authoritatively applying Jesus's teaching (7:12, "I not the Lord") to a situation Jesus did not address: the case of a follower of Christ married to an unbeliever (7:12–15). In such mixed marriages he commands the believing partner not to divorce, but permits remarriage if the unbelieving partner separates (7:15, "the brother or sister has not been bound in such cases"). Theologians refer to this permission as the "Pauline privilege." But this is in contrast with the absolutely indissoluble bond of a man and a woman united in Christ, which renders any subsequent union impossible while both spouses are still living (7:10–11; cf. 7:39). Thus Paul's gospel of the new family of God in Christ did not destroy or weaken the natural family but renewed and sanctified it, making the family indissoluble. The procreative dimension of marriage as the foundation of the family is implicit here and elsewhere in Paul (1 Cor 7:14; cf. Eph 6:1–4; Col 3:20–21), and is emphasized in the Pastoral Epistles (1 Tim 3:4–5, 12; 5:10, 14; Titus 2:3–5).

Paul's most full moral instructions regarding marriage are found in Ephesians 5. Here he exhorts husbands:

> [25]Husbands, love your wives, just as Christ loved the church and gave himself for her, [26]that he might sanctify her, purifying her through the

washing of water joined with the gospel proclamation, [27]that he himself might present the church to himself as glorious, not having a stain or wrinkle or any such thing, but that she might be holy and without blemish. [28]In this way husbands must love their wives as their own bodies. The one who loves his wife loves himself. [29]For no one ever hated his own flesh, but he nourishes and cherishes it, just as Christ does the church, [30]because we are members of his body. [31]"For this reason a man shall leave his father and his mother and be joined to his wife, and the two shall become one flesh." [32]This mystery is great—but I am speaking about Christ and the church. (Eph 5:25–32)

In this passage Paul transmits Jesus's understanding of marriage and sexuality as rooted in the original creation: "for this reason a man shall leave his father and his mother and be joined to his wife, and the two shall become one flesh" (Eph 5:31, quoting Gen 2:24; cf. Mark 10:7–8; Matt 19:5–6). Paul follows Jesus's teaching regarding the essential goodness of the body, of maleness and femaleness, and of sexual union (Mark 10:6, "from the beginning of creation God made them male and female"). But Paul here also *enriches* Jesus's teaching on marriage, for Paul understands the physical union of man and woman in marriage as a mysterious foreshadowing within the created order of the union of Christ with the church (Eph 5:31–32). The bodily complementarity of male and female, consummated in marriage, is in Paul's theology a divinely given sign of the mystery of redemption and the call to union with God in Christ (5:32, "This mystery is great—but I am speaking about Christ and the church"). Augustine believed that this Pauline doctrine of marriage as a transcendent bond revealed for the first time the inmost reason underlying the Lord's teaching of the indissolubility of Christian marriage.[13] This understanding of marriage—as a transcendent and indissoluble union of persons given as a sacrament or sign of the highest divine mystery—is the most exalted conception of marriage and sexuality that the world has ever known. Here, as throughout Paul's theology, the kingdom brings the restoration and fulfillment of creation.

This exalted understanding of marriage provides the key to understanding those elements of Paul's sexual ethic that are most controversial or misunderstood today—his teaching on sex outside marriage, homosexual activity, and celibacy. It follows from this new "law of Christ" regarding the sacred and indissoluble character of matrimony that this union must be exclusive, forbidding all sexual

---

13. Augustine, *Marriage and Concupiscence* 1.11. See Anthony J. Bevilacqua, "The History of the Indissolubility of Marriage," *Proceedings of the Catholic Theological Society of America* 22 (1967): 268–69, to whom I am indebted for this insight.

activity outside marriage (Rom 1:24–27; 1 Cor 5:1–13; 6:12–20; Eph 5:3–7; Col 3:5–7; 1 Thess 4:1–8). Consistent with the rest of the Bible, Paul's teaching also prohibits homosexual activity (Rom 1:26–27; 1 Cor 6:9; 1 Tim 1:10; cf. Gen 19:1–26; Lev 18:22; 20:13; Jude 7–8). This prohibition likewise has its source in the Pauline teaching on marriage we have explored. For according to Paul's marital ethic, derived from Jesus's teaching, sexual complementarity (rooted in creation) is the basis of marriage (Eph 5:31; cf. Mark 10:6, "from the beginning of creation God made them male and female"). Moreover, as in the Genesis creation account (Gen 1:28), the matrimonial union has in Paul's thought a procreative purpose—it is the source of children and the foundation of the family (1 Cor 7:14; Eph 6:1–4; Col 3:20–21; 1 Tim 3:4–5, 12; 5:10, 14; Titus 2:3–5). And above all, this complementary union of man and woman in marriage has a transcendent dimension, as a divinely given physical sign within creation of the mystery of the union of Christ and the church (Eph 5:25–32). Each of these essential dimensions of matrimony is necessarily absent from homosexual unions. In Paul's moral teaching, all forms of sexual activity outside the context of the sacred and indissoluble union of man and woman—whether extramarital sex, homoerotic unions, autoerotic behaviors, or divorce and remarriage—are dehumanizing and harmful to those who engage in them (Rom 1:24–27; 1 Cor 6:9–11; Gal 5:19–21; Eph 5:3–7; Col 3:5–7).

Paul's revolutionary conception of marriage is also the key to his much-misunderstood teaching on celibacy. Paul commends celibacy for those gifted by God for this calling, and teaches that celibacy is superior to marriage (1 Cor 7:1–9). The unmarried, widows, and widowers are free to marry, but "more blessed" if they remain unmarried (1 Cor 7:25–40). Contemporary readers sometimes assume that the reason for Paul's positive view of celibacy must be a "negative" or "low" view of sex and marriage.[14] (Readers of this chapter will appreciate the irony.) But in fact, the superiority of the celibate vocation in Paul's thought flows directly from his *exalted* understanding of marriage. For in this understanding, even the sacred union of marriage is not the ultimate, but is itself a sign of something greater—the call to union with Christ. Paul accordingly commends celibacy to both men and women as a way of more fully living out this union through maximal devotion to the service of Christ and to the mission of the church (1 Cor 7:35, "lovely, constant, and undistracted devotion to the Lord"). The motive of Paul's teaching on celibacy is missionary, not Manichean (cf. Jesus's teaching in Matt 19:10–12). Paul commends celibacy *on behalf of the kingdom*.

14. See, for example, J. Albert Harrill, *Paul the Apostle: His Life and Legacy in Their Roman Context* (Cambridge: Cambridge University Press, 2012), 106–7; Paula Fredriksen, *Paul: The Pagans' Apostle* (New Haven: Yale University Press, 2017), 132–33, 228n37.

Persons in our contemporary cultural context sometimes view Paul's moral teaching on sexuality and marriage as limiting and restrictive. The sexual ethic of Jesus for his followers transmitted by Paul is indeed a demanding one, no less for the earliest Christ followers than it is today. But for Paul's first hearers this new teaching had a powerful and liberating social effect. Paul's emphatic prohibition of all sexual activity outside marriage protected the vulnerable from sexual exploitation, especially women, slaves, and children. In sharp contrast with pagan social norms, Paul's commands and prohibitions regarding sexual morality applied equally to men and women (Rom 1:26–27; 1 Cor 7:8–9, 10–11, 12–16, 32–34; Gal 5:19–21; Eph 5:3–7). And in contrast with the ancient pagan philosophers and moralists, who focused exclusively on the sexual needs of the male, Paul emphasized mutuality within marriage, and the reciprocal needs of both partners for sexual intimacy (1 Cor 7:2–5).[15] Paul's sanctification of the family and prohibition of divorce fostered personal, emotional, and economic security for both women and children. And in brazen defiance of the ancient practice of arranged marriages, Paul's teaching that one must marry "only in the Lord" (1 Cor 7:39), and his commendation of celibacy as an alternative to marriage, placed the decision of *whether* to marry and *whom* to marry in the power of women themselves rather than in the power of their parents.[16]

But perhaps most profound, although impossible to quantify, was the liberating effect of this new teaching on the human heart, mind, and spirit. For this was a new vision of sexuality and marriage as not only rooted in the good creation but also a sacred and sacramental sign within the created order of the very mystery of Christ. It revealed the goodness of the human body as a created sign of the mystery of redemption, and bestowed a transcendent value upon maleness and femaleness—independent of its sexual expression in marriage—as an intrinsic aspect of human personhood created in the divine image. It sanctified marriage, and it opened the vista of a new path superior even to marriage—the vocation to celibacy on behalf of Christ and his kingdom. We find here in Paul's sexual ethics, as in his ethic of love, the inseparability of Paul's theology and his moral teaching. Take away one, and you abolish the other. Distort one, and you distort the other.

15. Cf. J. Paul Sampley, "The First Letter to the Corinthians," *NIB* 10:871–72; Anthony C. Thiselton, *The Living Paul: An Introduction to the Apostle's Life and Thought* (Downers Grove: InterVarsity, 2009), 73, 131.

16. There is no space in this little book to explore Paul's teaching on slavery, the relationship of men and women in marriage, or the roles of women and men in the church's life and ministry. However, were we to do so we would find that here, too, teachings of the apostle often misunderstood or even vilified in our contemporary world were in fact powerfully liberating for Paul's converts and churches.

Conclusion: The New Law of Christ in the Teaching of Paul

In Paul's theology, Christ followers are guided not by the law of Moses, which was abolished by Christ, but by the "law of Christ," the new way of life given by Jesus. And yet by following the law of Christ, the faithful in Christ fulfill the true intent of the law of Moses. Paul understood his apostolic role in his moral exhortation as the transmission, interpretation, and application of the law of Christ for the church of God. In both the new life bestowed by Christ and the new law he has given, Paul's divine and incarnational Christology is evident—for only the creator can renew the creation, and the only one who can replace the law of Moses is YHWH, who gave it.

In sharp contrast to the moral philosophers, for whom the gods were on the periphery of the moral life, in Paul's letters the love, worship, praise, and adoration of God are at the heart of Paul's ethical instruction. The goal of the moral life is "to please God in every way" (Col 1:10). This is truly a revolution in ethics. In Paul's transmission and application of Jesus's twofold love command, the command to love one's neighbor is grounded in God's love revealed in Christ. To a pagan world that believed that the gods could have nothing to do with suffering and death, Paul proclaimed the astonishing "message of the cross" (1 Cor 1:18): the creator had become human in order to undergo suffering, crucifixion, and death for humanity's salvation. Within Paul's moral exhortation, this divine love becomes in turn the model for human love. Imitation of God in Paul is always imitation of Christ, in his self-giving love to the point of death on a cross. In Paul's thought, the cross of Christ is the foundation of the command to love.

In his sexual ethics, Paul transmitted Jesus's revolutionary new teaching of the indissolubility of marriage. Paul's moral teaching forbids all divorce and remarriage for followers of Christ. In returning marriage to the original design of the creator, the kingdom brings the restoration and fulfillment of creation. But Paul also enriches Jesus's teaching through his doctrine of marriage as a mysterious sign within the created order of the union of Christ with the church. This understanding of marriage as an indissoluble union of persons given as a sacrament of the highest mystery of divine love is the most exalted conception of marriage, sexuality, and the body the world has ever known. This exalted conception is the true context for those aspects of Paul's sexual ethics that are so often misunderstood and even maligned today: the proscription in Paul's teaching of all extramarital sex, the prohibition of homosexual unions, and his teaching regarding celibacy on behalf of the kingdom. This Pauline ethical vision, which both sanctified marriage and opened the new path of celibacy for the sake of Christ, was a powerful liberating force, especially for women, slaves, and children.

In both Paul's ethic of love and his sexual ethics we discover the deep coherence—and thus the inseparability—of Paul's theology and his moral teaching, his "gospel" and his "ethics." Neither part of this seamless garment can be undone without unraveling the whole.

Part Five

Paul and Christian Origins

Chapter Thirteen

The Gospel of the Eyewitnesses

A familiar refrain in some recent popular-level books on ancient Christianity, and underlying a certain stream of scholarly work on Paul, is a particular narrative concerning the place of Paul within the historical origins of the Christian faith.[1] According to this view, the story of ancient Christianity is the story of an original diversity suppressed by the imposition of a later orthodoxy. This narrative has many variations, but in its standard form it usually goes something like this. Jesus's first disciples, the eyewitnesses of his ministry during his lifetime, revered him as a great prophet, but a mortal human being now dead. Many of them groped for some kind of divine purpose in Jesus's violent death. And soon some of them began to have experiences of the postmortem Jesus, which led them to believe that, although his body remained in the tomb, he had been spiritually exalted to heaven. Others began to regard this exalted Jesus as more than human, an angelic or supernatural being. Jesus's early followers, so the narrative goes, thus held no core beliefs, but a diversity of conflicting beliefs about Jesus. The "Gnostic" texts at Nag Hammadi, we are told, provide early firsthand evidence for this welter of divergent beliefs among the first Christ followers.

Into this ferment of conflicting beliefs and theological speculation (often called "pre-Pauline Christianity"), Paul came as a relative latecomer but a powerful theological innovator. Paul, the narrative goes on, knew little and cared less about the actual human Jesus who had walked the roads of Galilee (the "Jesus of

---

1. Among works aimed at a popular audience, see Bart Ehrman, *How Jesus Became God: The Exaltation of a Jewish Preacher from Galilee* (New York: HarperOne, 2014); Elaine E. Pagels, *Beyond Belief: The Secret Gospel of Thomas* (New York: Vintage, 2003); and Karen King, "The History of Christianity," in *The Gospel of Mary of Magdala: Jesus and the First Woman Apostle* (Santa Rosa, CA: Polebridge, 2003), 155–90. Classic versions of the narrative in scholarly works include P. M. Casey, *From Jewish Prophet to Gentile God: The Origins and Development of New Testament Christology* (Cambridge: James Clarke, 1991); J. M. Robinson, "Jesus—from Easter to Valentinus (or to the Apostles' Creed)," *JBL* 101 (1982): 5–37; and Hans Grass, *Ostergeschehen und Osterberichte* (Göttingen: Vandenhoeck & Ruprecht, 1962).

history"). The focus of his devotion was Jesus as a heavenly and glorified being (the "Christ of faith"). Influenced by ancient philosophical ideas and polytheistic myths, Paul powerfully molded the malleable faith of the early Christ followers by introducing (or popularizing) new teachings about Jesus as a preexistent heavenly figure who temporarily took on human form; the cross as a saving and atoning event; and Jesus's postmortem survival in a new "spiritual body" composed not of flesh and bones, but of spirit. Paul's teaching about Jesus, the scenario claims, contrasts with that of the four Gospels, which only much later would introduce legendary accounts of an empty tomb, and of the disciples' encounter, three days after his burial, with a Jesus risen from the dead in his physical body of flesh and bones.

In the second century the enforcers of an emerging self-styled "orthodoxy," suppressing the Gnostic texts and their witness to earlier Christ-less, cross-less, and resurrection-less forms of Christianity, would enshrine Paul's letters, alongside the four Gospels, at the center of the New Testament canon. But they would read into Paul's letters later legends and myths exalting Jesus as God incarnate and physically risen from the dead. And so (the scenario goes) the doctrines of Jesus's divinity, incarnation, atoning death, and bodily resurrection, drawn from a selective reading of Paul's letters, would become the basis for an arbitrarily imposed "orthodox" belief system in the second century and for the historic Christian creeds, such as the Nicene Creed and the Apostles' Creed, in the fourth century and beyond. In the radical metamorphosis that replaced the (historical) prophet of Galilee with the (fictional) crucified and risen Christ of Christian faith, Paul was thus the central figure. In this way, the narrative claims, Paul became "the second founder of Christianity."[2] For through the work of Paul, the real Jesus of history had become the mythical Christ of Christian dogma.

The thesis of an originally pluriform Christianity is extremely popular today, and many people assume it is an assured result of modern scholarship. That is why it may surprise many readers to learn that *every line of the scenario sketched above is profoundly unhistorical*. It is, in fact, a myth (in a peculiarly modern form) making pretensions to be serious history. That the claims of this scenario about what Paul actually taught involve a profound misreading of his letters will be evident to anyone who has read the first twelve chapters of this book. But this misreading of Paul begins with a false understanding of the origins of Christianity as a whole, and the place of Paul within those origins. This chapter will therefore be devoted to clarifying Paul's true place within the foundations of Christianity.

2. Wilhelm Wrede, *Paul*, trans. Edward Lummis (London: Green, 1907), 179.

Jesus was crucified on a Friday, on the eve of Passover, on either 14 Nisan (=our April 3) in 33 CE, or 14 Nisan (=our April 7) in 30 CE.[3] Which of these two possible dates is more likely is debated by scholars. Space precludes discussion, but I believe the evidence is strongly in favor of the date in 33 CE.[4] However, nothing in the argument of this chapter depends upon this question. In the discussion that follows, I will assume a date of 33 CE for Jesus's crucifixion.

What happened next? How did the Christian movement, which began with Jesus, get under way? Do the Gospels in the New Testament reflect the message about Jesus spread by the earliest apostles and eyewitnesses, or a different version invented decades later? How did Paul fit into it all? These are historical questions, which can be answered only by doing serious history. Serious history depends on the evidence of what historians call *primary sources*—the original, ancient documents written by those closest to the events. It depends on the testimony of eyewitnesses, and the veracity of that testimony. When we do rigorous history regarding Paul and the origins of the Christian movement, what do we find?

Our Earliest Historical Sources

The would-be historical scenario sketched above is advanced, in some popular-level books, by means of an uncritical and misleading approach that actually conceals from the reader our chief historical documents and evidence for the question. Readers accustomed to that scenario should therefore be prepared for a number of surprises. The first surprise is that *our earliest primary sources are the New Testament documents*. The Gospels of Matthew, Mark, and John, the letters of Paul, the letters of John, and other New Testament texts, by universal scholarly agreement, date to the first century. The "Gnostic" texts from Nag Hammadi date in fact to a much later period; they were composed anywhere from the second to the fourth century CE. We do not possess, contrary to a popular but unscholarly belief, writings "behind" or earlier than the New Testament documents. Our only first-century documents are the New Testament texts, together with a text called the Didache (date disputed, but probably around 75 CE) and an epistle by Clement, leader of the Christians at Rome (between 85 and 95 CE).

3. On the date of the crucifixion, see the seminal study of J. K. Fotheringham, "The Evidence of Astronomy and Technical Chronology for the Date of the Crucifixion," *JTS* 25 (1934): 146–62.

4. For detailed discussion, and the evidence supporting a date in 33 CE, see H. W. Hoehner, *The Chronological Aspects of the Life of Christ* (Grand Rapids: Eerdmans, 1977), and P. L. Maier, "Sejanus, Pilate, and the Date of the Crucifixion," *CH* 37 (1968): 3–13.

But among these first-century sources, *our earliest sources of all are the letters of Paul.* The narrative of Jesus's deeds and teachings was initially spread by Jesus's apostles and eyewitnesses orally, and only later put into written form in the Gospels. The letters of Paul are therefore our earliest written sources. Paul's first letter, 1 Thessalonians, is our earliest Christian document, composed in 50 or 51 CE, just seventeen or eighteen years after Jesus's crucifixion.[5] Paul's other letters followed at various points throughout the 50s and 60s, the great majority of them indisputably earlier than any other ancient Christian source. The earliest of the four Gospels, by contrast, does not appear until most likely the early 60s.

For the historian of the early church, Paul is therefore our most important source of information, and Paul's letters are our most important documents.[6] This is the case not only because of their astoundingly early date. Paul's letters are so crucial because they inform us not only regarding the teaching of Paul but also regarding the preaching of Peter, John, the Twelve, and the other disciples and eyewitnesses of Jesus. Moreover, as we will see, Paul's letters provide a direct window into the all-important period 33–49 CE, *the earliest period prior to the existence of written early Christian sources.* Paul's letters therefore provide firsthand information regarding the narrative of Jesus as it was proclaimed by the first apostles and eyewitnesses before being put into the written form of our gospels. Paul's letters are our only sources that can provide an answer to the question: Do our canonical gospels reflect the message of the earliest eyewitnesses—or later legends? This is an aspect of Paul's letters that is most likely unfamiliar to many readers of this book. Paul's epistles are not only of great theological importance as part of New Testament Scripture, but are of great historical importance for our understanding of the origins of the Christian faith. As our earliest historical sources, *Paul's letters are the key to the history of ancient Christianity.*

---

5. See Abraham J. Malherbe, *The Letters to the Thessalonians*, AB 32B (New York: Doubleday, 2000), 71–74. This is the near universal scholarly consensus concerning the date of 1 Thessalonians. However, Gerd Lüdemann argues that 1 Thessalonians should be dated much earlier, to the early 40s CE (*Paul, Apostle to the Gentiles: Studies in Chronology*, trans. F. Stanley Jones [Philadelphia: Fortress, 1984], 164–73). Other scholars follow the consensus date of 50 or 51 CE for 1 Thessalonians, but believe Galatians was Paul's earliest epistle, which they date to 46 or 47. None of these issues affects our historical conclusions in this chapter.

6. See Jeffrey R. Peterson, "The Extent of Christian Theological Diversity: Pauline Evidence," *RQ* 47 (2005): 1–12.

Our Most Valuable Source: 1 Corinthians 15:1–11

The richest passage of all for the historian is 1 Corinthians 15:1–11. Paul's letter to the Corinthians is a document of undoubted historical authenticity, written in 53 or 54 CE.[7] In this passage, Paul reminds the Corinthians of the gospel he first proclaimed to them, when he founded the church at Corinth:

> [1]And I make known to you, brothers and sisters, the good news which I proclaimed to you, which you also received, in which you stand, [2]through which you are being saved, if you hold fast to the message of the good news which I brought to you; unless, indeed, you have believed in vain. [3]For I transmitted to you from the first, that which I also received, that Christ died for our sins in fulfillment of the Scriptures, [4]and that he was buried, and that he rose again on the third day in fulfillment of the Scriptures, [5]and that he was seen by Peter, then by the Twelve; [6]then he was seen by more than five hundred brothers and sisters at the same time, of whom the majority remain until now, but some have fallen asleep; [7]then he was seen by James, then by all the apostles; [8]and last of all, as to one untimely born, he was seen by me as well. [9]For I am the least of the apostles, who am not worthy to be named an apostle, because I persecuted the church of God. [10]But by the grace of God I am what I am, and his grace toward me was not in vain; indeed, I labored more abundantly than them all, yet not I, but the grace of God which is with me. [11]Whether, then, it was I or they, this is what we proclaim, and this is what you believed. (1 Cor 15:1–11)

It is impossible to ignore the emphasis in these verses on the fixed, propositional content of the message. It is a message that Paul "transmitted" to them (15:3) and that they "received" (15:1). Moreover, it is clear that these beliefs are at the center of the Corinthians' (and Paul's) communal identity as Jesus followers. It is what the apostles "proclaim" and what the Christians at Corinth "believed" (15:11). They not only "received" this good news (15:1), but they "stand" by means of this teaching (15:1), and are being "saved" through this message (15:2)—but only if they continue to "hold fast" the good news they received (15:2). The claim that first-century Christians had no core beliefs is simply not consistent with the evidence of this passage.

7. On the dating of this letter, see J. Paul Sampley, "The First Letter to the Corinthians," *NIB* 10:776–77.

Moreover, the recitation of these core beliefs in verses 3–8 has a carefully structured, formulaic character. These verses have in fact a fourfold structure, delineated by the fourfold occurrence of the word "that" (Greek: *hoti*): (1) Christ died for our sins, (2) he was buried, (3) he rose again, and (4) he appeared to eyewitnesses (15:3–5). The fourth component of the structure, the appearances to eyewitnesses, has its own internal four-part structure, marked out by the fourfold repetition of the word "was seen" (Greek: *ōpthē*). In this way the different witnesses are carefully delineated into four groups: (1) Peter, then the Twelve; (2) over five hundred brothers and sisters at the same time; (3) James, then all the apostles; and (4) Paul last of all (15:5–8). The carefully structured, formulaic character of the body of teaching in 15:3–8 reveals not only its fixed, propositional character but also its central place and importance for the early Christians.

The specific content of this summary of the faith is equally striking. Jesus is the "Christ," the long-awaited King of Israel, come in fulfillment of the Scriptures (15:3–4). And although it is not explicit in this brief summary, Paul transmitted these core beliefs in the context of a gospel whose epicenter is, we saw in part 2 of this book, the incarnation—the mystery of the divine Son of God come in human flesh. The incarnation was not the temporary manifestation of a supernatural or angelic being but the union of God and man in the person of Christ, permanent and everlasting. Moreover, according to this brief confession, the cross is a saving event, or rather *the* saving event. The concept of Jesus's cross as a substitutionary atonement for human sin is at the center of this summary of the faith: "Christ died for our sins" (15:3). And at the climax of this "good news" is Jesus's resurrection from the dead (15:4–5). As we saw in chapter 10, this conviction that Jesus "rose again on the third day" (15:4) was not a belief merely in some sort of postmortem survival, or the assumption of Jesus to heaven in an ethereal or celestial body while his physical body remained in the tomb. Instead, it was the announcement that, three days after his death, Jesus had risen again from the tomb, an event in space and time involving Jesus's crucified body of flesh and bones, and corroborated by the list of eyewitnesses given in 15:5–8.[8] The coherence of this brief summary, in its shape, outline, and theology, with the narratives of Jesus's passion and resurrection in the four Gospels is striking. Can we trace the historical origins of this message?

---

8. For detailed discussion, see James Ware, "The Resurrection of Jesus in the Pre-Pauline Formula of 1 Cor 15.3–5," *NTS* 60 (2014): 475–98.

The Apostolic Origins of the Body of Teaching in 1 Corinthians 15:3–8

Fortunately for the historian, Paul wished to remind the Corinthians not only of the content of the gospel he proclaimed to them, but also of its historical foundations in the eyewitness testimony of the apostles. In so doing, Paul provides for the historian information about the beginnings of the Christian movement that, in its scope and significance, is truly mind-boggling.

First of all, when Paul says he "transmitted" (15:3) the content of verses 3–8 to them, he uses the ancient Greek word *paradidōmi*. This word was used in ancient Christianity as a technical term for *the authoritative transmission of the apostolic testimony to Jesus* (see, for example, Luke 1:2; Rom 6:17; 1 Cor 11:23; 2 Thess 2:15; Jude 3). The very word that Paul uses thus makes the claim that what he taught them was not his teaching alone, but the teaching of all the apostles. Paul makes this claim explicit in verse 11: "Whether, then, it was I or they, this is what we proclaim, and this is what you believed." The gospel he transmitted to the Corinthians, Paul claims, was identical with the teaching of all the other apostles and eyewitnesses of Jesus enumerated in 15:5–7. The Corinthians, for their part, were in a position immediately to discount Paul's claim if it were false—for, as many scholars have argued (in my view convincingly), Peter himself had visited and taught the church at Corinth.[9] Paul is writing to the Corinthians in 53 or 54 CE, recounting the core beliefs he transmitted to them when he founded the church at Corinth in (as all historians are agreed) 50 or 51.[10] This was only seventeen or

---

9. For the evidence in the primary sources, see 1 Cor 1:12; 3:22; 9:5; and the second-century testimony of Dionysius, bishop of Corinth, in Eusebius, *Ecclesiastical History* 2.25.8. Peter's visit to Corinth is a point of dispute among scholars. Oscar Cullmann considers such a visit a strong possibility but uncertain (*Peter: Disciple, Apostle, Martyr; A Historical and Theological Essay*, trans. Floyd V. Filson [Philadelphia: Westminster, 1953], 53–55). N. T. Wright, however, assumes (on my view rightly) that Peter had visited Corinth (*The Resurrection of the Son of God*, vol. 3 of *Christian Origins and the Question of God* [Minneapolis: Fortress, 2003], 318–19).

10. Paul's letters do not provide absolute dates but only relative chronological information for the events they describe (e.g., Gal 1:18, "after three years"). However, ancient historians are able to correlate this information in Paul's epistles with nonbiblical ancient sources to provide secure historical dates for many events in the life of Paul. Perhaps the most important of these ancient sources is the Gallio inscription discovered at Delphi in the previous century. For a translation of the text and discussion, see Everett Ferguson, *Backgrounds of Early Christianity*, 3rd ed. (Grand Rapids: Eerdmans, 2003), 585–86. Other important ancient sources for a chronology of Paul's mission include Josephus, *Jewish Antiquities* 19.343–54 (death of Herod Agrippa I, 44 CE); *Jewish Antiquities* 20.51–53, 101 (famine in Judea, from 44/45 to 46/47); Suetonius, *Claudius* 25.4 (edict of Claudius, most likely 49); and Josephus, *Jewish Antiquities* 20.169–72. Another important datable anchor is the rule of king Aretas of Damascus, on which see Douglas A. Campbell, "An Anchor of Pauline Chronology: Paul's Flight from 'The Ethnarch of King Aretas' (2 Corinthians 11:32–33)," *JBL* 121 (2002): 279–302.

eighteen years after Jesus's crucifixion, and while Peter and all the other apostles (except James the son of Zebedee) were still living. This is astounding historical evidence for the very early date and apostolic origins of belief in Jesus's redemptive death and bodily resurrection.

But the evidence Paul provides permits the historian to trace these core beliefs back even further. For Paul tells the Corinthians that he himself "received" the body of teaching he had transmitted to them (15:3). Paul here uses the word *paralambanō*, the technical term in early Christianity for the *reception* of the apostolic testimony to Jesus (see, for example, 1 Cor 11:23; Gal 1:9; Phil 4:9; 1 Thess 2:13; 4:1; 2 Thess 3:6). Paul uses the same word here in verse 3 that he used of the Corinthians "receiving" the apostolic message in verse 1. To see how and when Paul received this body of teaching, we must explore Paul's conversion and apostolic call. In this pivotal event, Paul, the onetime persecutor, had seen the risen Christ, and had been commissioned by him as an apostle to the gentiles (cf. 1 Cor 9:1; Phil 3:2–11; 1 Tim 1:12–17; Acts 9:1–22; 22:1–16; 26:9–23). We learn more about this event from another document of undoubted authenticity, Paul's letter to the Galatians, written most likely in 56:

> [15]But when God, who set me apart from my mother's womb and called me by his grace, was pleased [16]to reveal his Son to me, that I might proclaim the good news about him among the nations, I did not immediately confer with any human being, [17]nor did I go up to Jerusalem to those who were apostles before me, but I first went away into Arabia, and then I returned back again to Damascus. (Gal 1:15–17)

When did this event take place? It is beyond debate among historians that Paul's conversion and call near Damascus occurred, at the latest, in late 34 or early 35.[11] This was only one and a half years after Jesus's crucifixion in 33, and only two or three months after the first Christ followers, due to persecution, had been scattered from the community led by the apostles in Jerusalem (cf. Gal 1:13 with Acts 8:1–4; 9:1–22). This is a crucial historical datum, which reveals that Paul received the body of teaching he passed on to the Corinthians, and was on the scene and active as an apostle within the early Christian movement, within one and a half to two years of its inception.

11. See conveniently Stanley Porter, "The Chronology of Paul's Ministry and His Imprisonments," in *The Apostle Paul: His Life, Thought, and Letters* (Grand Rapids: Eerdmans, 2016), 50. For fuller discussion, see Robert Jewett, *A Chronology of Paul's Life* (Philadelphia: Fortress, 1979); Rainer Riesner, *Paul's Early Period: Chronology, Mission, Strategy, Theology*, trans. D. Scott (Grand Rapids: Eerdmans, 1998); and Lüdemann, *Paul*.

But in what way did Paul "receive" the content of 1 Corinthians 15:3–7? Paul is clear in the Galatians passage that in the event on the road to Damascus he had received direct, spoken revelation from Jesus (cf. Acts 9:3–8; 22:6–11; 26:12–18). But when he speaks in 1 Corinthians 15:3 of "receiving" the same message that he "transmitted" to the Corinthians, he is not speaking of this direct revelation from Christ, but of the core teachings transmitted by the apostles to the community of Christ followers. Paul tells us that he did not go up immediately to the apostles in Jerusalem (Gal 1:16–17), and hence it is clear that he first received this teaching from the Christ followers in Damascus, who had in turn received it from the apostles in Jerusalem ("the apostles who were before me" [Gal 1:17]). Paul thus received the core beliefs he later transmitted to the Corinthians at an amazingly early date, within approximately eighteen months after the first Easter. However, Paul first received the content of 1 Corinthians 15:3–7, not firsthand from the twelve apostles, but secondhand from those who had heard the apostles.

But, three years after his conversion, Paul would also make direct, firsthand contact with the apostles themselves:

> Then after three years I went up again to Jerusalem to talk with Peter directly, and I stayed with him for fifteen days. But I did not see any of the other apostles, except James the brother of the Lord. (Gal 1:18–19)

In this crucial event, Paul met and talked with Peter, the foremost among the twelve apostles, over a period of fifteen days. The Greek verb *historeō*, which I have translated as "talk with directly," is an unusual and strong word. It means to see someone face-to-face in order to make inquiry of the facts. We, in fact, derive our English word "history" from the noun form (*historia*) of this stem. It means that Paul went with the purpose of seeing Peter face-to-face, and hearing his eyewitness testimony to Jesus directly.[12] Over this fifteen-day period, Paul and Peter would not only have met together, but also would have come together at least twice on "the first day of the week" or "the Lord's day" (i.e., Sunday) to join in worship and share in the Eucharist or Lord's Supper together (cf. 1 Cor 11:17–24; 16:1–2; Acts 20:7–12; Rev 1:10; Didache 14.1). Far from a casual meeting to get acquainted, Paul's visit to Peter and James was more along the lines of an ancient fifteen-day "summit conference" among these three great apostles.

---

12. See William R. Farmer, "Peter and Paul and the Tradition concerning 'The Lord's Supper' in 1 Cor 11:23–26," in *One Loaf, One Cup: Ecumenical Studies of 1 Cor 11 and Other Eucharistic Texts*, ed. Ben F. Meyer (Macon, GA: Mercer University Press, 1993), 38–43.

Paul's conference with Peter and James occurred, historians are agreed, at the latest in 37 or 38.[13] This meeting thus took place within five years of the founding events of the first Good Friday and Easter. Paul had received in 34 or 35 the apostolic teaching from the Christ followers at Damascus, who had received it from the apostles, and now at his conference with Peter three years later Paul had the opportunity to verify this tradition. It is thus beyond historical controversy that Paul had heard the content of the apostolic testimony that he shares in 1 Corinthians 15:3-8 from the lips of the apostles themselves.

Paul most likely had numerous further contacts with the Twelve and with other apostles, many more than those he tells us about in his letters. But another important contact about which he does tell us is the Apostolic Council (also called "the Jerusalem Council"), held in Jerusalem sometime between 47 and 51 (thus, approximately two to five years prior to the time Paul wrote 1 Corinthians).[14] At this conclave, Paul met for extensive discussions with Peter, John the son of Zebedee, James, and other apostles and eyewitnesses of Jesus (Gal 2:1-10; cf. Acts 15:1-35). It is critical to grasp that the issue the council met to discuss did not involve what sociologists call "basic" beliefs (core beliefs shared in common by a community) but "consequent" beliefs (convictions regarding the consequences and implications of those core beliefs). That is, the question at hand did not involve the core beliefs we see expressed in 1 Corinthians 15:1-11, but the implications of these core beliefs for gentile followers of Jesus. The council met to decide whether gentiles who had become Christ followers needed also to adopt the age-old markers of Jewish covenant identity: circumcision, purity laws, and Sabbath keeping. Paul in his apostolic mission received gentiles into the church apart from these markers, and the council affirmed Paul's theology and practice (Gal 2:3, 6-10; cf. Acts 15:7-29).[15] Why this issue was controversial, and the importance of Paul's theological response, were discussed in part 3 of this book. Here we note that this council was another occasion on which Paul had direct contact, at the highest level, with the earliest apostles and eyewitnesses of Jesus's ministry, passion, death, and resurrection. And it was another occasion on which the agreement of their

13. See Porter, "Chronology" (he places the event in 37 CE); Jewett, *Chronology* (37 CE); Lüdemann, *Paul* (36 CE).

14. See Porter, "Chronology" (he places the event in 47 CE); Jewett, *Chronology* (51 CE); Lüdemann, *Paul* (50 CE).

15. Some scholars do not identity Gal 2:1-10 with Paul's visit to Jerusalem in Acts 15:1-35 (as assumed here), but with the visit of Paul to Jerusalem narrated in Acts 11:27-30 and 12:25. Nothing in regard to the historical importance of the information provided in Gal 2:1-10 hinges on this debate.

and Paul's gospel was explicitly expressed: "And recognizing the grace given to me, James and Peter and John, who were recognized as pillars, gave to me and Barnabas the right hand of partnership, that we might go to the gentiles, and they to the Jewish people" (Gal 2:9).

When we take the historical information Paul's letters provide concerning his contacts with the original apostles and compare it with the list of eyewitnesses in 1 Corinthians 15:5–8, we see an astounding historical reality. The eyewitnesses Paul lists are Peter, the Twelve, the five hundred brothers and sisters, James, all the apostles, and himself. Paul had, as we have seen, multiple contacts with Peter, the first-named apostle on the list (Gal 1:18–19; 2:9). Of the Twelve, Paul had met with John the son of Zebedee (Gal 2:9), and most likely with others as well. Of the five hundred brothers and sisters, Paul's statement that "the majority remain alive until now, but some have fallen asleep" (1 Cor 15:6) presumes his knowledge of who among them were alive and who had died, and thus suggests that he was personally acquainted with at least the majority of them. And Paul, as we have seen, had multiple contacts with James, the other named apostle on the list besides Peter (Gal 1:19; 2:9). What is crucial for the historian is that, *when Paul in 1 Corinthians 15:1–11 informs us of the content of the teaching of the earliest apostles and eyewitnesses, he was in a position to know*. It is fascinating to peruse the list of eyewitnesses to the resurrection in 1 Corinthians 15:5–8 and to realize that Paul had extensive and direct contacts with most of the people on that list!

Further Evidence from Paul's Letters

Extensive evidence elsewhere in Paul's epistles converges with our findings from 1 Corinthians 15:1–11. I will focus only on two important pieces of that evidence.

A crucial moment in the narrative of all three Synoptic Gospels (Matthew, Mark, and Luke) is the words and actions of Jesus during the Passover meal he shared with the twelve apostles on the night prior to his crucifixion.[16] According to these gospel texts, in the midst of this meal with his disciples, Jesus, taking bread and wine, identified them with his body given for them and his blood

---

16. The discussion below is indebted at several points to the groundbreaking essay of William R. Farmer, "Reflections on Isaiah 53 and Christian Origins," in *Jesus and the Suffering Servant: Isaiah 53 and Christian Origins*, ed. William H. Bellinger and William R. Farmer (Harrisburg, PA: Trinity, 1998), 260–80.

shed for them (Matt 26:26–29; Mark 14:22–25; Luke 22:19–20; cf. John 6:51–59). These words express Jesus's own self-understanding of his death as a sacrifice for sins, and his intention to give his life as an offering for sin in Jerusalem. These gospel texts thus indicate that the understanding of the cross as a sacrificial, atoning event goes back to the earliest origins of Christianity, indeed to the mind and teaching of Jesus himself. According to the Gospels, the Christian celebration of the Eucharist or Lord's Supper has its source in the extraordinary words and actions of Jesus on this occasion. However, proponents of the thesis of an originally Christ-less Christianity claim that these words of Jesus in the Gospels are a "cult legend," that is, a mythical retrojection of later beliefs about the Eucharist onto the lips of Jesus. It was not until decades after Jesus's death, according to this scenario, that some early Jesus followers invented these words of Jesus in order to explain to themselves why they celebrated this meal of bread and wine.

Did Jesus say and do what Matthew, Mark, and Luke claim he said and did on the night he was betrayed? This question is crucial for the origins of Christian belief in the sacrificial character of Jesus's death, and the basis of this in Jesus's own self-understanding and teaching. This question is crucial for the origins of the church's sacramental enactment of these beliefs in its celebration of the Eucharist. And this question also has powerful implications for the authenticity of the Gospels. For if Jesus's "words of institution" (as theologians call them) on this occasion are a cult legend, this portion of the narrative of the Gospels is theological fiction, and there would be good reason to assume this is true of the gospel narratives as a whole. On the other hand, if Jesus said and did on this occasion what the Gospels claim he said and did, this portion of the narrative is eyewitness history, based on the testimony of the apostles who shared the table with Jesus, and there would be every reason to assume that this is true of the gospel narratives as a whole. Do we have a source whereby we can historically verify, independently of the Gospels, what Jesus said and did on the night before his crucifixion?

Yes, we do: the letters of Paul. In 1 Corinthians 11:23–25 Paul reminds the Christ followers at Corinth of the words and actions of Jesus on the night in which he was betrayed, as transmitted to them by the apostle. For purposes of comparison, I have given this passage side by side with the accounts of Jesus's words in Mark and in Luke:

MARK 14:22–24	LUKE 22:19–20	1 COR 11:23–25
And as they were eating Jesus took bread, blessed it, broke it and gave it to them and said, "Take, this is my body." And he took a cup, gave thanks and gave it to them, and they all drank from it. And he said to them, "This is my blood of the covenant, which is poured out for many."	And he took bread, gave thanks, broke it, and gave it to them, saying "This is my body which is given for you; this do in remembrance of me." And the cup likewise after supper, saying, "This cup is the new covenant in my blood, which is poured out for you."	For I received from the Lord, what I also transmitted to you, that the Lord Jesus on the night in which he was betrayed took bread, gave thanks, broke it and said, "This is my body which is for you; do this in remembrance of me." Likewise also the cup after supper, saying, "This cup is the new covenant in my blood. Do this, as often as you drink it, in remembrance of me."

These three accounts of Jesus's words and actions on the night he was betrayed vary in wording, but they are in agreement in their basic content (Paul's wording is closest to that of Luke). When Paul says he transmitted to the Corinthians what he himself "received from the Lord" (1 Cor 11:23), he is most likely referring not to Jesus's self-revelation to him on the road to Damascus, but to his reception of the apostolic tradition of Jesus's words as transmitted by Peter and the other apostles, who had received them from the Lord. Two factors make Paul's testimony invaluable for the historian. First, Paul's account of the words and actions of Jesus on that night is *independent* of the Gospels, for he transmitted it to the Corinthians in 50 CE, only seventeen years after the event, and before Matthew, Mark, or Luke had been written. Second, as we have seen, *Paul had extensive and direct contacts with apostles who had shared the table with Jesus on that night.* Paul met with Peter for a fifteen-day conference in 37/38, for the specific purpose of hearing his eyewitness testimony to Jesus, and at the Apostolic Council in 48/49, Paul had met with Peter, John, and other apostles. It is historically certain that Paul had the opportunity to verify with Peter and the other eyewitnesses what Jesus had actually said and done on that night. After all, on these occasions Paul not only had extensive discussions with Peter and other members of the Twelve, but, as we have seen, he also *shared in the celebration of the Eucharist with them.*

Paul's letters provide striking and explosive evidence that, beyond a reasonable historical doubt, the words of Jesus identifying the bread with his body and the wine with his blood go back to the eyewitness testimony of the apostles who reclined with Jesus at table on that night. The conception of the cross as a sacrificial, atoning event, and the Christian celebration of the Eucharist, do not have their origins in myth or legend, but in the words and actions of Jesus on the night he was betrayed. Moreover, this confirmation of the eyewitness origins of the account of the Last Supper in the canonical gospels (considered alongside the coherence of 1 Cor 15:1–11 with the narrative of Jesus's death and resurrection in these same gospels) strongly suggests that the narrative of Jesus's deeds and teaching in the Gospels as a whole has its origins in the eyewitnesses' testimony of the apostles.

The confines of this little chapter will permit us to look at only one more piece of evidence. In Paul's letter to the Romans (c. 57 CE), another document of undoubted authenticity, Paul reminds the Roman Christians of the transformation of life brought about through their baptism:

> Or do you not know that all of us who were baptized into Christ Jesus were baptized into his death? We were buried with him through baptism into death, in order that just as Christ was raised from the dead through the glory of the Father, so we too might walk in newness of life. (Rom 6:3–4)

Paul's phrase "or do you not know?" is what may be called a "transmission indicator."[17] Paul regularly uses phrases like this to reference some aspect of the basic body of Christian teaching his readers have received (cf. Rom 6:9, 16; 7:1; 1 Cor 3:16; 6:2–3, 9, 15, 16, 19; Eph 5:5; 1 Thess 5:2). What is striking about this instance is that the church at Rome was one the apostle did not found and (at the time of the writing of Romans) had never visited (see Rom 1:8–15; 15:22–33). And yet he could take for granted that his readers not only had been baptized, but also shared a particular theological understanding of the meaning of their baptism. The understanding that Paul assumes they share is that in their baptism they have been united to *Christ*, they have *died* with him, they have been *buried* with him, and they have been *raised* with him to newness of life. In the theology of baptism in Romans 6:3–4, we find the identical underlying narrative about Jesus we saw in 1 Corinthians 15:3–8: his identity as the Christ, his death, his burial, and his resurrection.[18] Once again, the evidence is incompatible with the thesis of an originally pluriform Christianity (that is, a Christianity without core beliefs transmitted by the apostles). Paul here assumes that the Roman Christians, whom he

---

17. For this concept I am indebted to David Wenham, *Paul: Follower of Jesus or Founder of Christianity?* (Grand Rapids: Eerdmans, 1995). Wenham prefers the term "tradition indicator."

18. Cf. Peterson, "Extent of Christian Theological Diversity," 9–10.

had never visited, share the same core beliefs that he informs us in 1 Corinthians 15:1–11 were the shared teaching of all the apostles. To be sure, misunderstandings and corruptions of the apostolic teaching would arise within Paul's churches (cf. Rom 16:17–20; Col 2:1–23; 2 Tim 2:14–21; Acts 20:29–31). But these were later divergences from the body of teaching transmitted by the earliest apostles and eyewitnesses, which Paul himself received within approximately eighteen months of the first Good Friday and Easter.[19]

Conclusion: The Evidence of Paul's Letters for Christian Origins

Much more evidence is available elsewhere in Paul's letters, other New Testament documents, and additional first-century texts regarding the teaching of the first disciples and eyewitnesses of Jesus. But for purposes of space I have focused primarily on 1 Corinthians 15:1–11, our richest resource for the historian seeking the origins of the Christian movement. This passage, the core beliefs it expresses, and the information it provides regarding the source of these beliefs are of great historical importance. The thesis of an originally Christ-less and confession-less Christianity claims that the historic Christian teachings regarding Jesus's redemptive death and bodily resurrection were an invention of Paul, the gospel writers, or Christian bishops in the late second century. On this view, during the earliest, "pre-Pauline" period a diversity of conflicting beliefs about Jesus existed, and Jesus's earliest disciples followed him as a now-dead prophet.

But 1 Corinthians 15:1–11 reveals that these claims are radically unhistorical. This key historical source reveals the content of the message preached by Paul to the Corinthians only seventeen years after Jesus's crucifixion. But even more importantly, this source provides us with breathtaking information regarding the message proclaimed by the earliest apostles and eyewitnesses of Jesus's ministry, passion, death, and resurrection. This passage provides firm, bedrock evidence for the existence, within one to two years of the first Easter, of a core set of beliefs carefully formulated and transmitted to the earliest Christ followers by Peter, the twelve apostles, James, Paul, and other apostles and eyewitnesses. It is therefore beyond a reasonable historical doubt that the gospel of the first Christians had a definite content, which was shared by all the apostles, and which had its source in the eyewitness testimony of these apostles to the events of the first Good Friday and Easter. This gospel focused on Jesus's identity as the Christ, the messianic King

---

19. For a classic and still unsurpassed study of the apostolic kerygma within the earliest church, see J. N. D. Kelly, *Early Christian Creeds*, 3rd ed. (Essex, UK: Longman, 1972), 1–29.

promised in the prophetic Scriptures; on his redemptive death as an atonement for human sin; and on the physical resurrection of his crucified body from the tomb on the third day, an event in space and time, verified by eyewitness testimony. Far from being consistent with the thesis of an originally pluriform Christianity, 1 Corinthians 15:1–11 reveals a continuity in the proclamation of Jesus's death and resurrection from the earliest message of the first eyewitnesses to the time of the written gospels.

Our earliest sources, the letters of Paul, thus provide decisive evidence regarding the origins of Christianity. The narrative of ancient Christianity as the story of an original diversity suppressed by the imposition of a later orthodoxy, of an original cross-less and resurrection-less Christianity, is simply unhistorical. The crucified and risen Christ of the four Gospels and of historic Christian faith is not a fiction devised in the second, third, or fourth century, nor an invention of Paul, but the Jesus proclaimed by the first eyewitnesses closest to the events. Paul's letters are explosive documents, for they reveal that the oft-claimed contrast between the "Jesus of history" and the "Christ of faith," that is, the crucified and risen Christ proclaimed in the New Testament, is an unhistorical fiction inconsistent with our earliest sources and eyewitness evidence. Paul's letters, in providing us access to the testimony of these earliest eyewitnesses, reveal that the Christ of faith *is* the Jesus of history.

Chapter Fourteen

Paul and Peter among the Apostles

In the previous chapter, Paul's letters, as our earliest Christian sources, enabled us to gain a grasp of the historical origins of Christianity. Will Paul's letters also enable us to build upon this knowledge in order to gain a fuller understanding of Paul's place within the foundations of Christianity? The answer is yes. And an understanding of Paul's unique role among the apostles will enable us to grasp the distinctive function of the Pauline epistles within the New Testament, and to gain a new and helpful perspective on the proper context for reading Paul's letters as part of New Testament Scripture.

Paul within the Apostolic College

We saw in the prior chapter that the "pluriform Christianity" scenario (which claims that the first Christ followers had no core beliefs) depicts Paul as a freewheeling theological inventor. This way of thinking about Paul is reflected in a certain stream of New Testament scholarship, which regards Paul's teachings as varying from letter to letter. To take one example: it is sometimes held that Paul's teaching on the resurrection changed between his writing of 1 Thessalonians and his writing of 1 Corinthians, and then again between 1 Corinthians and 2 Corinthians.[1] The picture assumed is one of an apostle freely adapting and changing his gospel from one letter to another. With many other scholars, I consider such an approach to Paul misguided. But I find that I, as a Pauline scholar, am also often all too prone to unwittingly think of Paul as an autonomous theologian or thinker working in splendid isolation. For scholars of Paul, who focus our study especially on Paul's letters, this is perhaps an easy trap to fall into.

But our investigation in the previous chapter revealed an important fact about Paul's apostleship: *Paul did not carry out his apostolic mission in isolation, but as a*

---

1. For a classic survey (and withering critique) of such theories, see Ben F. Meyer, "Did Paul's View of the Resurrection of the Dead Undergo Development?" *TS* 47 (1986): 363–87.

member of a college of apostles. Paul functioned as one member of an apostolic band that had a shared body of fixed core teachings. The depiction of Paul within the "pluriform Christianity" thesis as a theological inventor, whose teachings were in a continual state of flux, is the stuff of fantasy rather than serious history. And even the less radical tendency to view Paul as an autonomous theologian is less than adequate historically. Paul was, to be sure, the most creative of theologians, but his theological thought and work took place *in the context of the core teachings he shared with the other members of the apostolic college.*

Paul, then, was one among a body or college of apostles. But Paul had a unique role in the extraordinary events that formed the apostolic body, which made him different from the other apostles. When we triangulate the evidence of Paul's letters with that of the four Gospels and Acts, Paul's distinctive place among the apostles will become clear.

The Twelve as the Nucleus of the Apostolic College

Within the early church, the guarantors of the gospel proclamation about Jesus, and of the historical, space-and-time reality of Jesus's resurrection, were the apostles—disciples who had personally seen the risen Lord and been commissioned by him as eyewitnesses of his resurrection (see 1 Cor 9:1; 15:7; cf. Acts 1:21–22; 4:33). According to Paul's letters, this group was *wider* than the Twelve. The Twelve were the nucleus of a larger group of apostles, all of whom were likewise eyewitnesses of Jesus's ministry, the climactic events in Jerusalem, and Jesus's resurrection (1 Cor 15:7). This latter group included James, the brother of the Lord (Gal 1:19); Andronicus and Junia (Rom 16:7); and others whose names have not come down to us.

According to 1 Corinthians 15:5, at the center of this apostolic confraternity were Peter and the other eleven apostles. This Pauline evidence coheres with the much more detailed picture we get in the four Gospels and Acts, which tell us that the Twelve were chosen by Jesus at the beginning of his ministry, were with him throughout his ministry in Galilee, and were eyewitnesses of the events in Jerusalem culminating in his passion, death, and resurrection (see conveniently Acts 1:21–22; 10:37–42; 13:31). Acts informs us that the appearances of the risen Jesus to Peter, the Twelve, and the other apostles began on the first Easter Sunday and continued throughout the forty-day period between Jesus's resurrection and his ascension (Acts 1:1–3). Both Acts and the four Gospels indicate that these were extended encounters in which the disciples saw, heard, touched, and ate and drank with Jesus, demonstrating that he had risen from the tomb in his body of flesh and bones (Matt 28:8–20; Luke 24:39–43; John 20:11–29; Acts 1:3–4; 10:40–42).

Luke tells us that the apostles, at the end of this forty-day period of resurrection appearances, were also eyewitnesses of Jesus's bodily ascension into heaven (Luke 24:50–53; Acts 1:4–11). Witnesses of Jesus from the time of his baptism by John until his ascension, and authoritatively commissioned by the risen Lord, the Twelve formed the authoritative core of the apostolic body (1 Cor 15:5; cf. Acts 1:2, 21–26; 2:14). Their unique foundational role is strikingly expressed in the climactic vision of the book of Revelation, where the gates of the new Jerusalem are inscribed with "the twelve names of the twelve apostles of the Lamb" (Rev 21:14). The Twelve, then, according to all our New Testament documents, formed the nucleus of the apostolic body.

Paul's Unique Place among the Apostles

It is clear from Paul's own letters, as well as from the four Gospels and Acts, that Paul was unique within this apostolic body. Paul, in contrast with the other apostles, was not a follower of Jesus during his ministry, nor an eyewitness of the culminating events in Jerusalem. Nor was he among the disciples who witnessed Jesus's post-Easter appearances prior to his ascension (cf. Acts 13:31). Moreover, Paul had originally opposed and persecuted the new Christian movement (1 Cor 15:9; Gal 1:13–14; Acts 7:54–8:3). Nevertheless, Paul became an apostle when he too saw and was commissioned by the risen Christ (1 Cor 15:8–9; cf. Rom 1:1; 1 Thess 2:7; Acts 14:4, 14; 26:16–18). But Paul saw the risen Jesus in such a way that he was "born out of due time" (1 Cor 15:8). For in this extraordinary event, Paul saw the risen Jesus approximately eighteen months *after* his ascension into heaven (Gal 1:13–17; Acts 9:1–22; 22:1–16; 26:9–23). Alone among the apostles, Paul saw *the ascended and glorified Jesus* (1 Cor 9:1). Paul's seeing of Jesus thus had a very different character than Jesus's self-disclosures to the other apostles. This fact is reflected in the very different ways in which the same author, Luke, describes Jesus's resurrection appearance to the Twelve in his gospel and Jesus's resurrection appearance to Paul in the book of Acts:

> And as they were speaking these things, Jesus himself stood in their midst and said to them, "Peace be with you." Terrified and frightened, they were supposing that they were beholding a spirit. And he said to them, "Why are you troubled and why do doubts arise in your hearts? See my hands and my feet that it is I myself; handle me and see, because a spirit does not have flesh and bones as you see that I have." And when he had said this, he showed them his hands and his feet. And while they were still

disbelieving it from their joy and were amazed, he said to them, "Do you have something to eat here?" And they gave him a piece of a roasted fish. And he took it before them and ate it. (Luke 24:36–43)

And as Paul was journeying it happened that he was drawing near to Damascus, and suddenly there flashed around him a light from heaven, and when he had fallen to the ground he heard a voice speaking to him: "Saul, Saul, why do you persecute me?" And he said, "Who are you, Lord?" And he said, "I am Jesus whom you are persecuting." (Acts 9:3–5)

And yet, Paul's postascension encounter with the ascended and glorified Christ was nonetheless (in a mystery that none of our New Testament texts explain) an objective, physical event. This is evident in Acts, which reports that Paul's eyes were physically blinded by the divine effulgence emanating from the Lord (Acts 9:8–9; 22:11). Moreover, in *both* 1 Corinthians 15:1–11 and Luke-Acts the same verb of seeing (the Greek verb *horaō*) is used for both the preascension appearances of the risen Jesus to the Twelve and his postascension appearance to Paul (cf. 1 Cor 15:5–8; Luke 24:34, 39; Acts 9:17, 27; 26:16). And in 1 Corinthians 15:1–11, Paul's emphatically placed "last of all" (1 Cor 15:8) sharply distinguishes these physical, objective appearances of the risen Lord to the apostles in 15:5–8, including the appearance to Paul, from all later subjective visions and ecstatic experiences, including Paul's own later "visions and revelations of the Lord" (2 Cor 12:1).[2] According to 1 Corinthians 15:3–8, these appearances of the risen Lord are the unrepeatable foundation of the church, and the appearance to Paul was the last of them.

The list of witnesses to Jesus's resurrection in 1 Corinthians 15:5–8 thus has a fascinating composite character, due to the unique character of Paul's encounter with the risen Lord. The list consists primarily of appearances of Jesus, after his resurrection but prior to his ascension, to the apostles he had previously chosen, as well as to other disciples (1 Cor 15:5–7). This portion of the list corresponds to the resurrection narratives of the four Gospels (Matt 28; Mark 16; Luke 24; John 20–21) and the summaries in Acts (10:36–41; 13:26–37), which tell of the disciples seeing, hearing, touching, and eating and drinking with the risen Lord. But *linked to and yet distinguished from them* is a mysterious and final postascension appearance to Paul (1 Cor 15:8). This final member of the list corresponds to Luke's report in Acts of Jesus's appearance to Paul in an overwhelming (and debilitating) blaze of glorious light (Acts 9:1–22; 22:1–16; 26:9–23). Because of

2. Cf. Friedrich Lang, *Die Briefe an die Korinther* (Göttingen: Vandenhoeck & Ruprecht, 1986), 213–14, 216.

the unique character of his eyewitness encounter with the risen Lord, Paul had (as we will see) a distinctive place among the apostles. But first we must discuss the role of Peter.

Peter among the Apostolic Pillars

The Twelve, we have seen, formed the nucleus of the apostolic body. In their exercise of their unique commission from Jesus, the Twelve functioned collaboratively as a team or college. And yet, according to the picture drawn in the four Gospels, not all the members of the Twelve were of equal weight and authority. Within the Twelve was an inner circle of apostles with a unique position. When Jesus raised to life the daughter of Jairus, the ruler of the synagogue, he did not take all the apostles with him, but only Peter, James, and John (Mark 5:37; Luke 8:51). When Jesus's glory was manifested on the mountain at the transfiguration, the only eyewitnesses of this momentous event were the disciples Jesus had taken with him: Peter, James, and John (Matt 17:1; Mark 9:2; Luke 9:28). And at the garden of Gethsemane before his passion, the apostles Jesus took with him to pray were Peter, James, and John (Matt 26:37; Mark 14:33). Moreover, in the lists of the names of the apostles given in the four Gospels and Acts, the first four names are always either Peter, Andrew, James, and John (Matt 10:2; Luke 6:14) or Peter, James, John, and Andrew (Mark 3:16–17; Acts 1:13). The order in Mark and Acts is especially significant, as it breaks the expected linkage of Andrew with his brother Peter, in order to place Peter, James, and John at the head of the list. And in the narrative of Acts, Peter and John function with a unique charism and authority among the other apostles (Acts 3–4; 8:14–25; 9:32–43; 10–12). In the four Gospels and Acts, Peter and James and John form a core group of apostolic pillars within the larger college of apostles.

According to the four Gospels, within this apostolic inner circle Peter had a place of priority or primacy. According to Matthew, Jesus himself had bestowed on Peter, whose given name was Simon son of John, the new name of Peter or "Rock" (Greek: *petros*) and given him the keys of the kingdom of God (Matt 16:16–19). In Luke it was Peter for whom Jesus prayed that his faith not fail, in order that he might "strengthen his brothers" (Luke 22:31–32). And according to John, Jesus commissioned Peter to "shepherd my sheep" (John 21:15–19; cf. 1:41–42). Peter is always first on the evangelists' lists of the apostles (Matt 10:2; Mark 3:16; Luke 6:14; Acts 1:13). These lists always use the name betokening Simon's primacy, *Petros* or Peter; Matthew's list specifically designates Peter as the "first" (*prōtos*). Peter's name is likewise always first in the lists of the apostolic inner circle or pillars (Matt

17:1; 26:37; Mark 5:37; 9:2; 14:33; Luke 8:51; 9:28). And according to Luke 24:34, Peter was the first apostle to see the risen Christ. Peter's priority among the apostles is conspicuous in the narrative of Acts (Acts 1:15–26; 2:14–41; 3:1–4:31; 5:1–42; 8:14–25; 9:32–42; 10–12; 15:6–21). Peter's priority or leadership among the apostles was considered axiomatic within the ancient church (see Tertullian, *Monogamy* 8; *Modesty* 21; Origen, *Homilies on Exodus* 5.4; Cyprian, *The Unity of the Catholic Church* 4; *Letters* 33.1; 43.5; Jerome, *Against Jovinianus* 1.26). Peter clearly had a unique position not only among the Twelve, but also among the apostolic pillars.

And yet, according to the four Gospels, Peter did not carry out this function independently but collaboratively, as the head or first of a band or company of apostles. This is expressed in the apostolic lists themselves, where Peter is not alone, but the "first" (Matt 10:2) among the college of the Twelve. In the same way, Peter was not the only apostle who saw the risen Christ, but the first in a company of eyewitnesses (Luke 24:34–43; Mark 16:7). This collaborative context is precisely the way we see Peter's primacy functioning in the book of Acts, among both the inner circle and the wider body of the Twelve (Acts 1–12; 15).

According to Acts, an important shift among the apostolic pillars took place in 44 CE, approximately a decade after the first Easter. At that time Herod Agrippa I put James, the brother of John, to death (Acts 12:2). Thereafter in Acts we see James, the brother (or cousin) of Jesus, although not a member of the Twelve, functioning with a distinct authority among the inner circle of the apostles (Acts 12:17; 15:1–35).

What was the relationship of Paul to this apostolic inner circle?

Paul among the Apostolic Pillars

In any study of Paul's role among the apostles, Paul's report in Galatians 2:6–9 of the outcome of the Apostolic Council is fundamental:

> [6]But those who were recognized as authoritative—what they were makes no difference to me; God shows no partiality—in our conference added nothing to me. [7]But, to the contrary, having seen that I have been entrusted with taking the gospel to the gentiles, just as Peter has been entrusted with taking the gospel to the Jewish people [8](for the God who had worked powerfully in Peter in his apostleship to the Jewish people had also worked powerfully in me in my apostleship to the nations), [9]and recognizing the grace given to me, James and Peter and John, who were recognized as pillars, gave to me and Barnabas the right hand of

partnership, that we might go to the gentiles, and they to the Jewish people. (Gal 2:6–9)

We have seen that the four Gospels and Acts portray Peter, James, and John as the authoritative core of the apostolic body, with Peter having a position of unique priority or primacy. Advocates of the thesis (explored in chapter 13) of an originally pluriform Christianity (a Christianity without core beliefs transmitted by the apostles) routinely call the historicity of this portrayal into question. It is therefore significant that Galatians 2:6–9, a source independent of the four Gospels and Acts and of undoubted authenticity, corroborates this picture in several striking ways. Paul in Galatians 2:9 makes explicit reference to Peter, James (the brother of Jesus), and John as the authoritative center of the apostolic body; he informs us that Peter, James, and John were regarded as the "pillars" of the community of Christ followers. The metaphor of "pillars" envisions the church as a temple, the dwelling place of God, and describes Peter, James, and John as the support of the entire structure.[3] Peter's primacy among these pillar apostles is evident as well. Paul, here as elsewhere, always refers to Simon as "Cephas" ("Rock" in Aramaic, 1 Cor 1:12; 3:22; 9:5; 15:5; Gal 1:18; 2:9, 14) or "Peter" ("Rock" in Greek, Gal 2:7, 8), that is, by the name given to him by Jesus and signifying his primacy. And Galatians 2:7–8 ascribes to Peter a unique position not only among the Twelve but also among the apostolic pillars. For here the mission of James, Peter, and John to the Jewish people (2:9) is described as especially entrusted to Peter (2:7–8). Peter's unique role is also implicit in Paul's report concerning his fifteen-day conference with Peter in Galatians 1:18–20 (explored in the previous chapter). And just as in the four Gospels and Acts we saw Peter carrying out this function collaboratively, as the leader of a college of apostles, likewise in Galatians 2:6–9 Peter functions in concert with the other pillars, James and John (2:9; cf. 1:18–20). The picture Galatians 2:6–9 draws of a group of "pillar" apostles headed by Peter is in striking coherence with the portrayal of the four Gospels and Acts. Although the historicity of the four Gospels and Acts on this score is sometimes brought into question, Galatians 2:6–9 triangulates with the evidence from the four Gospels and Acts to show that this is a firm historical datum.

What is also striking in this passage is the unique position of Paul. These verses recognize not only a core group of apostolic pillars, James and Cephas and John, but also a kind of shared apostolic primacy between Peter and Paul, one the

---

3. On the metaphor, see Simon Gathercole, "The Petrine and Pauline *Sola Fide* in Galatians 2," in *Lutherische und Neue Paulusperspektive*, ed. Michael Bachmann and Johannes Woyke (Tübingen: Mohr Siebeck, 2005), 316–17.

apostle to the Jewish people, the other the apostle to the gentiles. Paul's apostleship is depicted as *parallel in charism and authority with that of Peter* ("I have been entrusted . . . just as Peter" [2:7]; "the God who had worked powerfully in Peter . . . worked powerfully in me" [2:8]). The "right hand of partnership" given to Paul (and his coworker Barnabas) by the apostolic pillars in 2:9 is commonly regarded as simply a recognition of Paul's apostleship.[4] But, given by the apostolic pillars Peter, James, and John, I believe this partnership clearly involved something greater: an equal (although distinct) authority together with them of witness, mission, and teaching. Thus Paul's conference with Peter, James, and John involved more, I would propose, than recognition of Paul's apostleship. It involved the recognition of Paul's inclusion, together with them, among the apostolic pillars.

This is a facet of Paul's apostleship that has not received extensive discussion in contemporary scholarship on Paul. And yet I believe this dimension of Paul's apostleship is critical for understanding Paul's place within Christian origins. Ernst Barnikol, in an article from the previous century, called attention to the preeminent place given to Paul among the apostles in Galatians 2:7–9. According to Barnikol, this passage describes Peter and Paul as "the two great figures high above all other Christian missionaries of the early period."[5] So striking is this conception of "the parallelism of the apostles Peter and Paul" that Barnikol believed it could not have arisen until "the proclamation of the early Catholic Church in the second century."[6] For this and other reasons he regarded verses 7–8 as a second-century interpolation into the text of Galatians.[7] The vast majority of Pauline scholars rightly reject this unfounded interpolation theory, and are in agreement that Galatians 2:7–8 is from the hand of Paul. As such, the passage provides bedrock evidence for a dimension of Paul's apostleship that in my view has been hitherto insufficiently recognized. I would propose that, just as James the brother of Jesus, although not one of the Twelve, was recognized as being among the apostolic inner circle by the middle 40s CE at the latest, so also Paul, at the latest by the time of the Apostolic Council in 49, was included with Peter, James, and John

---

4. Cf., for example, H. J. Schoeps, *Paul: The Theology of the Apostle in the Light of Jewish Religious History*, trans. Harold Knight (Philadelphia: Westminster, 1961), 72; Richard B. Hays, "The Letter to the Galatians," *NIB* 11:225–27.

5. Ernst Barnikol, "The Non-Pauline Origin of the Parallelism of the Apostles Peter and Paul: Galatians 2:7–8," *Journal of Higher Criticism* 5 (1988): 285–300 (English translation of 1931 German original).

6. Barnikol, "Non-Pauline Origin," 285–86.

7. William O. Walker has recently sought to revive Barnikol's interpolation theory ("Galatians 2:7b–8 as a Non-Pauline Interpolation," *CBQ* 65 [2003]: 568–87). Prominent among the arguments Walker puts forward is the shared apostolic primacy presupposed in Gal 2:7–8 (582–83).

among the core body of apostolic pillars. Moreover, Paul's apostolic charism was recognized as second only to that of Peter, and Peter and Paul were closely linked together as the twin pillars of the apostolic body.

As we have seen, Barnikol considered the picture drawn in Galatians 2:7–8 of Paul's unique authority alongside Peter to have no equivalent in the first century. But I believe this passage has previously unrecognized parallels, both within and outside Paul's letters. First, let us consider Luke's portrayal of the Jerusalem Council in Acts. Paul's report of the council focuses especially, as he tells us explicitly, on the private conference he held with the pillars, Peter, James, and John (Gal 2:2, 6–10). Luke's report, by contrast, concentrates on the public deliberations of the council (Acts 15:1–35). Nonetheless, Acts offers important corroborating evidence. For the narrative of Acts focuses on three key speeches, whereby "after much debate" (15:7) the council's deliberations were brought to an authoritative conclusion (15:6–21). These three speeches in Acts are given by Peter (15:6–11), Paul and Barnabas (15:12), and James (15:13–21). Paul here, once again, is linked with Peter and James, the two apostles with whom he met in his important visit to Jerusalem in 37 CE (Gal 1:18–20), and by whom in private conference at the council he was given the right hand of partnership (Gal 2:9).

Now to the evidence elsewhere in Paul's letters. First Corinthians 15:5–8, as we saw in the previous chapter, consists of a carefully structured account of the eyewitnesses of Jesus's resurrection:

> [5]He was seen by Peter, then by the Twelve; [6]then he was seen by more than five hundred brothers and sisters at the same time, of whom the majority remain until now, but some have fallen asleep; [7]then he was seen by James, then by all the apostles; [8]and last of all, as to one untimely born, he was seen by me as well.

Three apostles are given special prominence, as the only persons individually identified: Peter, James, and Paul. Here, once again, we see Peter, James, and Paul linked together, as the core of the apostolic body of witnesses to Jesus's resurrection. We see *Peter's* primacy as the first in the list, and (as in Luke 24:34) the first apostle to see the risen Christ (1 Cor 15:5). And the parallel prominence within the list of Peter, James, and Paul, consistent with our other evidence, functions to include *Paul* among the apostolic pillars. We also see in this ancient confession that these apostolic pillars work in concert and unity with one another, with the Twelve, and with the rest of the apostles and their coworkers. The collaborative nature of the work of the apostolic body is here implicit in the fact that, as in the four Gospels and Acts, Peter is not the only eyewitness of the risen Christ listed, but the first in a company of eyewitnesses (1 Cor 15:5–8; cf. Luke 24:34–43; Mark 16:7). This collegial character of the apostolic mission is a key focus of Paul's exhortation to unity in the first part of the letter, 1 Corinthians 1–4 (cf. esp. 1:12; 3:22). And it is explicit and emphatic in 1 Corinthians 15:11: "Whether, then, it was I or they, so we proclaim, and so you believed."

Peter and Paul in the Ancient Church

There is a fascinating feature of the list of witnesses to Jesus's resurrection in 1 Corinthians 15:5–8: each of the named apostles in this list of eyewitnesses, Peter, James, and Paul, would die as martyrs for their proclamation of the resurrection. Their martyrdoms are recorded nowhere in the New Testament, but we know of them from reliable primary source evidence from outside the Bible. Josephus, the Jewish historian, provides us with a precious account of the martyrdom of James in Jerusalem in 62 CE (*Jewish Antiquities* 20.200). At some point in the 60s (the precise dates are disputed), both Peter and Paul would come to Rome, teach and confirm the church there, and become martyrs for their proclamation of the gospel (1 Clement 5–6; Ignatius, *To the Romans* 4.3; Irenaeus, *Against Heresies* 3.1–3; Dionysius of Corinth, in Eusebius, *Ecclesiastical History* 2.25.8; the Roman presbyter Gaius, in Eusebius, *Ecclesiastical History* 2.25.6–7; Tertullian, *Prescription against Heretics* 36; *Against Marcion* 4.5).

Our sources thereafter, which include our very earliest sources outside the New Testament, reflect what appears to have been a virtually universal early Christian understanding of Peter and Paul as the twin pillars of the apostolic body. Writing between 85 and 95 CE, Clement—a leader of the Christ followers at Rome—recounts the martyrdoms of Peter and Paul at Rome, calling them "the greatest and most righteous pillars" of the church (1 Clement 5). Here Clement uses the word "pillar" (Greek: *stuloi*), the same word Paul employed in Galatians 2:9. In calling them the greatest of the pillars, Clement describes Paul and Peter as the core apostles within the apostolic body. Ignatius, writing to the Romans, similarly links the unique authority of the two apostles: "I do not give you commands, as did Peter and Paul" (*To the Romans* 4.3). Irenaeus (*Against Heresies* 3.3.2) likewise refers to "the two most glorious of the apostles, Peter and Paul" (*gloriosissimis duobus apostolis Petro et Paulo*).

There is a consistency in the data spanning well over a century, from Galatians 2:6–9 to 1 Corinthians to Acts to 1 Clement to Ignatius to Irenaeus, that is quite striking. Our earliest sources, both within and outside the New Testament, concur that Paul was more than an apostle. Along with Peter, James, and John, he was among the apostolic pillars who were the foundation of the apostolic body. His apostolic charism and authority were second only to that of Peter, the first among the apostles, with whom in all our sources he is closely linked.

In what did the preeminence of Paul's apostolate lie? According to Paul's own letters, his unique apostolic charism involved his distinctive role "to bring to the gentiles the good news of the riches of Christ" (Eph 3:8), and his accompanying revelatory "insight into the mystery of Christ" (Eph 3:4), that is, the mystery of the full inclusion of the gentiles in the people of God through union with Christ (Rom 16:25–27; Eph 3:1–13; Col 1:24–29). Here we find another link between Paul and Peter. For according to Acts, the revelation of the full inclusion of the gentiles by faith and baptism, apart from the Jewish identity markers of circumcision, food laws, and Sabbath keeping, was first vouchsafed to Peter, and gentiles were first brought into the church through Peter's proclamation of the gospel (Acts 10–11; 15:7–9). Within Acts, Paul's apostolic mission to the gentiles is the outworking of this initial work of Peter (Acts 11:19–26; 13–28).

Paul's Distinctive Role among the Apostolic Pillars

The unique place of Paul within ancient Christianity that we have explored in this chapter illumines many otherwise perplexing aspects of his letters. For example, the supposed contrast between the four Gospels, where we learn the first eyewitnesses of the resurrection were women, and the list of eyewitnesses in 1 Corinthians 15:1–11, where only male disciples are named, has seemed a difficulty to many. The consensus is that the names of women eyewitnesses were omitted from the list in 1 Corinthians for missionary purposes, to increase the credibility of the list within the ancient world, in which the validity of testimony by women was widely questioned. Scholars usually divide only on whether this was a commendable attempt at cross-cultural communication or a cowardly act of sexism. But, as the discussion above has shown, this analysis simply misses the point. None of the eyewitnesses, whether male or female, including the Twelve, are identified or named except Peter, James, and Paul. Their special prominence within the list reflects their function as the core or pillar apostles within the apostolic body.

Paul's unique apostolic role sheds light on the seemingly contradictory evidence in his letters regarding whether he was dependent upon or independent of the Twelve. The evidence is not in fact contradictory, but reflects the unique character of Paul's apostleship that we have explored in this chapter. As an apostle "born out of due time" (1 Cor 15:8), who was an eyewitness neither of Jesus's ministry nor of the culminating events in Jerusalem, Paul's apostleship was, on the one hand, dependent upon and subordinate to the Twelve. Paul's postascension inclusion in the apostolic body explains his conference with Peter in 37 CE; Paul wanted to talk with him face-to-face regarding Peter's eyewitness testimony to the Jesus events (Gal 1:18–19). And the unique role of the Twelve within the apostolic college explains why Paul, although himself an apostle, laid his gospel before the apostles in Jerusalem for their consideration at the Apostolic Council in 49 CE.

On the other hand, Paul's independent authority among the apostolic pillars is evident in his joint partnership with Peter, James, and John in the apostolic mission (Gal 2:9). This aspect of Paul's apostleship helps to illumine a core question. Scholars have long debated the reasons for Paul's seeming indifference (even insouciance) toward the apostolic pillars in Galatians 2:6, and his apparent disregard in Galatians 2:11–14 of the authority of Peter, whom Paul called out publicly for reversing his past practice and no longer eating with gentile Christ followers. But Paul's actions gain a new coherence when we read these passages in light of his consciousness of his own standing on an equal footing with Peter and James among the apostolic pillars, and his conviction of his unique commission among them to safeguard the mystery of the full inclusion of the gentiles in Christ (Gal 2:4). Paul is not questioning Peter's authoritative role, but exercising his own authority as the member of the apostolic inner circle granted unique revelatory insight into the mystery of Christ (Eph 3:1–19; Col 1:24–27).

The Apostolic Pillars and the New Testament

If we examine the relationship between the apostolic pillars and the writings that make up the New Testament, we see a fascinating picture. A large percentage of the books of the New Testament bear the name of one or another of this apostolic inner circle (Peter, Paul, James, or John).[8] The list is extensive: thirteen epistles of Paul, two epistles of Peter, one epistle of James, and for John, a gospel, three epistles, and the book of Revelation.

But the foundational role of the apostolic pillars within the infrastructure of the New Testament is more extensive than even the list above would imply. Let us begin with Peter. We have already seen that Peter was active in Rome in the 60s CE. Our ancient sources are unanimous that Mark, the coworker of Peter, served

8. In some cases, modern scholars dispute whether a given book was authored by the apostle to whom it is attributed or by a disciple or follower of that apostle. Space precludes a discussion of each of these cases (but see the introduction for a discussion of the authorship of Paul's letters). Such questions are in any case irrelevant to the point here, which is to tally the books attributed in our canonical New Testament to a member of this core group among the apostles.

as Peter's translator in Rome, and that Mark's Gospel is a digest of Peter's proclamation of the gospel (Papias, in Eusebius, *Ecclesiastical History* 3.39; Irenaeus, *Against Heresies* 3.1; Clement of Alexandria, in Eusebius, *Ecclesiastical History* 6.14; Tertullian, *Against Marcion* 4.5; cf. 1 Pet 5:13). One key source is Papias, who wrote in the first quarter of the second century, based on his interaction with apostles and eyewitnesses in the latter decades of the first century, and who specifically claims that he received his information regarding the origins of Mark's Gospel from the apostle John himself (Papias, in Eusebius, *Ecclesiastical History* 3.39.15). Another key source is Irenaeus, who received his information from Polycarp (who lived 70–156 CE), a disciple of the apostle John (Irenaeus, *Against Heresies* 3.1.1–2). These and further evidences for the Gospel of Mark as a digest of Peter's testimony have been explored insightfully by such scholars as Martin Hengel, Richard Bauckham, and William Lane.[9] To be sure, a number of New Testament scholars reject this convergence of evidence regarding the origins of Mark's Gospel, but on entirely insufficient grounds. Our historical evidence is in my view conclusive that this gospel is the work of Mark, and the foundations of its narrative lie in Peter's proclamation of the Jesus events.

We may note in passing that the origins of Mark's Gospel in Peter's testimony offers dramatically important historical information regarding the origins of the Gospels. We saw in the previous chapter that Paul's letters, our earliest sources, provide striking historical confirmation of the eyewitness origins of the passion and resurrection narratives of our canonical gospels, strongly suggesting that the Gospels as a whole have their origin, not in later myths, but in eyewitness testimony. The evidence regarding the Petrine origins of Mark's Gospel converges with our evidence from Paul's letters. Mark's narrative has its source not only in eyewitness testimony, but in the testimony of the central eyewitness, Peter himself.

But Peter's impact on the canonical gospels is most likely even more profound. Matthew, Mark, and Luke are called by scholars the Synoptic Gospels, because they tell the story of Jesus's deeds and teachings in a very similar way (John's Gospel tells the story in its own, distinctive way). Like the majority of New Testament scholars today, I hold to the theory of "Markan priority," the view that Mark was our earliest gospel, and that Matthew and Luke used Mark in composing their own gospels. In my view this theory requires modification, to factor in the existence of an earlier draft of Mark (called "proto-Mark" by scholars). But

---

9. For further discussion and evidence, see Martin Hengel, *Studies in the Gospel of Mark* (Philadelphia: Fortress, 1985), 1–84; Richard Bauckham, *Jesus and the Eyewitnesses: The Gospels as Eyewitness Testimony*, 2nd ed. (Grand Rapids: Eerdmans, 2017), 124–82; William L. Lane, *The Gospel according to Mark*, NICNT (Grand Rapids: Eerdmans, 1974), 7–12.

I believe the thesis that Matthew and Luke in their narratives follow Mark's basic outline has strong plausibility. If so, the core narrative of all three Synoptic Gospels, Matthew, Mark, and Luke, had its origins in Peter's eyewitness testimony to Jesus's deeds and teaching.

In regard to Paul's place within the canonical writings, the Pauline letter corpus itself takes up a good part of the New Testament. But more can be said about the Pauline foundations of the New Testament canon. The Gospel of Luke and the book of Acts are, all scholars agree, a single work by one author in two volumes. This two-volume work makes up over a quarter of the New Testament. The author clearly presents himself as a companion of Paul on his missionary journeys, in the so-called "we passages" of Acts (16:10–17; 20:5–15; 21:1–18; 27:1–28:16). All ancient readers of the book of Acts of whom we have evidence read the "we passages" as the author's artful signal to his readers that he himself was among Paul's coworkers and an eyewitness to the events of Paul's mission of which he wrote. And our early Christian sources unanimously identify the author of Luke and Acts as Paul's fellow worker Luke (Justin, *Dialogue with Trypho* 103.19; Irenaeus, *Against Heresies* 3.1.1; 3.14.1; Tertullian, *Against Marcion* 4.2.2; 4.5.3; Muratorian Canon 2–8; cf. Philem 24; Col 4:14). The evidence is in my view convincing that the author of this work was Luke, a coworker of Paul.[10] If Luke-Acts is the work of Paul's fellow laborer Luke, his gospel and Acts obviously have close and vital connections to Paul and the Pauline mission. And once again (we may note in passing) this evidence corroborates the evidence from Paul's letters regarding the reliability of the four Gospels that we surveyed in the previous chapter. For the "we passages" in the book of Acts make clear that, as Paul's coworker, Luke not only was an eyewitness of Paul's mission but also had direct and extensive contacts with apostles and eyewitnesses of Jesus's ministry such as James (Acts 21:18), and with companions and coworkers of the apostles such as Philip (Acts 21:8; cf. 6:5–7; 8:4–40) and Silas (Acts 16:6–40; cf. 15:22–35).

The Gospel of Luke and the book of Acts, then, are closely tied to Paul's apostleship and work. This is also true of the book of Hebrews. This anonymous work was probably not authored by Paul. However, scholars today agree that it was certainly written by someone within the Pauline circle, as its reference to "our brother Timothy" attests (Heb 13:23; cf. Rom 16:21; 1 Cor 4:17; 16:10–11; 2 Cor

---

10. For the most thorough scholarly case for Paul's coworker Luke as the author of Luke-Acts, see the masterful analysis of the evidence in Joseph A. Fitzmyer, *The Gospel according to Luke*, AB 28A (New York: Doubleday, 1981), 1:35–53. Advocates of the thesis discussed in chapter 13 of an originally pluriform Christianity (that is, a Christianity disconnected from the witness and teaching of the apostles) regularly dismiss this evidence, but offer in my judgment forced explanations of the historical data that are unconvincing.

1:19–20; Phil 2:19–24; 1 Thess 3:1–2). First Peter similarly has a connection with the Pauline mission, through its apparent coauthorship by Paul's coworker Silvanus (1 Pet 5:12; cf. 2 Cor 1:19–20; 1 Thess 1:1; 2 Thess 1:1). Likewise the book of Jude, with its assertion of authorship by "Jude, a slave of Jesus Christ, and brother of James" (Jude 1), claims close ties to the circle of James.

The table below summarizes the connections our various books of the New Testament have with the apostolic pillars. The list indicates the books that bear the name of a member of this core body, together with books that have a close connection (on the evidence considered above) to one or more of these pillars (marked with an asterisk). The following books of the New Testament either claim authorship by, or have strong connections with, the apostolic pillars Peter, Paul, John, and James:

PAUL	PETER	JOHN	JAMES
Romans	1 Peter	John	James
1 Corinthians	2 Peter	1 John	Jude*
2 Corinthians	Mark*	2 John	
Galatians		3 John	
Ephesians		Revelation	
Philippians			
Colossians			
1 Thessalonians			
2 Thessalonians			
1 Timothy			
2 Timothy			
Titus			
Philemon			
Luke*			
Acts*			
Hebrews*			

It is a striking fact that the table includes all but one of the twenty-seven books of the New Testament (the only exception being Matthew's Gospel). *Every book but one of the New Testament either claims authorship by, or can be argued to have close connections with, one of the apostolic pillars: Peter, Paul, John, or James.* The core role of these figures within the apostolic body, which is in evidence in all our early sources, is reflected in the very makeup of the New Testament itself. And *over half the New Testament is either authored by Paul or strongly connected with him.* The early

Christian understanding of the unique charism and authority of Paul's apostleship, as second only to that of Peter, corresponds to the dominant place of Paul within the New Testament canon.

Reading Paul's Letters within the New Testament

What are the implications of the historical foundations of the New Testament in the witness of the apostolic pillars for the reading and study of Paul's letters? I believe it is in Paul's distinctive function among the pillars of the apostolic body, as the apostle given unique comprehension of the mystery of Christ, that we discover the true synthesis between his collaborative work in transmitting the core teaching shared in common by the apostolic college (1 Cor 15:11), and his work as a creative theologian within his letters. And in so doing we discover the proper context in which Paul's letters are to be read, whether in the first century or the twenty-first. Paul's collaborative work among the apostolic pillars, that apostolic inner circle whose witness to Christ forms the body of the New Testament canon, reveals that Paul's letters are to be read in concert with the whole New Testament. By the same token, Paul's unique role among the apostolic pillars, which is reflected in the dominant position of his epistles within the canon, reveals that the whole New Testament is to be read in concert with Paul's letters. The traditional theological principle of reading Paul's epistles in light of the whole canon, and the whole canon in light of Paul's epistles, letting "Scripture interpret Scripture," is in fact indispensable for reading Paul's letters in their original *historical* context. To read Paul's letters in effective isolation from the other New Testament writings would be not only a theological but also a historical mistake.

Paul's historical place, then, among the apostles is mirrored in the place of Paul's letters within the New Testament. Paul is therefore not to be read as a free-wheeling theological inventor, nor is the theological contribution of his letters to be minimized. We may summarize the function of Paul's letters within the canon, and the proper context for reading Paul's epistles as part of New Testament Scripture, as follows: Paul's letters provide *the fullest theological elaboration within the New Testament* of the teaching he shared in common with Peter, John, James, and the other apostles and eyewitnesses of Jesus.

Conclusion: Paul among the Apostles and in the New Testament

Paul, we have seen, did not function independently, but as one member of a college of apostles. The Twelve were the nucleus of this apostolic body, and Paul's apostleship functioned differently from theirs, because of his unique historical relationship to the Jesus events. But Paul was more than an apostle. He functioned, together with Peter, James, and John, among a core nucleus of "pillars" within the apostolic college. Within this core group, Peter and Paul shared a unique status as the two "greatest and most righteous pillars" of the apostolic body. The relationship of this inner circle among the apostles to our canonical New Testament is profound. Every book but one of the New Testament either claims authorship by or has close connections to one of these four pillars among the apostles—Peter, Paul, John, or James. And Paul occupies a central place within the New Testament canon: over half of the New Testament is either authored by Paul or closely connected with him.

Paul's own letters describe his distinctive apostolic charism in terms of his identity as "apostle to the gentiles," and his unique revelatory insight into the mystery of the full inclusion of the gentiles in the Israel of God through incorporation into Christ. The function of Paul's epistles within the New Testament corresponds to this historical role of Paul among the apostolic pillars. Paul's letters provide the fullest theological elaboration within the New Testament of the body of doctrine shared in common by the apostolic college. But this elaboration is given its distinctive Pauline shape by Paul's unique apostolic charism to bring the good news of Christ to the gentiles, and to make known the mystery of the inclusion of the gentiles in Christ. Paul's unique role among the apostles is reflected in the twofold method we have employed in this book, studying Paul's gospel as the fulfillment of Israel's hopes and Scriptures in Christ, and in the context of the beliefs and thought systems of the ancient gentile world to which Paul believed he had been called. If we are to read Paul's letters in full perspective, both of these lenses are necessary, for he was and still remains "the apostle to the gentiles."

Acknowledgments

I am thankful to the following persons who read all of parts of the manuscript at various stages and offered helpful comments and suggestions: Mark Reasoner, Frank Thielman, Glen Thompson, David Chapman, Christopher Hutson, Christian Raab, Trevor Petty, Charles Reed, Joseph Miller, Douglas Low, and Thomas Fast. I am also grateful to Trevor Thompson, acquisitions editor at Eerdmans, for his enthusiasm for this project, to Tom Raabe for his skillful editorial work, and to Linda Bieze for shepherding the book through the process of publication. Above all, I am thankful beyond measure for my wife, Jan, and for her love, support, and encouragement. Finally, this book, which seeks to illumine Paul's theology by studying it in the context of the ancient world into which his gospel came, owes a special debt to Abraham J. Malherbe, from whom I learned the art and science of reading Paul in his ancient context. This book is dedicated to Abe, now at home with the Lord, beloved teacher, mentor, and friend.

Bibliography

Adeyemi, Femi. "The New Covenant Law and the Law of Christ." *BSac* 163 (2006): 438–52.

Aletti, Jean Noel. *Israël et la Loi dans la lettre aux Romains*. Paris: Cerf, 1998.

Altermath, Francois. *Du corps psychique au corps spirituel: Interprétation de 1 Cor. 15,35–49 par les auteurs chrétiens des quatre premièrs siècles*. BGBE 18. Tübingen: Mohr Siebeck, 1977.

Anderson, A. A. *The Book of Psalms*. London: Oliphants, 1977.

Avemarie, Friedrich. "Erwählung und Vergeltung. Zur Optionalen Struktur rabbinischer Soteriologie." *NTS* 45 (1999): 108–26;

———. *Tora und Leben: Untersuchungen zur Heilsbedeutung der Tora in der frühen rabbinischen Literatur*. Tübingen: Mohr Siebeck, 1996.

Barclay, John M. G. "'Neither Jew Nor Greek': Multiculturalism and the New Perspective on Paul." In *Ethnicity and the Bible*, edited by M. G. Brett, 197–214. Leiden: Brill, 1996.

———. *Obeying the Truth: A Study of Paul's Ethics in Galatians*. Edinburgh: T. & T. Clark, 1988.

Barnikol, Ernst. "The Non-Pauline Origin of the Parallelism of the Apostles Peter and Paul: Galatians 2:7–8." *Journal of Higher Criticism* 5 (1988): 285–300.

Bassler, Jouette M. *Navigating Paul: An Introduction to Key Theological Concepts*. Louisville: Westminster John Knox, 2007.

Bates, Matthew W. "A Christology of Incarnation and Enthronement: Romans 1:3–4 as Unified, Nonadoptionist, and Nonconciliatory." *CBQ* 77 (2015): 107–27.

Bauckham, Richard. *God Crucified: Monotheism and Christology in the New Testament*. Grand Rapids: Eerdmans, 1998.

———. *Jesus and the Eyewitnesses: The Gospels as Eyewitness Testimony*. 2nd ed. Grand Rapids: Eerdmans, 2017.

———. *Jesus and the God of Israel*. Grand Rapids: Eerdmans, 2008.

Bell, Richard H. *No One Seeks for God: An Exegetical and Theological Study of Romans 1:18–3:20.* WUNT 106. Tübingen: Mohr Siebeck, 1998.

———. "Sacrifice and Christology in Paul." *JTS* 53 (2002): 1–27.

Bevilacqua, Anthony J. "The History of the Indissolubility of Marriage." *Proceedings of the Catholic Theological Society of America* 22 (1967): 268–69.

Blass, Friedrich, Albert Debrunner, and Friedrich Rehkopf. *Grammatik des neutestamentlichen Griechisch.* 18th ed. Göttingen: Vandenhoeck & Ruprecht, 2001.

Blome, Peter. "Zur Umgestaltung griechischer Mythen in der römischen Sepulkralkunst." *MDAI/Römische Abteilung* 35 (1978): 435–57.

Borg, Marcus. *Jesus: A New Vision.* San Francisco: HarperCollins, 1987.

Bornkamm, Gunther. *Early Christian Experience.* London: SCM, 1969.

Bultmann, Rudolf. *Theologie des Neuen Testaments.* 9th ed. Tübingen: Mohr Siebeck, 1984.

Bynum, Caroline Walker. *The Resurrection of the Body in Western Christianity, 200–1336.* New York: Columbia University Press, 1999.

Campbell, Constantine R. *Paul and Union with Christ: An Exegetical and Theological Study.* Grand Rapids: Zondervan, 2012.

Campbell, Douglas A. "An Anchor of Pauline Chronology: Paul's Flight from 'The Ethnarch of King Aretas' (2 Corinthians 11:32–33)." *JBL* 121 (2002): 279–302.

———. *The Deliverance of God: An Apocalyptic Rereading of Justification in Paul.* Grand Rapids: Eerdmans, 2009.

Capes, David B. *Old Testament Yahweh Texts in Paul's Christology.* WUNT 2.47. Tübingen: Mohr Siebeck, 1992.

Carraway, George. *Christ Is God over All: Romans 9:5 in the Context of Romans 9–11.* LNTS 489. London: Bloomsbury, 2013.

Casey, P. M. *From Jewish Prophet to Gentile God: The Origins and Development of New Testament Christology.* Cambridge: James Clarke, 1991.

Cerfaux, Lucien. *Christ in the Theology of St. Paul.* New York: Herder and Herder, 1959.

———. "'Kyrios' dans les citations pauliniennes de l'Ancien Testament." In *Recueil Lucien Cerfaux,* 1:173–88. Gembloux: Duculot, 1954.

Chadwick, Henry. "Origen, Celsus, and the Resurrection of the Body." *HTR* 41 (1948): 83–102.

Cobb, John B., and David Ray Griffin. *Process Theology: An Introductory Exposition.* Philadelphia: Westminster, 1976.

Cooke, Bernard J. *Christian Sacraments and Christian Personality.* New York: Doubleday, 1968.

Craig, William Lane. *The Kalam Cosmological Argument.* New York: Macmillan, 1979.

Bibliography

Cranfield, C. E. B. *A Critical and Exegetical Commentary on the Epistle to the Romans.* 2 vols. ICC. Edinburgh: T. & T. Clark, 1975–1979.

Cremer, Hermann. *Biblico-Theological Lexicon of New Testament Greek.* 4th ed. Edinburgh: T. & T. Clark, 1895.

Crouzel, Henri. "La doctrine origenienne du corps réssuscité." *BLE* 31 (1980): 175–200, 241–66.

Cullmann, Oscar. *Peter: Disciple, Apostle, Martyr; A Historical and Theological Essay.* Translated by Floyd V. Filson. Philadelphia: Westminster, 1953.

Dahl, M. E. *The Resurrection of the Body: A Study of 1 Corinthians 15.* SBT 36. London: SCM, 1962.

Das, Andrew. *Paul, the Law, and the Covenant.* Peabody, MA: Hendrickson, 2001.

Destro, Adriana, and Mauro Pesce. "Self, Identity and Body in Paul and John." In *Self, Soul, and Body in Religious Experience,* edited by Albert I. Baumgarten, J. Assmann, and G. G. Stroumsa, 184–97. Leiden: Brill, 1998.

Dunn, James D. G. "The Dialogue Progresses." In *Lutherische und Neue Paulusperspektive,* edited by Michael Bachmann and Johannes Woyke, 389–430. WUNT 2.182. Tübingen: Mohr Siebeck, 2005.

———. "Did Paul Have a Covenant Theology? Reflections on Romans 9.4 and 11.27." In *The New Perspective on Paul,* 429–46. Rev. ed. Grand Rapids: Eerdmans, 2008.

———. "The New Perspective on Paul: Whence, What and Whither?" In *The New Perspective on Paul,* 1–99. Rev. ed. Grand Rapids: Eerdmans, 2008.

———. "Paul and the Torah: The Role and Function of the Law in the Theology of Paul the Apostle." In *The New Perspective on Paul,* 447–67. Rev. ed. Grand Rapids: Eerdmans, 2008.

———. *Romans 1–8.* WBC 38. Dallas: Word, 1988.

———. *The Theology of Paul the Apostle.* Grand Rapids: Eerdmans, 1998.

———. "Why 'Incarnation'? A Review of Recent New Testament Scholarship." In *Christology,* vol. 1 of *The Christ and the Spirit,* 405–23. Grand Rapids: Eerdmans, 1998.

———. "Works of the Law and the Curse of the Law (Galatians 3.10–14)." In *The New Perspective on Paul,* 121–40. Rev. ed. Grand Rapids: Eerdmans, 2008.

———. "Yet Once More—'The Works of the Law': A Response." In *The New Perspective on Paul,* 213–26. Rev. ed. Grand Rapids: Eerdmans, 2008.

Ehrman, Bart. *How Jesus Became God: The Exaltation of a Jewish Preacher from Galilee.* New York: HarperOne, 2014.

Ellis, Earle. "*Soma* in 1 Corinthians." *Int* 44 (1990): 132–44.

Engberg-Pedersen, Troels. *Cosmology and Self in the Apostle Paul: The Material Spirit.* Oxford: Oxford University Press, 2010.

Farmer, William R. "Peter and Paul and the Tradition concerning 'The Lord's Supper' in 1 Cor 11:23–26." In *One Loaf, One Cup: Ecumenical Studies of 1 Cor 11 and Other Eucharistic Texts*, edited by Ben F. Meyer, 38–43. Macon, GA: Mercer University Press, 1993.

———. "Reflections on Isaiah 53 and Christian Origins." In *Jesus and the Suffering Servant: Isaiah 53 and Christian Origins*, edited by William H. Bellinger and William R. Farmer, 260–80. Harrisburg, PA: Trinity, 1998.

Fatehi, Mehrdad. *The Spirit's Relation to the Risen Lord in Paul: An Examination of Its Christological Implications*. WUNT 2.128. Tübingen: Mohr Siebeck, 2000.

Fay, Ron C. "Was Paul a Trinitarian? A Look at Romans 8." In *Paul and His Theology*, edited by Stanley E. Porter, 327–45. Leiden: Brill, 2006.

Fee, Gordon D. *Pauline Christology: An Exegetical-Theological Study*. Peabody, MA: Hendrickson, 2007.

Fitzmyer, Joseph. *The Gospel according to Luke*. AB 28A–B. New York: Doubleday, 1981–1985.

———. *Pauline Theology: A Brief Sketch*. Englewood Cliffs, NJ: Prentice-Hall, 1967.

Florovsky, Georges. "The Concept of Creation in St. Athanasius." Edited by F. L. Cross. StPatr 6. TU 81. Berlin: Akademie Verlag, 1962. Pages 36–57.

Fotheringham, J. K. "The Evidence of Astronomy and Technical Chronology for the Date of the Crucifixion." *JTS* 25 (1934): 146–62.

Fredriksen, Paula. "Mandatory Retirement: Ideas in the Study of Christian Origins Whose Time Has Come to Go." In *Israel's God and Rebecca's Children: Christology and Community in Early Judaism and Christianity*, edited by David B. Capes, April D. DeConick, Helen K. Bond, and Troy Miller, 35–38. Waco: Baylor University Press, 2007.

———. *Paul: The Pagans' Apostle*. New Haven: Yale University Press, 2017.

———. "Vile Bodies: Paul and Augustine on the Resurrection of the Flesh." In *Biblical Hermeneutics in Historical Perspective*, edited by Mark S. Burrows and Paul Rorem, 75–87. Grand Rapids: Eerdmans, 1991.

Gabriel, Andrew C. "Pauline Pneumatology and the Question of Trinitarian Presuppositions." In *Paul and His Theology*, edited by Stanley E. Porter, 347–62. Leiden: Brill, 2006.

Gathercole, Simon. "The Petrine and Pauline *Sola Fide* in Galatians 2." In *Lutherische und Neue Paulusperspektive*, edited by Michael Bachmann and Johannes Woyke, 309–27. Tübingen: Mohr Siebeck, 2005.

———. *Where Is Boasting? Early Jewish Soteriology and Paul's Response in Romans 1–5*. Grand Rapids: Eerdmans, 2003.

Gibbs, John G. *Creation and Redemption: A Study in Pauline Theology*. Leiden: Brill, 1971.

Given, Mark D. "Paul and Writing." In *As It Is Written: Studying Paul's Use of Scripture*, edited by Stanley E. Porter and Christopher D. Stanley, 237–60. SBLSS 50. Atlanta: Society of Biblical Literature, 2008.

Gorman, Michael J. *Inhabiting the Cruciform God: Kenosis, Justification, and Theosis in Paul's Narrative Soteriology*. Grand Rapids: Eerdmans, 2009.

Gottfried, Nebe. "Creation in Paul's Theology." In *Creation in Jewish and Christian Tradition*, edited by Henning Graf Reventlow and Yair Hoffman, 111–37. JSOTSup 319. Sheffield: Sheffield Academic, 2002.

Grass, Hans. *Ostergeschehen und Osterberichte*. Göttingen: Vandenhoeck & Ruprecht, 1962.

Gunkel, Hermann. *The Influence of the Holy Spirit: The Popular View of the Apostolic Age and the Teaching of the Apostle Paul*. Philadelphia: Fortress, 1979.

Harrill, J. Albert. *Paul the Apostle: His Life and Legacy in Their Roman Context*. Cambridge: Cambridge University Press, 2012.

Hays, Richard. *Echoes of Scripture in the Letters of Paul*. New Haven: Yale University Press, 1989.

———. *First Corinthians*. Louisville: Westminster John Knox, 1997.

———. "Psalm 143 and the Logic of Romans 3." *JBL* 99 (1980): 107–15.

Heim, S. Mark. *The Depth of the Riches: A Trinitarian Theology of Religious Ends*. Grand Rapids: Eerdmans, 2000.

Heitmüller, Wilhelm. "Zum Problem Paulus und Jesus." *ZNW* 13 (1912): 320–37.

Hengel, Martin. "Das Begräbnis Jesu bei Paulus und die leibliche Auferstehung aus dem Grabe." In *Auferstehung—Resurrection*, edited by Friedrich Avemarie and Hermann Lichtenberger, 119–83. WUNT 135. Tübingen: Mohr Siebeck, 2001.

———. *Studies in the Gospel of Mark*. Philadelphia: Fortress, 1985.

Hermann, I. *Kyrios und Pneuma: Studien zur Christologie der paulinischen Hauptbriefe*. SANT 2. Munich: Koesel, 1961.

Hill, Wesley. *Paul and the Trinity: Persons, Relations, and the Pauline Letters*. Grand Rapids: Eerdmans, 2015.

Hoehner, H. W. *The Chronological Aspects of the Life of Christ*. Grand Rapids: Eerdmans, 1977.

Horn, Friedrich W. *Das Angeld des Geistes: Studien zur paulinischen Pneumatologie*. Göttingen: Vandenhoeck & Ruprecht, 1992.

Hurtado, Larry. *One God, One Lord: Early Christian Devotion and Ancient Jewish Monotheism*. 3rd ed. London: T. & T. Clark, 2015.

———. "YHWH's Return to Zion: A New Catalyst for Earliest High Christology?" In *God and the Faithfulness of Paul: A Critical Examination of the Pauline*

Theology of N. T. Wright, edited by Christoph Heilig, J. Thomas Hewitt, and Michael F. Bird, 417–38. Tübingen: Mohr Siebeck, 2016.

Jewett, Robert. *A Chronology of Paul's Life*. Philadelphia: Fortress, 1979.

Käsemann, Ernst. *Commentary on Romans*. Grand Rapids: Eerdmans, 1980.

Keck, Leander E. *Paul and His Letters*. 2nd ed. Philadelphia: Fortress, 1988.

Kelly, J. N. D. *Early Christian Creeds*. 3rd ed. Essex, UK: Longman, 1972.

King, Karen. "The History of Christianity." In *The Gospel of Mary of Magdala: Jesus and the First Woman Apostle*, 155–90. Santa Rosa, CA: Polebridge, 2003.

Kraftchick, Steve. "Paul's Use of Creation Themes: A Test of Romans 1–8." *ExAud* 3 (1987): 72–87.

Kreitzer, L. Joseph. *Jesus and God in Paul's Eschatology*. Sheffield: JSOT, 1987.

Laato, Timo. "'God's Righteousness'—Once Again." In *The Nordic Paul: Finnish Approaches to Pauline Theology*, edited by Lars Aejmelaeus and Antti Mustakallio, 40–44. LNTS 374. London: T. & T. Clark, 2008.

———. *Paul and Judaism: An Anthropological Approach*. Atlanta: Scholars Press, 1995.

———. "Paul's Anthropological Considerations: Two Problems." In *The Paradoxes of Paul*, vol. 2 of *Justification and Variegated Nomism*, edited by D. A. Carson, Peter T. O'Brien, and Mark A. Seifrid, 343–59. Grand Rapids: Baker, 2004.

Lampe, Peter. "Paul's Concept of a Spiritual Body." In *Resurrection: Theological and Scientific Assessments*, edited by Ted Peters, Robert John Russell, and Michael Welker, 103–14. Grand Rapids: Eerdmans, 2002.

Lane, William L. *The Gospel according to Mark*. NICNT. Grand Rapids: Eerdmans, 1974.

Lang, Friedrich. *Die Briefe an die Korinther*. Göttingen: Vandenhoeck & Ruprecht, 1986.

Lewis, C. S. *Miracles: A Preliminary Study*. New York: Macmillan, 1947.

Lindemann, Andreas. *Der Erste Korintherbrief*. Tübingen: Mohr Siebeck, 2000.

Lüdemann, Gerd. *Paul, Apostle to the Gentiles: Studies in Chronology*. Translated by F. Stanley Jones. Philadelphia: Fortress, 1984.

Macaskill, Grant. "Incarnational Ontology and the Theology of Participation in Paul." In *"In Christ" in Paul: Explorations in Paul's Theology of Union and Participation*, edited by Michael J. Thate, Kevin J. Vanhoozer, and Constantine R. Campbell, 87–101. Tübingen: Mohr Siebeck, 2014.

———. *Union with Christ in the New Testament*. Oxford: Oxford University Press, 2013.

MacMullen, Ramsay. *Paganism in the Roman Empire*. New Haven: Yale University Press, 1981.

Maier, P. L. "Sejanus, Pilate, and the Date of the Crucifixion." *CH* 37 (1968): 3–13.

Malherbe, Abraham J. *The Letters to the Thessalonians*. AB 32B. New York: Doubleday, 2000.

———. *Paul and the Popular Philosophers*. Minneapolis: Fortress, 1989.

Martin, Dale. *The Corinthian Body*. New Haven: Yale University Press, 1995.

Matera, Frank J. *God's Saving Grace: A Pauline Theology*. Grand Rapids: Eerdmans, 2012.

May, Gerhard. *Creatio ex Nihilo: The Doctrine of "Creation out of Nothing" in Early Christian Thought*. Edinburgh: T. & T. Clark, 1994.

McFarland, Ian A. *From Nothing: A Theology of Creation*. Louisville: Westminster John Knox, 2014.

McGrath, J. F. *The Only True God: Early Christian Monotheism in Its Jewish Context*. Urbana and Chicago: University of Illinois Press, 2009.

McLaren, Brian D. *Why Did Jesus, Moses, the Buddha, and Mohammed Cross the Road? Christian Identity in a Multi-Faith World*. New York: Jericho, 2012.

Meeks, Wayne A. *The First Urban Christians*. 2nd ed. New Haven: Yale University Press, 2003.

Meyer, Ben F. "Did Paul's View of the Resurrection of the Dead Undergo Development?" *TS* 47 (1986): 363–87.

Mitchell, Stephen, and Peter Van Nuffelen, eds. *One God: Pagan Monotheism in the Roman Empire*. Cambridge: Cambridge University Press, 2010.

Moo, Douglas J. *The Epistle to the Romans*. NICNT. Grand Rapids: Eerdmans, 1996.

Murphy-O'Connor, Jerome. *Becoming Human Together: The Pastoral Anthropology of St. Paul*. 3rd ed. Atlanta: Society of Biblical Literature, 2009.

The New Interpreter's Bible. Edited by Leander E. Keck. 12 vols. Nashville: Abingdon, 1994–2004.

Nilsson, Martin P. *Geschichte der griechischen Religion*. 2nd ed. Munich: Beck, 1961.

Novenson, Matthew V. *Christ among the Messiahs: Christ Language in Paul and Messiah Language in Ancient Judaism*. Oxford: Oxford University Press, 2015.

Oehler, G. F. *Theologie des alten Testaments*. 2nd ed. Stuttgart: Steinkopf, 1882.

Pagels, Elaine E. *Beyond Belief: The Secret Gospel of Thomas*. New York: Vintage, 2003.

———. "'The Mystery of the Resurrection': A Gnostic Reading of 1 Corinthians 15." *JBL* 93 (1974): 276–88.

Pelikan, Jaroslav. "Creation and Causality in the History of Christian Thought." *JR* 32 (1960): 246–55.

Peterson, Jeffrey R. "The Extent of Christian Theological Diversity: Pauline Evidence." *RQ* 47 (2005): 1–12.

Porter, Stanley. *The Apostle Paul: His Life, Thought, and Letters.* Grand Rapids: Eerdmans, 2016.

Reumann, John. *Creation and New Creation: The Past, Present, and Future of God's Creative Activity.* Minneapolis: Augsburg, 1973.

Ridderbos, Herman. *Paul: An Outline of His Theology.* Translated by John Richard De Witt. Grand Rapids: Eerdmans, 1975.

Riesner, Rainer. *Paul's Early Period: Chronology, Mission, Strategy, Theology.* Translated by D. Scott. Grand Rapids: Eerdmans, 1998.

Robinson, J. M. "Jesus—from Easter to Valentinus (or to the Apostles' Creed)." *JBL* 101 (1982): 5–37.

Romanides, John S. *The Ancestral Sin.* Translated by George S. Gabriel. Ridgewood, NJ: Zephyr, 2002.

Rowe, C. Kavin. "Biblical Pressure and Trinitarian Hermeneutics." *Pro Ecclesia* 11 (2002): 295–312.

Sanders, E. P. *Paul and Palestinian Judaism.* Philadelphia: Fortress, 1977.

Schoeps, H. J. *Paul: The Theology of the Apostle in the Light of Jewish Religious History.* Translated by Harold Knight. Philadelphia: Westminster, 1961.

Schrage, Wolfgang. *Unterwegs zur Einzigkeit und Einheit Gottes: Zum "Monotheismus" des Paulus und seiner alttestamentlich-früjüdischen Tradition.* Neukirchen-Vluyn: Neukirchener Verlag, 2002.

Schreiner, Thomas R. "Justification: The Saving Righteousness of God." *JETS* 54 (2011): 19–34.

———. *The Law and Its Fulfillment: A Pauline Theology of Law.* Grand Rapids: Baker Academic, 1993.

———. "An Old Perspective on the New Perspective." *CJ* 35 (2009): 141–55.

———. *Paul, Apostle of God's Glory in Christ: A Pauline Theology.* Downers Grove: InterVarsity, 2001.

———. "Paul's View of the Law in Romans 10:4–5." *WTJ* 55 (1993): 113–35.

———. *Romans.* BECNT 6. Grand Rapids: Baker Academic, 1998.

Schweitzer, Albert. *The Mysticism of Paul the Apostle.* Translated by W. Montgomery. Baltimore: Johns Hopkins University Press, 1998.

Scroggs, Robin. "Paul the Prisoner: Political Asceticism in the Letter to the Philippians." In *Asceticism in the New Testament,* edited by Leif E. Vaage and Vincent L. Wimbush, 187–207. New York: Routledge, 1999.

Snodgrass, Klyne. "Justification by Faith—to the Doers: An Analysis of the Place of Romans 2 in the Theology of Paul." *NTS* 32 (1986): 72–93.

Stowers, Stanley K. *A Rereading of Romans: Justice, Jews, and Gentiles.* New Haven: Yale University Press, 1994.

Tannehill, Robert C. "Participation in Christ: A Central Theme in Pauline Soteriology." In *The Shape of the Gospel: New Testament Essays*, 225–39. Eugene, OR: Wipf and Stock, 2007.

Tanqueray, Adolphe. *Synopsis Theologiae Dogmaticae*. Paris: Desclée, 1938.

Thate, Michael J., Kevin J. Vanhoozer, and Constantine R. Campbell, eds. *"In Christ" in Paul: Explorations in Paul's Theology of Union and Participation*. Tübingen: Mohr Siebeck, 2014.

Thielman, Frank. *Paul and the Law: A Contextual Approach*. Downers Grove: InterVarsity, 1994.

Thiselton, Anthony C. *The First Epistle to the Corinthians: A Commentary on the Greek Text*. NIGTC. Grand Rapids: Eerdmans, 2000.

—————. *The Living Paul: An Introduction to the Apostle's Life and Thought*. Downers Grove: InterVarsity, 2009.

Thurén, Lauri. *Derhetorizing Paul: A Dynamic Perspective on Pauline Theology and the Law*. WUNT 124. Tübingen: Mohr Siebeck, 2000.

Tilling, Chris. *Paul's Divine Christology*. Tübingen: Mohr Siebeck, 2012.

Vielhauer, Philipp. "On the 'Paulinism' of Acts." *PSTJ* 17 (1963): 5–18.

Waaler, Erik. *The Shema and the First Commandment in First Corinthians: An Intertextual Approach to Paul's Rereading of Deuteronomy*. WUNT 2.253. Tübingen: Mohr Siebeck, 2008.

Wagner, J. Ross. *Heralds of the Good News: Isaiah and Paul "in Concert" in the Letter to the Romans*. NovTSup 101. Leiden: Brill, 2002.

Walker, William O. "Galatians 2:7b–8 as a Non-Pauline Interpolation." *CBQ* 65 (2003): 568–87.

Walter, Nikolaus. "Leibliche Auferstehung? Zur Frage der Hellenisierung der Auferweckungshoffnung bei Paulus." In *Paulus, Apostel Jesu Christi*, edited by Michael Trowitzsch, 109–28. Tübingen: Mohr Siebeck, 1998.

Ware, James. "Euripides' Beatific Vision." *Touchstone* 26 (2013): 27–33.

—————. "Law, Christ, and Covenant: Paul's Theology of the Law in Romans 3:19–20." *JTS* 62 (2011): 513–40.

—————. "Moral Progress and Divine Power in Seneca and Paul." In *Passions and Moral Progress in Greco-Roman Thought*, edited by John T. Fitzgerald, 267–83. New York: Routledge, 2008.

—————. "Paul's Understanding of the Resurrection in 1 Corinthians 15:36–54." *JBL* 133 (2014): 809–35.

—————. "The Resurrection of Jesus in the Pre-Pauline Formula of 1 Cor 15.3–5." *NTS* 60 (2014): 475–98.

—————. "The Salvation of Creation: Seneca and Paul on the Cosmos, Human Beings, and Their Future." In *Paul and Seneca in Dialogue*, edited by Joseph R. Dodson and David E. Briones, 285–306. Leiden: Brill, 2017.

Watson, Francis. "The Triune Divine Identity: Reflections on Pauline God-Language, in Disagreement with J. D. G. Dunn." *JSNT* 80 (2000): 99–124.

Wenham, David. *Paul: Follower of Jesus or Founder of Christianity?* Grand Rapids: Eerdmans, 1995.

Westerholm, Stephen. "Finnish Contributions to the Debate on Paul and the Law." In *The Nordic Paul: Finnish Approaches to Pauline Theology*, edited by Lars Aejmelaeus and Antti Mustakallio, 3–15. LNTS 374. London: T. & T. Clark, 2008.

————. *Perspectives Old and New on Paul: The "Lutheran" Paul and His Critics.* Grand Rapids: Eerdmans, 2004.

Wood, Susan. "Alcestis on Roman Sarcophagi." *AJA* 82 (1978): 499–510.

Worthington, Jonathan D. *Creation in Paul and Philo.* WUNT 2.317. Tübingen: Mohr Siebeck, 2011.

Wrede, Wilhelm. *Paul.* Translated by Edward Lummis. London: Green, 1907.

Wright, N. T. *The Climax of the Covenant: Christ and the Law in Pauline Theology.* Minneapolis: Fortress, 1991.

————. *Jesus and the Victory of God.* Vol. 2 of *Christian Origins and the Question of God.* Minneapolis: Fortress, 1996.

————. *Justification: God's Plan and Paul's Vision.* Downers Grove: InterVarsity, 2009.

————. "Monotheism, Christology and Ethics: 1 Corinthians 8." In *The Climax of the Covenant: Christ and the Law in Pauline Theology*, 120–46. Minneapolis: Fortress, 1991.

————. *Paul and the Faithfulness of God.* Vol. 4 of *Christian Origins and the Question of God.* Minneapolis: Fortress, 2013.

————. *Paul in Fresh Perspective.* Minneapolis: Fortress, 2005.

————. *The Resurrection of the Son of God.* Vol. 3 of *Christian Origins and the Question of God.* Minneapolis: Fortress, 2003.

————. *What Saint Paul Really Said: Was Paul of Tarsus the Real Founder of Christianity?* Grand Rapids: Eerdmans, 1997.

Yeago, David. "The New Testament and the Nicene Dogma: A Contribution to the Recovery of Theological Exegesis." *Pro Ecclesia* 3 (1994): 157–58.

Ziesler, John. *The Meaning of Righteousness in Paul: A Linguistic and Theological Inquiry.* Cambridge: Cambridge University Press, 1972.

Index of Authors

Aelian, 2n4
Aeschylus, 25, 142
Aletti, Jean Noel, 104
Ambrose, 87
Anacreon, 142
Anderson, A. A., 105
Aquinas, Thomas, 17n18, 22n22, 31n6
Aristotle, 2n4, 27, 118, 166, 186
Arrian, 2n4, 27
Athenagoras, 191n10
Augustine, 13n14, 31, 159, 191n10, 193
Avemarie, Friedrich, 99

Barbour, Ian, 13n12
Barclay, John M. G., 83
Barnikol, Ernst, 224
Bates, Matthew W., 57n11
Bauckham, Richard, 52n6, 229
Buddha, 9, 14, 25, 27, 47, 78, 141, 143
Bultmann, Rudolf, 78, 161

Campbell, Douglas A., 130
Capes, David B., 66n5
Cerfaux, Lucien, 66n5
Chesterton, G. K., 144
Childs, Brevard, 74
Chrysippus, 27, 140
Cicero, 2n4, 9, 14, 17, 25, 27, 29n4, 31, 34, 47, 78, 118, 140, 141
Clement of Alexandria, 2n4, 191n10
Cobb, John B., 13n12
Collins, Adela Yarbro, 167
Craig, William Lane, 17n18
Cullmann, Oscar, 207n9
Cyprian, 179n2, 222
Cyril of Alexandria, 86–87

Dahl, M. E., 160
Das, Andrew, 104
Dio Cassius, 2n4
Dio Chrysostom, 2n4
Diodorus Siculus, 2n4
Diogenes Laertius, 2n4, 140
Dunn, James D. G., 8n5, 98, 102, 127n4, 133n12

Ehrman, Bart, 70n9
Engberg-Pedersen, Troels, 161
Epictetus, 141, 143, 166
Epicurus, 9, 78, 143
Epiphanius, 87
Euripides, 64, 143–44
Eusebius, 207n9, 226, 229

Fitzmyer, Joseph, 180n5
Fredriksen, Paula, 155n4, 161, 167

Gathercole, Simon J., 99
Gautama Buddha, 9, 14, 25, 27, 47, 78, 141, 143
Gregory of Nyssa, 86, 87
Griffin, David Ray, 13n12

Hays, Richard, 1n2, 108–9n24, 160
Heim, S. Mark, 88
Hengel, Martin, 229
Hermas, 191n10
Hesiod, 9, 14, 63
Hilary, 87
Hippolytus, 179n2
Homer, 25, 63, 119, 142
Hume, David, 19

Index of Subjects

Abrahamic covenant. *See* covenant
Acts, authorship, 230
adultery, 190–91
afterlife. *See* death and suffering;
  resurrection
Anacreon, 142
ancient Christianity. *See* Christianity,
  ancient
ancient Judaism. *See* Jewish theology
ancient pagans. *See* pagan worldviews
Andronicus and Junia, 218
anointing, 179
anthropology. *See* humanity
apostles: apostolic college, 217–19; and
  apostolic origins of Pauline theology,
  207–11; New Testament writings of,
  228–32; Paul as distinct among, 219–21,
  227–28; role of Paul, 222–28; role of
  Peter, 221–22
Apostolic Council (48/49 CE), 210, 222–25
Aquinas, Thomas, 22n22
argument from design, 16–17
Aristotle, 118, 186
atonement: in Mosaic v. new covenant,
  114–15; through sacrifice of Jesus Christ,
  116–17
Augustine, 31, 159

baptism, 179–80, 214
binary sex difference, 29–30
body: ancient pagan denial of bodily resurrection, 140, 141–42; bodily resurrection
  of Jesus Christ, 147–49, 154–56, 171–72;
  corruption of, 167–69; *egeirō* term,
  169–70; flesh/spirit distinction, 35–38;
  Jewish hope for bodily resurrection,
  146–47; made incorruptible in resurrec-

tion, 167–69; materiality of resurrected
  body, 167–68; perspectives on Paul's
  understanding of bodily resurrection,
  159–65; sex and gender, 29–30; spiritual
  body, 165–67; union with God, 30–31;
  union with soul, 27–28
Buddha and Buddhists: on body and soul,
  27, 31; on cosmos and divinity, 9, 14, 78,
  141; on death and suffering, 25, 34, 143;
  on history, 47

cause and effect, 19–20
celibacy, 194
ceremonial law, 98–99, 101
chrismation, 179n2
Christ. *See* Jesus Christ
Christianity, ancient: apostolic college,
  217–19; apostolic origins of Pauline
  theology, 207–11; apostolic role of Paul,
  222–28; apostolic role of Peter, 221–22;
  and authorship of New Testament
  books, 228–32; earliest historical sources
  for, 203–4; historical witness of Pauline
  epistles, 205–6, 211–15; impact of Pauline
  theology on, 74–75, 159–60; Paul as
  distinct among apostles, 219–21, 227–28;
  pluriform Christianity thesis, 201–2
Christology: debates on Pauline, 43, 66–67,
  70–71, 73, 74; defined, 43. *See also* incarnation; Jesus Christ
church: as new temple, 77, 82; union with
  Jesus Christ, 29, 80, 82, 192–93
Cicero, 118, 140
communion. *See* participation
confirmation, 179n2
consummated v. inaugurated kingdom, 48,
  175

humanity: fall of, 31–34; flesh/spirit distinction, 35–38; as image of God, 30–31; of Jesus Christ, 48–49, 56–57, 59, 70–71; participatory union with God, 76–82; sex and gender, 29–30; union of body and soul, 27–28. *See also* body; resurrection
Hume, David, 19
hypostatic union, 64

identity, Jewish, 98–99, 101, 133n12, 210
image of God, 30–31, 32
imitation of Christ, 188–89
imperishability, of resurrected body, 167–69
imputed v. infused righteousness, 129–31, 178
inaugurated v. consummated kingdom, 48, 175
incarnation: in ancient pagan context, 62–65; as epicenter of Pauline theology, 88–89; as fulfillment and foundation of covenantal promise, 108–10, 116–17; Jesus Christ as human, 48–49, 56–57, 59, 70–71; Jesus Christ as Messiah, 47–48, 56–60; Jesus Christ as YHWH, 52, 54–55, 56–60, 65–70, 71–73, 154–56; Nicene use of Pauline theology of, 74–75; and participatory union with God, 76–82; and renewal of creation, 150–51, 171–72, 176–79; and resurrection of Jesus Christ, 147–49, 154–56, 171–72; as revelation of creation's goodness, 65, 171–72; as revelation of Trinity, 83–85; and sacrificial love, 117–20
indwelling, of Jesus Christ, 79–80, 82, 120–21
intellect, transformation of, 181
Irenaeus, 159, 229

James, brother of Jesus, 209, 210, 211, 218, 222, 223, 224, 226
James, son of Zebedee, 221, 222
Jerome, 159
Jerusalem Council (48/49 CE), 210, 222–25
Jesus Christ: as agent of creation, 52–53; command to love, 185–89; divine title v. divine name, 73–74; as fulfillment and foundation of covenantal promise, 108–10, 116–17; Holy Spirit as Spirit of, 85–88; as human, 48–49, 56–57, 59, 70–71; incarnation in ancient pagan

context, 62–65; Last Supper, 211–14; law of, 183–85; love of, 83, 89, 117–20; as Messiah, 47–48, 56–60; new life in, 176–81; participatory union with, 79–82, 120–21; rejection of, 83; renewal of creation through, 150–51, 171–72, 176–79; resurrection of, 147–49, 154–56, 171–72; teaching on marriage, 190–91; union with church, 29, 80, 82, 192–93; witnesses of resurrected, 206, 218–21; as YHWH, 52, 54–55, 56–60, 65–70, 71–73, 154–56
Jewish theology: debates on Pauline approach to, 95, 96–100, 133; divine name for God, 45–46; expectation of Messiah's coming, 46–49; expectation of YHWH's dwelling, 49–51, 145–47; flaws in debates on Pauline approach to, 100–104; fulfilled expectations of, 56–60, 108–10, 116–17; Mosaic v. new covenant, 114–15; righteousness within v. apart from covenant, 110–12, 134; solution to problem of Pauline approach to, 104–10
John, Gospel of, 229
John, son of Zebedee, 210, 211, 221, 223
Judaizers, 111
Jude, authorship of, 231
judgment, 150
justification: defined, 126; faith and ethics, 132; and fulfillment of law, 133–35; and righteousness of God, 126–31, 178. *See also* law and works

kingdom: and bodily imperishability, 167–69; and command to love, 185–89; and debates on Pauline resurrection theology, 160–62; and early church use of Pauline resurrection theology, 159–60; *egeirō* term, 169–70; and ethics of marriage and sexuality, 189–95; and God's victory over death, 152–54; inaugurated v. consummated, 48, 175; Jewish expectation of, 46–51, 145–47; and law of Christ, 183–85; and renewal of creation, 150–51, 171–72, 176–79; and resurrection of Jesus Christ, 147–49, 154–56, 171–72; and sacraments, 179–80; and spiritual body, 165–67; and structure of Pauline resurrection theology, 162–65

Last Supper, 211–14

Index of Scripture and Other Ancient Texts